PREPARING ACCOUNTS FOR LLPS
Third edition

PREPARING ACCOUNTS FOR LLPS
Third edition

Iain Storey and Catherine Willshire

© 2016 Wolters Kluwer

Wolters Kluwer
145 London Road
Kingston upon Thames KT2 6SR
United Kingdom
Tel: 0844 561 8166
Fax: 0208 547 2638
E-mail: cch@wolterskluwer.com
www.cch.co.uk

ISBN 978-1-78540-259-3

British Library Cataloguing-in-Publication Data
A catalogue record for this book is available from the British Library.

Typeset by Innodata Inc., India

Printed by Sowa Sp. z o.o. Warsaw, Poland, 2016.

About the authors

Iain Storey

Iain works in Price Bailey's technical team in a role that includes giving advice on technical accounting matters. As part of this role, he has been involved in the firm's preparations for the switch to FRS 102. Before joining the technical team, Iain worked in audit for many years.

Catherine Willshire

Catherine qualified as a chartered accountant with Ernst & Young in 1997. She joined Price Bailey in 2003 and became a partner in 2014, heading up the technical and compliance team. She has significant experience of working with a broad range of corporate and not for profit clients.

Founded in 1938, Price Bailey (www.pricebailey.co.uk) is a leading firm of chartered accountants and business advisers operating throughout the UK, with global connections. Clients range from high net worth individuals to publicly listed businesses. Price Bailey has built a reputation as one of the market leaders in business advice to the professional services sector many of which are Limited Liability Partnerships.

Preface

Preparing Accounts for LLPs Third edition represents the third edition of this title.

The *Limited Liability Partnerships Act* 2000 (the Act) came into force on 6 April 2001, introducing a new form of legal entity known as a limited liability partnership (LLP). In the first few years following the Act's introduction, only a relatively small number of LLPs were established, but since then the number of LLPs has increased significantly.

The current accounting requirements for LLPs are based on the requirements for companies. In 2008, three Statutory Instruments were issued to apply the *Companies Act* 2006 (CA 2006) to LLPs and to set out the accounting requirements for both small LLPs and large and medium-sized LLPs.

These Statutory Instruments and UK GAAP (generally accepted accounting practice) remain the basis of the content of this book. In addition the CCAB (the Consultative Committee of Accountancy Bodies) has developed a Statement of Recommended Practice (SORP) *Accounting by Limited Liability Partnerships*. The current LLP SORP was published in July 2014. The accounting guidance given in the LLP SORP is also discussed within this book.

In itself, implementation of CA 2006 was a major landmark. However, the dawn of this new era of company legislation has now been followed by the end of another – UK GAAP in the form many of us have grown up with.

The period since the first edition of this book has seen the issue of the new UK financial reporting standard (FRS 102 *The Financial Reporting Standard applicable in the UK and Republic of Ireland*) and has had significant 'knock on' effects on the LLP SORP.

There have also been changes to the financial reporting regime for companies for periods commencing on or after 1 January 2016, radically reducing the disclosures required by small companies but increasing the complexity of their accounting by withdrawing the Financial Reporting Standard for Smaller Entities. Whilst the legislation implementing these changes specifically excluded LLPs, the Government has announced that LLPs will be brought within its scope from the same effective date, although the legislation to implement this has yet to be published.

The main objective of the book is to be a companion, rather than a comprehensive technical treatise in its own right – a quick and relatively straightforward guide, simplifying where possible, concentrating on basic principles, suggesting appropriate tools, and illustrating changes and opportunities. The book is primarily aimed at those smaller LLPs which are preparing accounts in accordance with UK GAAP and aims to highlight where there are differences in disclosure requirement for small LLPs compared to large and medium-sized LLPs.

As always, we would be grateful to readers for any comments and helpful suggestions.

We are indebted to our colleagues Anthony DeMartino and Hannah Crisp for their help in editing the book.

Catherine Willshire and Iain Storey
January 2016

Contents

Contents

Abbreviations

AAC	Audit and Assurance Council (part of the FRC)
APB	Auditing Practices Board (disbanded in July 2012, replaced by the FRC's Audit and Assurance Council)
ASB	Accounting Standards Board (disbanded in July 2012, replaced by the FRC's Accounting Council)
BIS	Department for Business, Innovation and Skills
CA 2006	Companies Act 2006
CCAB	Consultative Committee of Accountancy Bodies
EEA	European Economic Area
EU	European Union
EU Regulation	Regulation (EC) No. 1606/2002 of the European Parliament (dated 19 July 2002) on the application of international accounting standards
FASB	US Financial Accounting Standards Board
FRC	Financial Reporting Council
FRED	Financial Reporting Exposure Draft
FRRP	Financial Reporting Review Panel
FRS	Financial Reporting Standard
FRS 100	Application of financial reporting requirements
FRS 101	Reduced Disclosure Framework – Disclosure exemptions from EU-adopted IFRS for qualifying entities
FRS 102	The Financial Reporting Standard applicable in the UK and Republic of Ireland
FRS 103	Insurance Contracts – Consolidated accounting and reporting requirements for entities in the UK and Republic of Ireland issuing insurance contracts
FRS 104	Interim Financial Reporting
FRS 105	The Financial Reporting Standard applicable to the Micro-entities Regime
FRSSE	Financial Reporting Standard for Smaller Entities (being the 'FRSSE (effective April 2008)' unless otherwise indicated or as the circumstances dictate)
FSMA 2000	Financial Services and Markets Act 2000
GAAP	Generally accepted accounting practice (or principles) (see also 'UK GAAP')
IAASB	International Auditing and Assurance Standards Board
IAS	International accounting standards issued or adopted by IASB
IASB	International Accounting Standards Board
IFRIC	International Financial Reporting Interpretations Committee (an IASB committee)
IFRS	International Financial Reporting Standards (including IAS and interpretations adopted by IASB)
IFRS for SMEs	International Financial Reporting Standard for Small and Medium-sized Entities
ISA	International Standard on Auditing ('ISA (UK and Ireland)': an ISA applicable within UK and Ireland)
iXBRL	Inline Extensible Business Reporting Language
LLP	Limited Liability Partnership (as defined by the Limited Liability Partnership Act 2000)
LLP SORP	Statement of Recommended Practice – Accounting by Limited Liability Partnerships (2014)
NIC	National Insurance contributions
MiFID	MiFID investment firm – an investment firm within the meaning of Article 4.1.1 of Directive 2004/39/EC of the European Parliament and of the Council of 21 April 2004 on markets in financial instruments (but see CA 2006, s. 474)

P & L account	Profit and loss
account PAYE	Pay as you earn
PN	APB Practice Note
POB	Professional Oversight Board (part of the FRC)
Reg.	Regulation (for example, SI 2008/1913, reg. 4(2) means regulation 4(2) of SI 2008 No. 1913)
s.	section (unless otherwise stated, section references refer to CA 2006 as applied to LLPs and as amended or inserted from time to time)
Sch.	Schedule (for example: 'CA 2006, Sch 7.7(2)' means Companies Act 2006, Schedule 7, paragraph 7(2))
SI	Statutory instrument
SME	Small or medium-sized entity (or enterprise)
	Abbreviations
SORP	Statement of Recommended Practice
SSAP	Statement of Standard Accounting Practice
STRGL	Statement of total recognised gains and losses
UCITS	Undertaking for Collective Investment in Transferable Securities (see CA 2006, s. 471(1))
UITF	Urgent Issues Task Force (part of FRC since July 2012, previously part of the ASB)
UK GAAP	Financial reporting requirements (as specified by the FRC/ASB) in the United Kingdom and the Republic of Ireland (see 'GAAP')
VAT	Value added tax

Statutory instruments

SI 2013/2005	Companies and Partnerships (Accounts and Audit) Regulations 2013
SI 2013/1971	Companies (Revision of Defective Accounts and Reports) (Amendment) Regulations 2013
SI 2013/618	Limited Liability Partnerships (Application of Companies Act 2006) (Amendment) Regulations 2013
SI 2012/2301	Companies and Limited Liability Partnerships (Accounts and Audit Exemptions and Change of Accounting Framework) Regulations 2012
SI 2009/1833	Limited Liability Partnerships (Amendment) Regulations 2009
SI 2009/1804	Limited Liability Partnerships (Application of Companies Act 2006) Regulations 2009
SI 2008/1913	Large and Medium-sized Limited Liability Partnerships (Accounts) Regulations 2008
SI 2008/1912	Small Limited Liability Partnerships (Accounts) Regulations 2008
SI 2008/1911	Limited Liability Partnerships (Accounts and Audit) (Application of Companies Act 2006) Regulations 2008
SI 2008/489	Companies (Disclosure of Auditor Remuneration and Liability Limitation Agreements) Regulations 2008
SI 2008/373	Companies (Revision Of Defective Accounts And Reports) Regulations 2008

Summary of implementation dates

Limited Liability Partnerships Act 2000

The Limited Liability Partnerships Act came into force on 6 April 2001 (SI 2000/3316 *The Limited Liability Partnership Act 2000 (Commencement) Order* 2000).

Companies Act 2006 as applied to LLPs

The *Companies Act* 2006 was applied to LLPs by various statutory instruments.

Accounts provisions – effective for accounts and reports of companies for **periods beginning on or after 6 April 2008**.

Audit provisions – applicable to the audits of accounts of companies for **financial years beginning on or after 6 April 2008**.

The provisions of the *Companies Act* 2006 were not applicable to LLPs until 1 October 2008 when the LLP regulations below were introduced.

SI 2008/1911 The *Limited Liability Partnerships (Accounts and Audit) (Application of Companies Act* 2006) *Regulations* 2008: *www.legislation.gov.uk/uksi/2008/1911/contents/made*

SI 2008/1912 The *Small Limited Liability Partnerships (Accounts) Regulations* 2008: *www.legislation.gov.uk/uksi/2008/1912/contents/made*

SI 2008/1913 The *Large and Medium-sized Limited Liability Partnerships (Accounts) Regulations* 2008: *www.legislation.gov.uk/uksi/2008/1913/contents/made*

Note: the versions of the statutory instruments shown on the legislation website are in the form that they were originally issued. SI 2008/1911 has been amended several times and reference should be made to a copy containing the amendments.

Within this publication these three statutory instruments are referred to as 'The Regulations'.

Financial Reporting Standard for Smaller Entities (FRSSE)

Members choosing to adopt the FRSSE must ensure that accounts are prepared in accordance with the appropriate version. The current version is:

- FRSSE (effective January 2015) – accounts prepared under CA 2006.

The FRSSE (effective January 2015) is available free of charge on the FRC website at:

www.frc.org.uk/Our-Work/Codes-Standards/Accounting-and-Reporting-Policy/FRSSE.aspx

and hard copies are available from FRC Publications.

FRSSE (effective January 2015)

The Financial Reporting Standard for Smaller Entities (effective January 2015) is applicable to small LLPs, as an option, for financial statements relating to accounting periods beginning on or after 1 January 2015, in compliance with SI 2008/1912 *Small Limited Liability Partnerships (Accounts) Regulations* 2008.

LLP SORP

The current version of the Statement of Recommended Practice for LLPs *Accounting by Limited Liability Partnerships* was issued by the Consultative Committee of Accounting Bodies (CCAB) in July 2014. It is effective for all accounting periods commencing on or after 1 January 2015.

LLP size thresholds

Accounting and audit exemption thresholds for small and medium-sized companies, as set by SI 2008/393 (*Companies Act 2006 (Amendment) (Accounts and Reports) Regulations* 2008) and subsequently applied to LLPs by SI 2008/1911 (*Limited Liability Partnerships (Accounts and Audit) (Application of Companies Act 2006) Regulations* 2008), are set out below.

These thresholds apply to LLPs in relation to financial years beginning on or after 1 October 2010. These thresholds are currently under review and the table shows the proposed revised thresholds expected to apply to LLPs for periods beginning on or after 1 January 2016 (see **Chapter 13**).

	Thresholds applicable from	
	1 October 2010	*1 January 2016*
Small LLPs		
Small LLP		
Turnover	£6.5m	£10.2m
Balance sheet total	£3.26m	£5.1m
Average number of employees (on a monthly basis)	50	50
Small group		
Aggregate turnover	£6.5m net* (£7.8m gross**)	£10.2m net* (£12.2m gross**)
Aggregate balance sheet total	£3.26m net (£3.9m gross)	£5.1m net (£6.1m gross)
Average number of employees (on a monthly basis)	50	50
Medium-sized LLPs		
Medium-sized LLP		
Turnover	£25.9m	£36m
Balance sheet total	£12.9m	£18m
Average number of employees (on a monthly basis)	250	250
Medium-sized group		
Aggregate turnover	£25.9m net (£31.1m gross)	£36m net (£43.2m gross)
Aggregate balance sheet total	£12.9m net (£15.5m gross)	£18m net (£21.6m gross)
Average number of employees (on a monthly basis)	250	250

*'Net' basis – Aggregate figures for turnover and balance sheet totals after any set-offs and consolidation adjustments made for the elimination of group transactions

**'Gross' basis – Aggregate figures for turnover and balance sheet totals without such set-offs and consolidation adjustments.

Note on scope of book

Scope and contents of book

This third edition of *Preparing Accounts for LLPs* concentrates on matters most relevant to the preparation of accounts for smaller LLPs.

Changes to legislation and to accounting standards issued up to 31 December 2015 have been considered in the writing of this edition of *Preparing Accounts for LLPs*.

The following topics are considered peripheral to this main objective and are not therefore covered in detail:

International accounting standards (IAS): Only a very small proportion of LLPs prepare IAS accounts; the vast majority of accounts are non-IAS accounts prepared in accordance with UK GAAP and therefore this book focuses on the accounting requirements of UK GAAP.

At present, IAS impinge on LLPs generally only to the extent of 'convergence' (that is, harmonisation) of domestic UK and international financial reporting standards. Under the new UK GAAP regime it is possible that LLPs that meet certain conditions choose to apply FRS 101 *'Reduced Disclosure Framework – Disclosure exemptions from EU-adopted IFRS for qualifying entities'* rather than FRS 102. Under FRS 101 an entity applies the measurement principles of IFRS but is able to take certain disclosure exemptions. This will only arise for LLPs that are themselves parent entities preparing group accounts under IFRS (who can take the exemptions only in their individual accounts) or those LLPs with a corporate member, because of the need to have a parent that prepares consolidated financial statements, so is not relevant to, for instance, stand alone professional services firms where the partners are all individuals. Therefore only a small subset of LLPs might consider applying FRS 101, so this standard is not addressed in this book. Readers can find further information in the CCH Publication 'FRS 101 The Reduced Disclosure Framework'

Consolidated accounts: Small parent LLPs (as defined) are not required to prepare group accounts. However, as well as preparing individual accounts for a year, they may prepare group accounts if they wish to do so. **Chapter 7** provides details of the exemption opportunities and also the requirements where a small parent entity prepares group accounts. As noted in **Chapter 7** groups which are not classified as small are required to prepare consolidated accounts. *Preparing Accounts for LLPs Third Edition* does not cover the detailed mechanics of consolidations and group accounting.

Audit and assurance: Preparing Accounts for LLPs Third Edition does not purport to provide professional guidance on auditing or the provision of assurance services by auditors. The book does comment on audit exemption, audit reports and on the reporting requirements of auditors in circumstances where an audit may be appropriate. Reference should be made to **Chapter 9** (Determining LLP audit exemption) and **Chapter 12** (LLP audit and assurance reports).

Future developments: Changes to the financial reporting and auditing regime that will apply to LLPs for periods commencing on or after 1 January 2016 are currently under consideration. A summary of the likely changes is given in **Chapter 13**. The key changes and impact on LLPs from the adoption of New UK GAAP, specifically FRS 102, are set out in **Chapter 14**.

Chapter 1 Introduction

1.1 Purpose of the book

1.1.1 Accounts of Limited Liability Partnerships

When the *Limited Liability Partnerships Act* 2000 (the Act) came into force on 6 April 2001, it introduced a new form of legal entity known as a limited liability partnership (LLP).

As defined by the Act, a limited liability partnership is a body corporate (with legal personality separate from that of its members) which is formed by being incorporated under the *Limited Liability Partnerships Act* 2000.

Since inception, this form of legal entity has been adopted by many organisations which previously would have operated under partnership law, such as accountancy firms or legal practices, and has been adopted by many financial services organisations. The number of LLPs has grown significantly and therefore this book is essentially concerned with setting out the legal and accounting provisions applicable when preparing a set of financial statements for an LLP.

The main legal provisions set out in this book are those set out in the *Companies Act* 2006 (CA 2006) as applied to LLPs and therefore the legal provisions are those applicable for accounting periods starting on or after 1 October 2008.

The book also considers the disclosure requirements of the LLP SORP (Statement of Recommended Practice) (July 2014) which is applicable for accounting periods starting on or after 1 January 2015.

There are some differences in accounting and auditing requirements of small LLPs compared with those of large or medium-sized LLPs. This book aims to highlight the key differences in legislation and accounting standards. **Chapter 4** explains the size classification for LLPs and explains the circumstances when the small LLPs regime will not be applicable to an entity regardless of the size of the entity.

The book endeavours to simplify the complex requirements for LLPs accounts. While not purporting to give comprehensive coverage of all accounting provisions, the aim of the book is to explain many of the accounting requirements that affect LLPs preparing their accounts in accordance with UK GAAP and the exemptions (both accounting and audit) that are available to some small or medium-sized LLPs. The book concentrates on those matters of practical relevance as far as accounts are concerned. In essence, it aims to resolve the following issues:

- What sort of statutory accounts are required?
- Preparing and filing abbreviated accounts (applicable to small and medium-sized LLPs).
- The disclosure requirements of the LLP SORP.
- The adoption of the FRSSE (Financial Reporting Standard for Smaller Entities).
- Is an audit necessary or required?

1.2 Legislation – Accounting regime under the *Companies Act 2006* as applied to LLPs

The *Companies Act* 2006 received Royal Assent on 8 November 2006.

The accounts provisions of CA 2006, Pt. 15 became effective for all accounting periods of companies commencing on or after 6 April 2008.

However, for CA 2006 to be applicable to LLPs supplementary legislation was required. The *Limited Liability Partnerships (Accounts and Audit) (Application of the Companies Act 2006) Regulations* 2008 (SI 2008/1911) were made on 17 July 2008, thus making CA 2006 applicable to LLPs. The implementation date for the accounting requirements of Pt. 15 of CA 2006 as applied to LLPs was later than for companies. The requirements became applicable for LLPs for accounting years starting on or after 1 October 2008.

Reference should always be made to the actual legislation itself (CA 2006 as applied to LLPs) in order to ensure full adherence to current and up-to-date legislation.

As explained in subsequent chapters of this book, the Accounts Regulations for small LLPs and large and medium-sized LLPs are set out in SI 2008/1912 and SI 2008/1913 respectively. These two statutory instruments are reproduced in full in **Appendices C** and **D**.

Those familiar with the Companies Act will recognise that many of the requirements of CA 2006 in relation to the accounts and audit of companies are also applicable to LLPs. As a quick reference guide, **Appendix B** sets out which sections of Pt. 15 'Accounts and Reports' and Pt. 16 'Audit' of CA 2006 are applicable to LLPs. However, as there have been some amendments to sections, to ensure that they are appropriately worded for LLPs reference should always be made to SI 2008/1911 for the amended text for each of the CA 2006 sections which are applicable to LLPs.

This book brings the legislation currently in force up to date to December 2015, having regard, where possible, to known or anticipated changes in the law or accounting standards and practice. Changes under consideration are covered in **Chapter 13**.

1.3 New UK GAAP and FRS 102

The UK Financial Reporting Council (FRC) has issued a suite of new standards to replace all existing UK general accounting standards for periods commencing on or after 1 January 2015. The main standard applicable to all LLPs, other than those preparing their accounts in accordance with the FRSSE (see below), is FRS 102 *The Financial Reporting Standard applicable in the UK and Republic of Ireland*. The key changes and impact on LLPs from the adoption of FRS 102 are set out in **Chapter 14**.

Following the issue of FRS 102, the LLP SORP was also updated with effect from the same date, to apply the requirements of the new standard in areas of specific concern to LLPs.

1.4 Financial Reporting Standard for Smaller Entities (FRSSE)

To reduce the burden for smaller entities of considering and complying with the requirements relating to large entities while producing clear financial reporting, the FRC issued the FRSSE. The current version of the FRSSE is the amended version issued by the FRC in July 2013, effective January 2015. The key impact on a set of LLP accounts of adopting the FRSSE is discussed in **Chapter 8**.

The FRSSE applies to all smaller entities (as defined) – including LLPs – which prepare accounts showing a true and fair view and which choose to adopt the stand-alone document containing all the relevant standards. In essence, the FRSSE aims to be a 'one-stop shop FRSSE' in the sense of incorporating all relevant existing requirements of small entities legislation and including, for example, statutory accounts formats.

For companies, the FRSSE has been withdrawn for periods commencing on or after 1 January 2016. This is likely to also apply the LLPs from the same date (see **Chapter 13**).

1.5   International Accounting Standards

In July 2003, the UK Government announced its intention to permit (but not require) all companies subject to CA 2006 (other than those automatically covered by the EU Regulation) to use International Accounting Standards as an alternative to UK domestic accounting standards. This option also applied to LLPs; however, only a very limited number of LLPs have adopted IASs.

The impact of international accounting standards is explained more fully in **Chapter 3** (for IAS generally).

1.6   Changes for 2016

In November 2015, the Government issued a consultation on proposed changes to the financial reporting regime for LLPs for periods commencing on or after 1 January 2016 (it is likely that some early adoption will be permitted). In addition, there is a separate consultation on the audit requirements for companies, the results of which are expected to also be applied to LLPs. The expected effects of these proposals are considered in **Chapter 13**.

Chapter 2 General accounting provisions

2.1 Introduction

This chapter summarises the accounting provisions which are applicable to LLP accounts including the prescriptive formats of accounts, the content of accounts and principles and rules for determining amounts to be included in the accounts.

The chapter summarises accounts provisions of CA 2006, as applied to LLPs insofar as they relate to accounts (individual accounts) which the members of the LLP have a duty to prepare. 'Abbreviated' accounts (modified statutory accounts) are considered separately in **Chapter 6**. Matters relating to groups headed by LLPs are covered in **Chapter 7**.

Annual accounts may be prepared:

- as 'non-IAS individual accounts' (CA 2006, s. 396) or 'non-IAS group accounts' (CA 2006, s. 404); or
- in accordance with international accounting standards (IAS individual accounts or IAS group accounts).

The LLP SORP applies to non-IAS individual and group accounts but not to IAS accounts. Unless otherwise indicated, this chapter summarises and comments upon the accounts provisions for non-IAS accounts set out in the Regulations.

2.2 Accounts

Full accounts must be prepared for all LLPs, irrespective of size.

s. 394

The full accounts of a 'small' LLP, however, may be less detailed with reduced disclosure requirements (see **Chapter 5**). A small LLP may also take advantage of the FRSSE (being replaced by FRS 102 section 1A) (see **Chapters 3** and **13**).

An LLP qualifying as 'small' or 'medium-sized' (see **Chapter 4**) may, in addition, prepare 'abbreviated' accounts for filing with the Registrar of Companies.

LLP accounts are produced from the entity's underlying financial records (adequate accounting records) as explained at **2.8** (CA 2006, s. 386–389 'Accounting Records').

Table 2.1 Individual accounts (s. 396)

Non-IAS individual accounts must comprise a balance sheet (as at the last day of the financial year) which gives a true and fair view of the state of affairs of the LLP and a profit and loss account which gives a true and fair view of the profit or loss of the LLP for the financial year.

The form and content of the accounts and the notes to the accounts must comply with the provisions of reg. 3 of SI 2008/1912 or reg. 3 and 4 of SI 2008/1913. The LLP should also comply with the disclosure requirements of the LLP SORP. Where there are any contradictions between the Regulations and the LLP SORP, the Regulations take precedence.

2.3   'True and fair' view

There is a fundamental requirement for full accounts (individual accounts or group accounts) to show a 'true and fair' view. The members of an LLP must not approve accounts unless they are satisfied that they give a true and fair view of the LLP's assets, liabilities, financial position and profit or loss.

s. 393

The requirement for full accounts to show a 'true and fair' view applies irrespective of whether or not the accounts are subject to audit. Any decision concerning the method of accounting or means of disclosing information must take this basic requirement into account.

The basic accounting principle is that annual accounts should show a 'true and fair' view, a term that has never been defined in statute or case law.

In essence, accounts are deemed to present a 'true and fair view' if they:

- comply with any relevant legislation or regulatory requirement;
- comply with accounting standards and generally accepted accounting practice (GAAP – see **Chapter 3**);
- provide an unbiased (fair and reasonable) presentation;
- are compiled with sufficient accuracy within the bounds of materiality; and
- faithfully represent the underlying commercial activity (the concept of 'substance over legal form').

The requirement for accounts to give a 'true and fair view' is also embodied within European Accounting Directives. In the case of IAS accounts, there is a requirement under International Accounting Standards that such accounts must achieve a 'fair presentation'.

'True and fair view accounts' (not a statutory term or specifically defined but used in this book for convenience) are financial statements intended to give a true and fair view of the financial position and profit or loss (or income and expenditure) of an entity.

A 'true and fair view' is required to be given of the state of affairs of the LLP (and/or consolidated undertakings) as at the end of the financial year and of the profit or loss of the LLP (and/or consolidated undertakings so far as concerns members of the parent entity) for the financial year.

Where compliance with the provisions of the Regulations as to the matters to be included in 'annual accounts' ('individual accounts' or 'group accounts') or the notes would not be sufficient to give a true and fair view, the necessary additional information must be given in the accounts or in a note to them.

If, in special circumstances, such compliance with any of the provisions of the Regulations is inconsistent with the requirement to show a 'true and fair view', the members must depart from the relevant provision to the extent necessary to show a 'true and fair view' and must explain the particulars of any such departure in a note to the accounts (the true and fair 'override' principle).

The 'true and fair view' has the ultimate legal override; an entity may override accounting standards only to give a 'true and fair view' and this would be only in exceptional circumstances. A departure from an accounting standard must be justified and explained.

2.4   Format of accounts

The form and content of accounts is governed by the Regulations made under CA 2006, which apply the Companies Act to LLPs.

The form and content of non-IAS individual accounts is determined in accordance with:

- SI 2008/1912 (*Small Limited Liability Partnerships (Accounts) Regulations* 2008) for small LLPs; and
- SI 2008/1913 (*Large and Medium-sized Limited Liability Partnerships (Accounts) Regulations* 2008) for medium-sized and large LLPs.

SI 2008/1912 and SI 2008/1913 are set out in full in **Appendices C and D** and they are discussed in greater detail in **Chapter 5**.

Schedules within SI 2008/1912 and SI 2008/1913 prescribe the required formats from which an LLP may choose for non-IAS individual and group accounts. Formats which are most commonly used are illustrated in **Chapter 5**. There are additional disclosure requirements for LLPs which are set out in the LLP SORP; these are discussed in **Chapter 8**.

Once a format has been adopted, the LLP must use the same format for subsequent years unless, in the members' opinion, there are special reasons for changing; these must be disclosed in the year of change. *Sch 1.2*

Every balance sheet and profit and loss account must show the items listed in the adopted format, if they apply either in the financial year or the preceding year. *Sch 1.1*

Adopting a particular format is not as restricting as it may seem, as there are a variety of options, for example: *Sch 1.3*

- departure is allowed if it is made to ensure a true and fair view (see above); *Sch 1.10(2)*
- certain arabic numbered headings may be combined (provided combination is disclosed); *Sch 1.4*
- immaterial items may be disregarded;
- information can be given in greater detail than prescribed and items not listed in a format may be included; and
- certain information may be given in notes instead of on the face of the accounts.

Where there is no amount to be shown for a format item for the financial year, a heading or sub-heading corresponding to the item must not be included, unless an amount can be shown for the item in question for the immediately preceding financial year under the relevant format heading or sub-heading. *Sch 1.5*

For every balance sheet or profit and loss account item, the corresponding amount for the immediately preceding financial year must also be shown. Where that corresponding preceding year amount is not comparable, the former amount may be adjusted, but particulars of the non-comparability and of any adjustment must be disclosed in a note to the accounts. *Sch 1.7*

Every profit and loss account must show the amount of an LLP's profit or loss on ordinary activities before taxation (See **5.5**). *Sch 1.6*

2.5 Accounting principles

Accounts are required to be prepared in accordance with the principles set out in the Regulations. These principles are the fundamental accounting concepts that underlie accounts and are also incorporated within accounting standards (FRS 102 for LLPs generally or Section 1A of FRS 102 (to replace the FRSSE) for small LLPs adopting it). *Sch 1.10-15*

The basic statutory accounting principles are as follows:

- *Going concern* – The reporting entity is to be presumed to be carrying on business as a going concern.
- *Consistency* – Accounting policies must be applied consistently within the same accounts and from one financial year to the next.

- *Prudence* – The amount of any item must be determined on a prudent basis.
- *Accruals* – All income and charges relating to the financial year to which the accounts relate must be taken into account, without regard to the date of receipt or payment.

Sch 1.15
- *Individual determination* – In determining the aggregate amount of any item, the amount of each individual asset or liability that is taken into account must be determined separately.
- *Netting* – Amounts in respect of items representing assets or income must not be set off against amounts in respect of items representing liabilities or expenditure (as the case may be), or vice

Sch 1.8
versa.
- *Substance of transactions* – In determining how amounts are presented within the accounts, regard should be had to the substance of the reported transaction or arrangement in accordance

Sch 1.9
with GAAP.

With regard to prudence, the basic principle is that unrealised profits are not included in the profit and loss account for the year but unrealised losses are (Sch. 1.13). However, this is modified in respect of financial instruments, investment properties and living animals and plants to allow unrealised profits in respect of these to be included in the profit and loss account (Sch. 1.40).

If it appears to the LLP's members that there are special reasons for departing from any of the accounting principles in preparing the LLP's accounts in respect of any financial year, they may do so. Particulars of the departure, the reasons for it and its effect must be given in a note to the accounts.

FRS 102
FRSSE
Accounting standards enhance the above principles by determining that accounting policies adopted should be relevant, reliable, comparable and understandable.

For fixed assets, stocks, investments and goodwill, rules regarding valuation, accounting and *Sch 1.17–29* disclosure are laid down in the Regulations.

Historical cost principles are stated as the normal method of accounting but alternative bases (e.g. revaluation and current cost) are allowed provided that details and related historical cost figures *Sch 1.30–35* are disclosed. The 'alternative accounting rules' are illustrated in **Appendix A section 6**.

In principle, the regulations only allow 'realised' profits to be included in the profit and loss account, however, where fair values are used, the unrealised gains on these can also be included.

Sch 1.36–41 Financial instruments, including derivatives, may be included at fair value.

It should be noted, however, that LLPs adopting 'fair value accounting' rules cannot apply the FRSSE, although this does not preclude accounting for fixed assets and investments at valuation.

2.6 Members' report – requirements

For a company, the requirement to prepare a Directors' Report is set out in CA 2006, s. 415. However, as shown in SI 2008/1911 (*Limited Liability Partnership (Accounts and Audit) (Application of Companies Act 2006) Regulations* 2008), s. 415 of the Act is not applied to LLPs. Previous versions of the LLP SORP included a requirement to prepare a Members' Report. This requirement has been removed from the current version, however, certain information which was previously required to be disclosed in the Members' Report is still required and the LLP SORP suggests the voluntary inclusion of a Members' Report as one way in which this could be achieved.

Large and medium-sized companies are also required to prepare a Strategic Report, however, this requirement has not been extended to LLPs either by the legislation or in the LLP SORP.

2.7 Group accounts

A parent entity (other than a small parent entity (see **7.1**)) which has 'subsidiary undertakings' is required (with certain exceptions) to prepare group accounts in the form of consolidated accounts of the parent entity and its subsidiary undertakings, as if they were a single entity.

Group accounts (when prepared) are required to comply with the provisions of CA 2006 as applied to LLPs as to the form and content of consolidated accounts and additional information to be given.

Regulations under CA 2006 provided by SI 2008/1912, Sch. 4 (Small LLPs) and SI 2008/1913, Sch. 3 (large and medium-sized LLPs), require the following accounting for consolidations:

- elimination of group transactions;
- provisions for acquisition and merger accounting;
- treatment and disclosure of 'minority interests'; and
- joint ventures and associated undertakings.

CA 2006 sets out certain circumstances under which subsidiary undertakings may be excluded from consolidation. However, FRS 102 sets out requirements for how these exemptions are to be used, with the result that a subsidiary may be excluded from consolidation on the grounds of immateriality and *must* be excluded in the following circumstances: *s. 405(2)*

- severe long-term restrictions; or   *FRS 102*
- temporary control – holding with a view to subsequent resale.   *Para 9.9*

FRS 102 does not allow the exclusion of a subsidiary because the information necessary for the preparation of the consolidated accounts cannot be obtained without disproportionate expense or   *FRS 102* undue delay, unless its inclusion is immaterial.   *Para 9.8A*

The exemptions available for small and medium-sized groups are explained in **Chapter 7**.

Exemptions otherwise available for groups generally are under:

- CA 2006, s. 400 (LLP included in EEA accounts of larger group);
- CA 2006, s. 401 (LLP included in non-EEA accounts of larger group); and
- CA 2006, s. 402 (LLP where no subsidiary undertakings need be included in the consolidation).

2.8 Adequate accounting records

Every LLP is required to keep 'adequate accounting records' in accordance with CA 2006, s. 386. LLP accounts are produced from these underlying financial records.

CA 2006, s. 386 as applied to LLPs is summarised in **Table 2.2**.

> **Table 2.2   Adequate accounting records**
>
> An LLP is required to keep accounting records ('adequate accounting records') which are sufficient to show and explain the LLP's transactions. The accounting records must:
>
> - disclose with reasonable accuracy, *at any time*, the financial position of the LLP *at that time*;
>
> - enable the members of the LLP to ensure that any accounts required to be prepared comply with the requirements of the Act;
>
> - contain entries from day to day of all receipts and expenditure (with sufficient identifying detail); and
> - contain a record of assets and liabilities of the LLP.
>
> If the LLP deals in goods, the accounting records must also contain statements of:
>
> - stock held at the year end;
>
> - stocktaking (records and procedures) underlying the year end stock; and
> - all goods sold and purchased (except for retail sales), in sufficient detail to identify the goods and the buyers and sellers.
>
> A parent entity must ensure that any subsidiary undertaking also keeps such accounting records.

Accounting records are required by CA 2006, s. 388(4) to be preserved for three years from the date on which they are made although, having regard to other legislation, it is generally considered that documents should be kept for at least six years (and 12 years in the event of contracts under seal).

2.9   Approval and signature of accounts

The members' report, statutory accounts and the auditor's report all require appropriate approval and signature.

s. 414   An LLP's annual accounts must be approved by the members and signed on behalf of the members by a designated member of the LLP. The signature must be on the LLP's individual balance sheet and the name of the signatory must be stated.

For a company, there is a requirement in CA 2006 for the directors' report to be signed by a director or the company secretary. As s. 419 of CA 2006 does not apply to LLPs, there is no similar requirement for the members' report where an LLP chooses to produce one. However, the general convention which is followed is that the members' report is signed and dated by the designated member who signs the balance sheet. As with the balance sheet, their name should also be printed.

s. 450(3)   The above requirements also apply to the approval and members' signature of abbreviated accounts.

s. 503   The auditor's report must state the name of the auditor and be signed and dated. Where the auditor is an individual, the report must be signed by him or her. Where the auditor is a firm, the report delivered to the members must be signed by the senior statutory auditor in his or her own name, for and on behalf of the firm of auditors.

s. 414(3)   The balance sheet of a small LLP which has been prepared in accordance with the provisions for LLPs subject to the small LLPs regime must contain a statement by the members to that effect in a prominent position above the signature (see **5.10**).

2.10 Publication of statutory and non-statutory accounts

If an LLP publishes any of its statutory accounts, they must be accompanied by the auditor's report on those accounts (unless the LLP is exempt from audit and the members have taken advantage of that exemption). An LLP that prepares statutory group accounts for a financial year must not publish its statutory individual accounts for that year without also publishing with them its statutory group accounts

s.434

If an LLP publishes non-statutory accounts, it must publish with them a statement indicating:

s. 435(1)

- that they are not the LLP's statutory accounts;
- whether statutory accounts dealing with any financial year with which the non-statutory accounts purport to deal have been delivered to the Registrar of Companies; and
- whether an auditor's report has been made on the LLP's statutory accounts for any such financial year, and if so whether the report:
  - (a) was qualified or unqualified, or included a reference to any matters to which the auditor drew attention by way of emphasis without qualifying the report; or
  - (b) contained a statement under s. 498(2) (accounting records or returns inadequate or accounts not agreeing with records and returns), or s. 498(3) (failure to obtain necessary information and explanations).

An LLP must not publish with any non-statutory accounts the auditor's report (i.e. a full audit report) on the LLP's statutory accounts.

s. 435(2)

'Non-statutory accounts' are accounts or other published financial information that are not the LLP's statutory accounts, e.g. simplified accounting information such as an account in any form purporting to be a balance sheet or profit and loss account relating to the financial year of an LLP or group.

s. 435(3)

Chapter 3 Accounts and accounting standards

3.1 Basic contents of financial statements

Section 2 of FRS 102 sets out the concepts and pervasive principles that underlie the preparation and presentation of financial statements. This states that the objective of financial statements is:

> 'to provide information about the financial position, performance and cash flows of an entity that is useful for economic decision-making by a broad range of users who are not in a position to demand reports tailored to meet their particular information needs.' (FRS 102 para 2.2)

To meet this objective, accounting information is normally presented in the form of a structured set of financial statements comprising:

* primary statements; and
* supporting notes, related to the primary statements.

Together these will form the true and fair view 'accounts' (as the term is used in this book).

3.2 Primary statements

As set out in the LLP SORP, the primary statements within a set of LLP accounts comprise (SORP para. 26):

* a statement of financial position;
* either:
  - a single statement of comprehensive income displaying all items of income and expense recognised during the period including those items recognised in determining profit or loss and items of other comprehensive income; or
  - a separate income statement and a separate statement of comprehensive income;
* a statement of changes in equity;
* a statement of cash flows.

The names of the financial statements are based on those used in FRS 102, however LLPs are allowed to use other names for the statements, provided these are not misleading. Therefore, they can continue to use balance sheet (for the statement of financial position) and profit and loss account (for the income statement).

It should be noted that the FRSSE requires presentation of a separate profit and loss account and statement of total recognised gains and losses, so LLPs adopting the FRSSE will not be able to combine these.

Notes to the financial statements amplify or explain items in the primary statements (for example, principal accounting policies).

The formats of the primary statements, as they apply to LLPs, are determined as in **Table 3.1**.

Table 3.1   Formats of the primary statements under FRS 102

Primary statements	Format
Financial performance	
Income statement (profit and loss account)	Small LLPs regime – SI 2008/1912, Sch. 1 (Small LLPs) amplified by FRS 102 and the LLP SORP
	Large and Medium-sized – SI 2008/1913, Sch. 1 (Large and medium-sized LLPs) amplified by FRS 102 and the LLP SORP
Other comprehensive income	FRS 102
(These may be combined into a single statement of comprehensive income)	
Financial position	
Balance sheet	Small LLPs regime – SI 2008/1912, Sch. 1 (Small LLPs) amplified by FRS 102 and the LLP SORP
	Large and Medium-sized – SI 2008/1913, Sch. 1 (Large and medium-sized LLPs) amplified by FRS 102 and the LLP SORP
Cash flow	
Statement of cash flows	FRS 102 and the LLP SORP

Table 3.2   Formats of the primary statements under the FRSSE

Primary statements	Format
Financial performance	
Profit and loss account	SI 2008/1912, Sch. 1 (Small LLPs) amplified by the FRSSE and the LLP SORP
Statement of total recognised gains and losses	FRSSE
(These must be shown as separate statements)	
Financial position	
Balance sheet	SI 2008/1912, Sch. 1 (Small LLPs) amplified by the FRSSE and the LLP SORP
Cash flow	
Cash flow statement (voluntary)	FRSSE and the LLP SORP

3.3   Other comprehensive income

Other comprehensive income includes those items, being gains or losses that are recognised in the period, which do not pass through the profit and loss account. Gains, such as revaluation surpluses on fixed assets (other than investment properties) that are recognised but are not necessarily realised in the period, are dealt with in this statement. In the FRSSE these are required to be shown in a separate primary statement called the statement of total recognised gains and losses.

3.4 Statement of changes in equity

FRS 102 requires a statement of changes in equity, showing movements in the components of the LLP's equity to be presented as a primary statement. See **Chapter 8** for details of which elements of members' interests are classified as equity.

As an alternative to presenting a statement showing only changes in equity, the LLP SORP allows LLPs to present a reconciliation of members' interests, showing changes in all elements of members' interests (including those classified as liabilities), providing that the equity interests are separately identified in the statement.

In either case, an equivalent statement for the comparative year must also be included.

3.5 Statement of cash flows

FRS 102 in section 7 requires, with exceptions, all entities producing true and fair view accounts to include a statement of cash flows within the accounts.

Small LLPs are exempt from the requirement to produce a statement of cash flows (but are, nevertheless 'encouraged' by the FRSSE to provide such a statement on a voluntary disclosure basis). Subsidiary undertakings, provided that consolidated financial statements in which the subsidiary undertakings are included are publicly available, are also exempted (see **14.3.10**). However, FRS 102 makes the exemption for subsidiaries conditional on the 'shareholders' being informed that the entity intends to use the exemption and objections not having been received from the holders of 5% of the entity's allotted shares or 50% of those not held by the parent. For an LLP the reference to shareholders should be read as referring to the members.

FRS 102 para 1.12(b)

A parent LLP preparing consolidated accounts can also take exemption from presenting its own statement of cash flows on the same basis as for subsidiaries above. However, it must include a consolidated statement of cash flows.

The parent entity of a small group, entitled to the exemption from preparing group accounts, is (subject to the voluntary provisions of the FRSSE, if applicable) exempted from preparing a statement of cash flows (whether its own individual statement or a consolidated one), whether or not group accounts are actually prepared.

Medium-sized and large LLPs, and small ineligible LLPs (including, for example, a banking LLP or insurance company or certain authorised entities under FSMA 2000), are required to prepare a statement of cash flows in accordance with FRS 102.

The form of a statement of cash flows, including the guidance from the LLP SORP is set out in **Chapter 5 (Table 5.6)**.

3.6 Accounting standards

3.6.1 True and Fair

The basic accounting principle (and statutory requirement) is that annual accounts should show a 'true and fair' view, a term that has never been defined precisely in statute or case law, although eminent authority has been given over the years in the form of legal opinion.

To provide a 'true and fair view', in all but highly exceptional cases, requires compliance with UK accounting standards.

UK tax legislation requires that the profits of a trade, profession or vocation be computed in accordance with generally accepted accounting practice on an accounting basis which gives a true and fair view, subject to any adjustment required by tax law in computing those profits.

3.6.2 Accounting standards

s. 464

Accounting standards are defined as 'such standards as are, in accordance with their terms, relevant to the LLP's circumstances and to the accounts'.

For the purposes of LLPs the term 'Accounting standards' means the financial reporting standards issued by the FRC. For periods commencing on or after 1 January 2015 there are seven accounting standards in issue: FRS 100, 101, 102, 103, 104, 105 and the FRSSE; however, the main accounting standards that LLPs will refer to are the FRSSE (for small LLPs which choose to adopt it) and FRS 102.

'Accounting standards', in the context of this chapter, are UK (FRC) accounting standards considered on the basis discussed in **3.6.1**, particularly the requirement to show a 'true and fair' view of its state of affairs at the balance sheet date and of its profit or loss (or income and expenditure) for the financial period ending on that date.

In its *Foreword to Accounting Standards (March 2015)*, the FRC has stated that:

> 'Accounting standards are applicable to the financial statements of a reporting entity that are required to give a true and fair view of its financial position at the reporting date and of its profit or loss (or income and expenditure) for the reporting period.'.

Accounting standards do not need to be applied to items judged to be immaterial.

In preparing accounts giving a true and fair view, an LLP should therefore follow as applicable the requirements of the FRSSE or FRS 102 and any other accounting standard unless there are good reasons for not doing so.

Recent years have seen a programme of increasing convergence (that is, harmonisation) of domestic UK and international (including US) financial reporting on the basis of globally accepted accounting standards (see **3.8**).

The Regulations require individual accounts, other than those prepared by small or medium-sized LLPs, to state whether they have been prepared in accordance with applicable accounting standards and to give particulars of any material departure from those standards and the reasons for it. The reference to disclosing that the accounts have been prepared in accordance with applicable accounting standards is contained in paragraph 45 of SI 2008/1913, Sch. 1 *Large and Medium-sized Limited Liability Partnerships (Accounts) Regulations* 2008, however there are exemptions for medium-sized LLPs which are set out in reg. 4(2) of SI 2008/1913.

An LLP subject to the small LLPs regime may choose to adopt the FRSSE instead of FRS 102 which is more appropriate to larger entities (see **Chapter 8**).

3.6.3 Generally accepted accounting practice (GAAP)

There is no precise technical or legal definition of 'GAAP' in the UK. 'Generally accepted' means a practice that is accepted by accountants generally as being permissible in the particular circumstances of a business – the practice may not necessarily be the 'best' or 'only' accounting method available. GAAP may therefore be regarded as encompassing:

- accounting principles contained in 'Accounting Standards';
- Companies Acts and supporting regulations;
- industry-specific accounting treatments, including SORPs; and

- any other acceptable accounting treatment, including treatments for which there is currently no adopted Accounting Standard.

3.6.4 Statement of Recommended Practice, Accounting by Limited Liability Partnerships ('the LLP SORP')

Certain industries or sectors have distinguishing features such that it is appropriate to have guidance issued on how to interpret accounting standards for those special circumstances. LLPs are one such case. In the UK, such guidance is issued by way of a Statement of Recommended Practice (SORP), interpreting UK accounting standards for those special circumstances.

SORPs are not issued by the FRC itself, they are issued by an appropriate body that the FRC authorises for the purpose. SORPs are not 'approved' by the FRC but a SORP should contain a 'negative assurance' statement from the FRC that it (the FRC) has no reservations concerning the contents of a SORP.'

SORPs have been issued for, amongst others, LLPs, charities, pension schemes, banks, insurance companies and the oil and gas industry.

SORPs set out recommended practice, both in terms of accounting and disclosure, and although their application is not strictly mandatory, FRS 100 *Application of Financial Reporting Requirements* makes it quite clear that entities are expected to follow a SORP where one exists for the particular industry or business sector.

The LLP SORP is unusual in that it does not apply to a particular industry or sector but rather a type of business entity.

The body responsible for the development of the LLP SORP is the Consultative Committee of Accountancy Bodies (CCAB).

The CCAB is the umbrella organisation for the five major accountancy bodies in the UK:

- the Institute of Chartered Accountants in England and Wales (ICAEW);
- the Institute of Chartered Accountants of Scotland (ICAS);
- the Institute of Chartered Accountants in Ireland (ICAI);
- the Association of Chartered Certified Accountants (ACCA); and
- the Chartered Institute of Public Finance Accountants (CIPFA).

The LLP SORP provides guidance for LLPs on the application of UK GAAP and the accounting requirements of the Companies Act as applied to LLPs.

The LLP SORP was first published in May 2002, a year after LLPs were introduced as a corporate body. The SORP has been updated several times to provide further guidance for LLPs on changes to UK GAAP since the SORP was first published. The most recent edition, taking account of the issue of FRS 102 and the FRSSE (2015) was published in July 2014 and is effective for years commencing on or after 1 January 2015.

The LLP SORP should not be used as a standalone document as it does not contain all the disclosure requirements that relate to LLPs. In the event of any conflict, accounting standards or the provisions of the Companies Act take precedence over the LLP SORP.

FRS 100 requires that where financial statements comply with a SORP this fact should be stated, together with the name of the SORP.

If an LLP decides it is not going to comply with all the recommended treatments and disclosures set out in the LLP SORP, FRS 100 requires the entity to give a brief description of how the financial statements depart from the recommended practice set out in the SORP, which shall include:

(a) for any treatment that is not in accordance with the SORP, the reasons why the treatment adopted is judged more appropriate to the entity's particular circumstances; and

(b) brief details of any disclosures recommended by the SORP that have not been provided, and the reasons why they have not been provided.

For the avoidance of doubt, the LLP SORP does not carry any authority within the IFRS framework although it may still provide useful guidance in the interpretation of IFRS, particularly as UK GAAP and IFRS become more aligned.

Chapter 8 contains more detail of accounting treatments recommended by the LLP SORP.

3.7 Application of accounting standards to smaller LLPs

It is frequently recognised that the burden of complying with accounting standards falls proportionally more heavily upon the smaller entities. While it is correct that the *principles* of accounting (in terms of accounting methods and treatment, measurement criteria and estimation techniques) should apply equally to all LLPs, the application of certain accounting standards (particularly their disclosure requirements) is seen as inappropriate, cost-inefficient, immaterial or simply not applicable to small LLPs. Alleviation is achieved in three ways:

- exemptions and concessions;
- the small LLPs regime; and
- the FRSSE.

Under UK GAAP prior to the introduction of FRS 102 small LLPs which chose not to use the FRSSE were still entitled to various disclosure exemptions. These exemptions, other than the statutory exemption from the requirement to prepare consolidated accounts (see **Chapter 7**), have not been carried forward into FRS 102. Therefore small LLPs which, for example, wish to continue not to include a statement of cash flows may need to adopt the FRSSE.

However, for periods commencing on or after 1 January 2016 significant exemptions from the disclosure requirements in FRS 102 have been introduced in conjunction with the withdrawal of the FRSSE. The Government intends to issue regulations to allow LLPs to choose to adopt these early (see **Chapter 13**).

A small LLP can alternatively choose to adopt the stand-alone FRSSE. However, an LLP is not able to take advantage of the significant exemptions which now exist for the smallest companies – the so-called micro-entities – however, the Government intends to introduce this option.

A small or medium-sized LLP is not required to state in its non-IAS individual accounts whether they have been prepared in accordance with applicable accounting standards and to give particulars of and reasons for any material departure from those standards. However, this exemption relates only to disclosure – it does not diminish in any way the obligation of a small or medium-sized LLP to adopt and comply with appropriate accounting standards.

3.7.1 Accounting standards and the FRSSE

While the principles of accounting standards explained in the earlier part of this chapter apply to LLPs generally, small LLPs can currently have regard to the single Financial Reporting Standard for Smaller Entities (FRSSE).

The FRSSE is designed to provide smaller entities with a single accounting standard that is focused on their particular circumstances. The FRSSE applies to all smaller entities (as defined) which prepare true and fair view accounts and which choose to adopt the FRSSE. Generally, accounts complying with the SORP of a particular industry or sector should not, however, be prepared in accordance with the FRSSE, other than in the circumstances specified in the SORP.

As noted in the LLP SORP, LLPs can opt to apply the FRSSE and in the event of conflicting requirements, those in the Regulations or accounting standards (including the FRSSE) should take precedence over the SORP. The SORP should not be interpreted as removing or not permitting exemptions for certain smaller entities in legislation or accounting standards, including those from the need to prepare group accounts or cash flow statements.

On other matters, the SORP sometimes includes references to specific sections of FRS 102. Those preparing financial statements in accordance with the FRSSE should interpret these as referring to the related requirements that are generally included in the FRSSE. In particular, LLPs entitled to use the FRSSE should note that while the main part of the requirements of section 22 of FRS 102 have not been incorporated into the FRSSE, the definition of financial liabilities and a requirement to present those separately from equity (paragraph 12.1 of the FRSSE) have been included and these are important for the accounting for members' participation rights.

With certain exceptions, for example small groups, compliance with the FRSSE grants exemption from other accounting standards. Nevertheless, in the absence of guidance on a particular accounting practice within the FRSSE, the FRC stated that the preparers and auditors of accounts of small entities should have regard to FRSs (including FRS 102) , not as mandatory documents, but as a means of establishing current accepted accounting practice (FRSSE Appendix IV para. 41).

3.8 International Accounting Standards

3.8.1 Arrival of IAS

The year 2005 saw the arrival of an EU requirement to adopt international accounting standards (IAS). Recent years have seen a continuing programme aiming at convergence (that is, harmonisation) of domestic UK, international and US financial reporting on the basis of globally accepted accounting standards.

Despite the fact that changes from 2005 onwards (in the UK) have impacted primarily on the consolidated accounts of quoted (that is, publicly traded) groups of companies, there has been an inevitability about the cascading effect of international harmonisation so that all companies and LLPs, including small companies and LLPs, will sooner or later have to embrace new procedures or principles. The content of FRS 100 *Application of Financial Reporting Requirements*, FRS 101 *Reduced Disclosure Framework* and FRS 102 *The Financial Reporting Standard applicable in the UK and Republic of Ireland* confirm that UK GAAP will continue, albeit in a different form, although one which has been derived from international GAAP, for the foreseeable future.

3.8.2 IAS accounts and the option to choose

Within the UK, SI 2004/2947 (*Companies Act 1985 (International Accounting Standards and Other Accounting Amendments) Regulations* 2004) implemented changes to bring UK accounting into line with EU requirements. The changes applied to financial years beginning on or after 1 January 2005 and the adoption of IAS can now be broadly illustrated as in **Table 3.3**.

Table 3.3   The adoption of IAS accounts by British companies and LLPs

	IAS accounts	Non IAS accounts
Group accounts of publicly traded companies (trading on an EU regulated market)	Required	Not permitted
	Permitted (if not otherwise required by EU regulation)	Required (unless IAS accounts adopted)
Non-publicly traded companies	Permitted	Required (unless IAS accounts adopted)
Limited Liability Partnerships	Permitted	Required (unless IAS accounts adopted)
Incorporated charities	Not Permitted	Required

As part of the preparations for adoption of the new financial reporting framework set out in FRS 100, CA 2006, s. 395 was amended by the *Companies and Limited Liability Partnerships (Accounts and Audit Exemptions and Change of Accounting Framework) Regulations* 2012 (SI 2012/2301) such that for financial years ending on or after 1 October 2012, LLPs that have voluntarily converted to IAS accounts in previous periods may choose to revert back to preparing non IAS (UK GAAP) accounts (provided they have not changed to non IAS accounts in the period of five years preceding the first day of that financial year (s. 395(4))). Prior to this a change to IAS accounts was (with certain exceptions) largely irrevocable; reverting to non IAS accounts was only allowed in special circumstances.

Small LLPs (as defined) should be alert to various factors if considering a move to full IAS accounts:

- no equivalent exemptions as afforded by CA 2006 or the FRSSE are available under IAS;
- the determinants to define a 'small LLP' are different within IAS formats;
- abbreviated accounts are not available for filing (although a small entity is not required to file its IAS profit and loss account); and
- exemptions concerning audit exemption and group accounts continue to be available.

3.9   The new financial reporting framework for small LLPs

The Government has announced that the new framework to be applied by small UK companies for periods commencing on or after 1 January 2016 will be extended to LLPs. This is discussed in **Chapter 13**.

Chapter 4 Size classification for LLPs

4.1 The 'small limited liability partnerships regime'

CA 2006 as applied to limited liability partnerships by the *Limited Liability Partnerships (Accounts and Audit) (Application of Companies Act 2006) Regulations* 2008, provides for different provisions to apply in certain respects to different kinds of LLP. As far as the smaller LLP is concerned, the main distinction is between:

- LLPs subject to the 'small limited liability partnerships regime'; and *s. 381*
- other LLPs (LLPs that are not subject to that regime). *s. 380(3)*

The small LLPs regime applies to an LLP for a financial year in relation to which the LLP:

- qualifies as small; and *s. 382-383*
- is not excluded from the regime. *s. 384*

The small limited liability partnerships regime does not apply to the following LLPs: *s. 384(1)*

(a) an LLP whose securities are admitted to trading on a regulated market in an EEA State;

(b) an LLP that:
  (i) is an authorised insurance company*, a banking LLP, an e-money issuer, a MiFID investment firm or a UCITS management company, or
  (ii) carries on insurance market activity, or

(c) a member of an ineligible group**.

* As defined by FSMA 2000, s. 316(3) 'insurance market activity' means a regulated activity relating to contracts of insurance written at Lloyd's.

** A group is ineligible if any of its members is a public company, a body corporate (other than a company) whose shares are admitted to trading on a regulated market in an EEA State, a person (other than a small company or small LLP) who has permission under Pt. 4A of FSMA 2000 to carry on a regulated activity, a small company or small LLP that is an authorised insurance company, a banking company or banking LLP, an e-money issuer, a MiFID investment firm or a UCITS management company, or a person who carries on insurance market activity.

4.2 Qualifying conditions – 'small' and 'medium-sized' LLPs

Two classifications of LLPs – 'small' and 'medium-sized' – are entitled to certain provisions with regard to the contents of the statutory accounts for filing with the Registrar of Companies.

Companies Act 2006, s. 382(3) and 465(3) set out the conditions to be met by an LLP to qualify as 'small' or 'medium-sized' as appropriate.

s. 382(3) and
s. 465(3)

An LLP is currently treated as small or medium-sized if it does not exceed more than one of the following criteria:

	Small	Medium-sized
Turnover	£6.5m	£25.9m
Balance sheet total	£3.26m	£12.9m
Average number of employees (on a monthly basis)	50	250

s. 382(4) and
s. 465(4)

Turnover figures should be proportionately adjusted where the financial 'year' is not in fact 12 months.

s. 382(5) and
s. 465(5)

'Balance sheet total' means the aggregate of the amounts shown as assets in the LLP's balance sheet (i.e. gross assets before deduction of liabilities, accruals and provisions; that is, the aggregate of headings A to C in Format 1 or the 'Assets' headings in Format 2).

As a general rule, for an LLP to qualify as small or medium-sized, the criteria must be met for the current and previous year. If the criteria are not met for the following year, an LLP may continue to be treated as small or medium-sized, as appropriate, for that year. However, if the criteria are not met in the year after that, then the LLP must file accounts according to its size.

4.3   Small LLP size criteria examples

In order to demonstrate the 'drop in-drop out' rules, where an LLP must fail to meet the size criteria for two years in a row before moving up to being a medium-sized LLP, it is helpful to set out an example to illustrate the way this works.

The below example is an LLP incorporated on 1 January 20X2. This LLP is not in a group and is not ineligible in any other way (see **4.1** above).

For each period, the '"size" this period' line in the table below applies the size criteria just to the period in question, and applying the test to establish if the LLP meets two out of the three limits in that period alone.

The last line in the table, 'Qualify as small?', applies the 'drop in-drop out' rule, where criteria are not met for the following year (Y2), an LLP may still continue to be treated as small for that following year.

	31 December 20X2	31 December 20X3	31 December 20X4	31 December 20X5	30 June 20X6 (six months)
Turnover	£7m	£8m	£10m	£15m	£6m
Balance sheet total	£3m	£4m	£3m	£6m	£3m
Employees	40	45	49	55	55
'Size' this period	Small	Medium	Small	Medium	Medium
Qualify as small?	Yes	Yes	Yes	Yes	No

In the example above, for the year ended 31 December 20X4, the LLP qualified as small in the previous year (bottom row of 20X3). In 20X4, it is 'small-sized' as only one of the three criteria (penultimate row) has been breached. It did not breach the medium criteria for two years in a row. Therefore it continues to qualify as small.

For the period ended 30 June 20X6, the LLP fails the turnover limit as this has been pro-rated for the shorter period to £3.25m for six months.

4.4   Parent entities and small groups

Companies Act 2006, s. 383(4), 466(4) set out the conditions to be met by a group for the parent entity to qualify as 'small' or 'medium-sized' as appropriate.

A parent LLP qualifies as a small LLP in relation to a financial year only if the group headed by it qualifies as a small group.   *s. 383*

The size classification of a parent entity is determined with regard to the aggregate qualifying criteria of the group taken as a whole (parent entity and subsidiary undertakings), irrespective of the actual size qualification of the parent entity itself (see **Chapter 7**).

4.5   Future developments

The small and medium-sized criteria applicable to companies have been increased for periods commencing on or after 1 January 2016 and the Government has recently announced that it will extend these changes to LLPs.

Unusually, companies have the option of early adopting these new criteria (for accounting purposes but not for audit exemption) for any accounting period commencing on or after 1 January 2015, provided they also adopt other accounting changes with the same effective date. Again, the Government has announced that it will extend this option to LLPs.

Further details on these developments are covered in **Chapter 13**.

Chapter 5 Contents of LLP accounts

5.1 Introduction

This chapter summarises accounts provisions of the Regulations, insofar as they relate to individual LLP accounts ('Non-IAS individual accounts') that are prepared in accordance with CA 2006, s. 396. 'Abbreviated accounts' (modified statutory accounts for filing purposes) are considered separately in **Chapter 6**. Group accounts, which the Regulations refer to as 'non-IAS group accounts' are considered in **Chapter 7**.

'Regulations' refers to SI 2008/1911 (*Limited Liability Partnerships (Accounts and Audit) (Application of Companies Act 2006) Regulations* 2008), SI 2008/1912 (*Small Limited Liability Partnerships (Accounts) Regulations* 2008) and SI 2008/1913 (*Large and Medium-Sized Limited Liability Partnerships (Accounts) Regulations* 2008).

All LLPs are required to keep 'adequate accounting records' in accordance with CA 2006, s. 386.

This chapter also explains where the LLP SORP includes additional disclosure requirements above those set out in the Regulations.

5.2 Accounts – provisions for LLPs

For each financial year, accounts must be prepared for all LLPs, irrespective of size. However, a small LLP may take advantage of the FRSSE (see **Chapter 3**).

s. 394 et seq

In addition, an LLP qualifying as 'small' or 'medium-sized' (see **Chapter 4**) may prepare 'abbreviated' accounts for filing with the Registrar of Companies (see **Chapter 6**).

A category of small company called a 'micro-entity' was introduced in 2013 by the *Small Companies (Micro-Entities' Accounts) Regulations* 2013. This legislation specifically excludes LLPs from the 'micro-entities regime', however, the Government has announced that this will change (see **Chapter 13**).

Certain small LLPs may be exempt from the requirement for audit, as explained in **Chapter 9**. Dormant LLPs may also take advantage of audit exemption.

By virtue of the provisions for small LLPs under CA 2006, a small LLP is therefore entitled to prepare:

- annual accounts for members – with a balance sheet and reduced disclosure requirements for the notes to the accounts (as determined by SI 2008/1912 – see Chapter 2); and
- abbreviated accounts for filing and delivery to the Registrar of Companies – under CA 2006, s. 444 (as applied to LLPs).

Small LLP accounts with simplified provisions and reduced disclosure provided by CA 2006, s. 396 and Regulations contained in Sch. 1 of SI 2008/1912 are referred to as 'small LLP accounts' in this book.

An LLP wishing to file abbreviated accounts with the Registrar of Companies has to produce two sets of accounts: the annual accounts for members and the abbreviated accounts.

However, a small LLP does not have to take advantage of all the exemptions and modifications permitted if it does not wish to do so. For example, SI 2008/1912 provides that individual accounts 'are treated as having complied with any provision of Sch. 1 to these Regulations (i.e. the *Small Limited Liability Partnership (Accounts) Regulations* 2008 (SI 2008/1912)) if they comply instead with the corresponding provision of Sch. 1 to the *Large and Medium-Sized Limited Liability Partnership (Accounts) Regulations* 2008 (SI 2008 /1913)'.

SI 2008/1912, reg. 3(3)

Similarly, non-IAS group accounts 'are treated as having complied with any provision of Part 1 to Schedule 4 (of SI 2008/1912 – 'Form and content of Non-IAS group accounts') if they comply instead with the corresponding provision of Schedule 6 to the Large and Medium-Sized LLP Accounts Regs (SI 2008/1913)'.

SI 2008/1912, reg.6(1), 8(2)

The provisions for small LLPs apply not only to the individual accounts of such LLPs but also to the group accounts where a small LLP produces them. If at the end of a financial year an LLP subject to the small LLPs regime is a parent entity the members, as well as preparing individual accounts for the year, have the option to prepare group accounts for the year, if they so wish.

s. 399

There is no provision for 'abbreviated group accounts' within CA 2006 and therefore small or medium-sized groups are unable to file abbreviated accounts.

5.3   Format of LLP accounts

5.3.1   Form and content of accounts prepared by LLPs

The form and content of individual accounts prepared by LLPs are determined in accordance with the LLP SORP and regulations provided by SI 2008/1912 (*Small Limited Liability Partnerships (Accounts) Regulations* 2008) and in particular Sch. 1 or SI 2008/1913 (*Large and Medium-sized Limited Liability Partnerships (Accounts) Regulations* 2008), Sch. 1.

The LLP SORP sets out the primary statements to be included within the accounts, two of which are also requirements of the Regulations (although the Regulations use different names for these).

The statements required by the LLP SORP and the Regulations are:

- Statements of financial position (balance sheet in the Regulations);
- Income statement (profit and loss account in the Regulations).

The other required statements in the LLP SORP are:

- Statement of comprehensive income (for FRSSE LLPs this is called a statement of total recognised gains and losses);
- Statement of changes in equity;
- Statement of cash flows.

Where the statements have different names in the LLP SORP and the Regulations, either name may be used. Further details of the requirements for the primary statements in the LLP SORP are given in **Chapter 3**.

The Regulations prescribe the required formats for the balance sheet and profit and loss account from which LLPs may choose. Once a format has been adopted, the LLP must use the same format for subsequent years unless, in the members' opinion, there are special reasons for changing; these must be disclosed in the year of change.

Sch 1.2(1)

Schedule 1 (Non-IAS individual accounts) of both SIs is structured as in **Table 5.1**.

Table 5.1   Schedule 1 Non-IAS individual accounts – SI 2008/1912 (Small LLPs) and SI 2008/1913 (Large and Medium-sized LLPs)

Part 1 General rules and formats

Section A	General rules
Section B	Required formats for accounts

- Balance sheet formats (Formats 1 and 2) and notes thereon
- Profit and loss account formats (Formats 1 and 2) and notes thereon

Part 2 Accounting principles and rules

Section A	Accounting principles
Section B	Historical cost accounting rules

- Fixed assets
- Depreciation and diminution in value
- Development costs
- Goodwill
- Current assets
- Miscellaneous and supplementary provisions *(including excess of money owed over value received as an asset item, assets included at a fixed amount, determination of purchase price or production cost, and substitution of original stated amount where price or cost unknown)*

Section C	Alternative accounting rules

- Alternative accounting rules
- Application of the depreciation rules
- Additional information to be provided in case of departure from historical cost account rules
- Revaluation reserve

Section D	Fair value accounting

- Inclusion of financial instruments at fair value
- Determination of fair value
- Hedged items
- Other assets that may be included at fair value
- Accounting for changes in value
- The fair value reserve

Part 3 Notes to the accounts

- Reserves
- Disclosure of accounting policies
- Information supplementing the balance sheet *(Loans and other debts due to members, fixed assets, investments, fair values, reserves and provisions, indebtedness, and guarantees and other financial commitments)*
- Information supplementing the profit and loss account *(including particulars of turnover)*
- Miscellaneous matters *(including foreign currencies and dormant LLPs acting as agents)*

SI 2008/1912, Sch. 1 is reproduced in full in **Appendix C**

SI 2008/1913, Sch. 1 is reproduced in full in **Appendix D**

5.3.2 The statutory formats

The accounts formats from which a small LLP may choose are given in SI 2008/1912, Sch. 1 (Part 1 Section B – 'The required formats for accounts'). There is a choice of two profit and loss account formats and two balance sheet formats.

A small LLP must adopt in its annual (individual) accounts one of the formats of balance sheet set out in SI 2008/1912, Sch. 1 (Part 1 Section B). If applicable, it must show the items listed in either of the formats, as set out in **Tables 5.2** and **5.3**. The individual balance sheet of a small LLP which adopts Format 1 would be as set out in **Table 5.2**.

The choice of profit and loss account formats for a small LLP is set out in SI 2008/1912, Sch. 1 (Part 1 Section B) and is reproduced in **Appendix C**. They are also illustrated in **Table 5.3**. The principles governing the formats are as set out in **3.4 (Chapter 3)**.

Sch 1.10–15 Small LLP accounts are prepared in accordance with the principles set out in SI 2008/1912, Sch. 1 (Part 2 Section A). These principles are the fundamental accounting concepts that underlie accounts and are also incorporated within FRS 102 and the FRSSE for small entities.

Accounting principles are explained further in **2.5 (Chapter 2)**.

5.4 LLP balance sheet

The formats of balance sheet set out in Sch. 1 (Part 1 Section B) of SI 2008/1912 (Small LLPs) and of SI 2008/1913 (Large and Medium-sized LLPs) from which an LLP must choose for its annual (individual) accounts are set out in **Appendices C** and **D**. **Table 5.2** illustrates Format 1 (most commonly used by LLPs) showing the differences between small and not small accounts. All of the main 'letter' headings are the same for both small and not-small accounts and therefore the basic format of the balance sheet will be the same for all LLPs preparing Non-IAS accounts. As can be seen below it is only the level of detail under some of these headings that differs depending on the size of the organisation.

Table 5.2

FORMAT 1

Small LLP accounts as per SI 2008/1912	Large and medium-sized LLP accounts as per SI 2008/1913
A Fixed assets	A Fixed assets
I. Intangible assets	I. Intangible assets
1. Goodwill	1. Development costs
2. Other intangible assets	2. Concessions, patents, licences, trade marks and similar rights and assets
	3. Goodwill
	4. Payments on account
II. Tangible assets	II. Tangible assets
1. Land and buildings	1. Land and buildings
2. Plant and machinery, etc.	2. Plant and machinery etc.
	3. Fixtures, fittings, tools and equipment
	4. Payments on account and assets in course of construction

Table 5.2 (cont'd)

III.	Investments	III. Investments

III. Investments

1. Shares in group undertakings and participating interests
2. Loans to group undertakings and undertakings in which the LLP has a participating interest
3. Other investments other than loans
4. Other investments

III. Investments

1. Shares in group undertakings
2. Loans to group undertakings
3. Participating interests (*note 1*)
4. Loans to undertakings in which the LLP has a participating interest
5. Other investments other than loans
6. Other loans

B Current assets

I. Stocks

1. Stocks
2. Payments on account

B Current assets

I. Stocks

1. Raw materials and consumables
2. Work in progress
3. Finished goods and goods for resale
4. Payments on account

II. Debtors (*note 2*)

1. Trade debtors
2. Amounts owed by group undertakings and undertakings in which the LLP has a participating interest
3. Other debtors

II. Debtors (*note 2*)

1. Trade debtors
2. Amounts owed by group undertakings
3. Amounts owed by undertakings in which the LLP has a participating interest
4. Other debtors
5. Prepayments and accrued income (*note 3*)

III. Investments

1. Shares in group undertakings
2. Other investments

III. Investments

1. Shares in group undertakings
2. Other investments

IV. Cash at bank and in hand

IV. Cash at bank and in hand

C. Prepayments and accrued income (*note 3*)

C. Prepayments and accrued income (*note 3*)

D. Creditors: amounts falling due within one year

1. Bank loans and overdrafts
2. Trade creditors
3. Amounts owed to group undertakings and undertakings in which the LLP has a participating interest
4. Other creditors (*note 4*)

D. Creditors: amounts falling due within one year

1. Debenture loans (*note 6*)
2. Bank loans and overdrafts
3. Payments received on account (*note 7*)
4. Trade creditors
5. Bills of exchange payable
6. Amounts owed to group undertakings
7. Amounts owed to undertakings in which the LLP has a participating interest
8. Other creditors including taxation and social security (*note 8*))
9. Accruals and deferred income (*note 4*)

E. Net current assets (liabilities)

E. Net current assets (liabilities)

F. Total assets less current liabilities

F. Total assets less current liabilities

G. Creditors: amounts falling due after more than one year

1. Bank loans and overdrafts
2. Trade creditors
3. Amounts owed to group undertakings and undertakings in which the LLP has a participating interest

G. Creditors: amounts falling due after more than one year

1. Debenture loans (*note 6*)
2. Bank loans and overdrafts
3. Payments received on account (*note 7*))
4. Trade creditors
5. Bills of exchange payable

Table 5.2 (cont'd)

4.	Other creditors *(note 4)*	6. Amounts owed to group undertakings
		7. Amounts owed to undertakings in which the LLP has a participating interest
		8. Other creditors including taxation and social security *(note 8)*
		9. Accruals and deferred income *(note 4)*

H.	Provisions for liabilities	H. Provisions for liabilities
		1. Pensions and similar obligations
		2. Taxation, including deferred taxation
		3. Other provisions
I.	Accruals and deferred income *(note 4)*	I. Accruals and deferred income *(note 4)*
	Net assets attributable to members (note 9)	*Net assets attributable to members (note 9)*
J.	Loans and other debts due to members *(note 5)*	J. Loans and other debts due to members *(note 5)*
K.	Members' other interests	K. Members' other interests
	I. Members' capital	I. Members' capital
	II. Revaluation reserve	II. Revaluation reserve
	III. Other reserves	III. Other reserves
	Total members' interests (note 9)	*Total members' interests (note 9)*

Note 1 Where a small LLP prepares group accounts, in a consolidated balance sheet the format for 'Investments' is:

1. shares in group undertakings;
2. interests in associated undertakings;
3. other participating interests;
4. loans to group undertakings and undertakings in which a participating interest is held;
5. other investments other than loans; and
6. others.

*SI 2008/1912
Sch. 4.1(2)
SI 2008/1913,
Sch. 3,
para. 20(3)*

Where a large or medium-sized LLP prepares group accounts, in a consolidated balance sheet the format for the heading 'participating interests' in the investment section should be replaced with two headings 'Interests in associated undertakings' and 'Other participating interests'.

Note 2 An LLP must disclose the total of 'debtors falling due after more than one year' but such disclosure (if the amount is not material) may be in the notes to the accounts rather than in the balance sheet.

Note 3 Prepayments and accrued income can be disclosed as part of debtors rather than as a separate heading.

Note 4 Accruals and deferred income may also be shown under 'other creditors' The amount of any creditors in respect of taxation and social security and convertible debt should be shown separately.

Note 5 The following amounts must be shown separately under 'loans and other debts due to members'–

(a) the aggregate amount of money advanced to the LLP by the members by way of loan,

(b) the aggregate amount of money owed to members by the LLP in respect of profits,

(c) any other amounts

Note 6 The amount of any convertible loans must be shown separately.

Note 7 Payments received on account of orders must be shown for each of these items in so far as they are not shown as deductions from stocks.

Note 8 The amount of any creditors in respect of taxation and social security should be shown separately.

Table 5.2 (cont'd)

Note 9 These two lines are a requirement of the LLP SORP rather than the Regulations. Paragraph 58 of the LLP SORP states that the face of the balance sheet should show the 'Net assets attributable to members' of the LLP (that is the sum of items B to I). In addition, 'Total members' interests', being the total of items J and K less any amounts due from members in debtors, should be disclosed as a memorandum item on the face of the balance sheet. (As generally only Balance Sheet Format 1 is used by LLPs the LLP SORP does not provide guidance on how Balance Sheet Format 2 should be amended.)

5.5 LLP profit and loss account

The choice of profit and loss account formats for an LLP, as set out in SI 2008/1912, Sch. 1 (Part 1 Section B) or SI 2008/1913 (Part 1 Section B), is illustrated in **Table 5.3**. The formats are the same in both of the Statutory Instruments.

In practice, care needs to be taken in the choice of format and presentation of the profit and loss accounts. **Table 5.3** presents a comparison of the two formats (Formats 1 and 2) showing the differences in presentation and disclosure. It is particularly relevant to note:

- *gross profit or loss* is specifically disclosed only in Format 1; and
- *depreciation* may require allocation over various cost headings in Format 1 but needs only to be shown as one item in a Format 2 profit and loss account.

The amount of an LLP's 'profit or loss on ordinary activities before taxation' must be included on every profit and loss account. (This item is not specified in the formats.)

All other items in the profit and loss account formats (being represented by Arabic numbers) could be combined and given in the notes to the accounts, provided the profit and loss account contains a summarised linking figure.

For small LLPs which are able and intend to file abbreviated accounts, the choice of profit and loss account formats may be of less consequence.

Table 5.3   LLP profit and loss account formats (SI 2008/1912 and SI 2008/1913, Sch. 1 (Part I Section B))

Expenses classified by function	Expenses classified by type
Format 1	Format 2
1 Turnover	1 Turnover
2 Cost of sales	2 Change in stocks of finished goods and work in progress
3 Gross profit or loss	3 Own work capitalised
4 Distribution costs	
5 Administrative expenses	
6 Other operating income	4 Other operating income
	5 (a) Raw materials and consumables
	(b) Other external charges
In Format 1 staff costs must be allocated over items 2, 4 and 5. (Staff costs disclosure in the notes is not applicable for a small LLP (s. 411))	6 Staff costs:
	(a) Wages and salaries
	(b) Social security costs
	(c) Other pension costs
In Format 1 depreciation must be allocated over items 2, 4 and 5 (Sch. 1, Part I Section B note 9) and disclosed separately in Notes (Sch 1.19)	7 (a) Depreciation and other amounts written off tangible and intangible fixed assets
	(b) Exceptional amounts written off current assets
	8 Other operating charges

Table 5.3 (cont'd)

7	Income from shares in group undertakings	9	Income from shares in group undertakings
8	Income from participating interests *(note 3)*	10	Income from participating interests *(note 3)*
9	Income from other fixed asset investments	11	Income from other fixed asset investments
10	Other interest receivable and similar income	12	Other interest receivable and similar income
11	Amounts written off investments	13	Amounts written off investments
12	Interest payable and similar charges	14	Interest payable and similar charges
12A	Profit or loss on ordinary activities before taxation *(Sch. 1.6 and FRSSE) (note 2)*	14A	Profit or loss on ordinary activities before taxation *(Sch 1.6 and FRSSE) (note 2)*
13	Tax on profit or loss on ordinary activities	15	Tax on profit or loss on ordinary activities
14	Profit or loss on ordinary activities after taxation	16	Profit or loss on ordinary activities after taxation
15	Extraordinary income *(note 1)*	17	Extraordinary income *(note 1)*
16	Extraordinary charges *(note 1)*	18	Extraordinary charges *(note 1)*
17	Extraordinary profit or loss *(note 1)*	19	Extraordinary profit or loss *(note 1)*
18	Tax on extraordinary profit or loss	20	Tax on extraordinary profit or loss
19	Other taxes not shown under the above items	21	Other taxes not shown under the above items
20	Profit or loss for the financial year before members' remuneration and profit shares	22	Profit or loss for the financial year before members' remuneration and profit shares
	**Members' remuneration charged as an expense		**Members' remuneration charged as an expense
	**Profit or loss for the financial year available for discretionary division among the members		**Profit or loss for the financial year available for discretionary division among the members

Note 1 – Extraordinary items, although included within the statutory formats, are now viewed as being extremely rare.

Note 2 – 'Profit and loss on ordinary activity before taxation' must also be disclosed – see SI 2008/1912, Sch. 1.6 or SI 2008/1913, Sch. 1.6 and FRSSE.

Note 3 – Where an LLP prepares group accounts, the items in **Table 5.3** headed 'Income from participating interests' in the above formats (item 8 (Format 1) and item 10 (Format 2)) become two items:

SI 2008/1912, Sch 4.1(3) & SI 2008/1913, Sch. 3.20(2)

- Income from interests in associated undertakings; and
- Income from other participating interests.

** Required by the LLP SORP paragraph 51

5.6 Cash flow statements

The inclusion of a cash flow statement as one of the primary statements within a set of accounts is a requirement of FRS 102 rather than legislation. The LLP SORP provides guidance on how the cash flow statement format set out in section 7 of FRS 102 should be adapted for LLPs.

FRS 102 exempts 'qualifying entities' from preparing a cash flow statement, subject to a requirement to inform their members about their proposed use of the exemption and the ability of a certain proportion of members to prohibit use of the exemption (as noted in **3.5**).

A 'qualifying entity' is a member of a group where the parent of that group prepares publicly available consolidated financial statements which are intended to give a true and fair view (of the assets, liabilities, financial position and profit or loss) and that member is included in the consolidation.

This therefore means that, unless the members object, subsidiaries are not required to include a cash flow statement in their accounts and parent companies are not required to include their own cash flow statement, although they are required to include one covering their group as a whole.

The cash flow statement shows changes in cash and cash equivalents. This is a change from FRS 1 where only movements in cash and bank overdrafts were included. Cash equivalents are defined as 'short-term, highly liquid investments that are readily convertible to known amounts of cash and that are subject to an insignificant risk of changes in value'. The most common form of cash equivalent would be bank accounts with a notice period (provided the period is short, FRS 102 suggests no more than three months).

The format of the cash flow statement in FRS 102 is substantially different from that shown in the previous standard, FRS 1. All cash flows are now shown in one of three categories: operating, investing or financing.

FRS 102 does not include an example of the format of a cash flow statement, however the FRC has also issued guidance in the form of Staff Education Note 1 and the cash flow statement format below is based on the example included in the Staff Education Note, modified to show the amendments required by the LLP SORP. This example is for a single entity.

Example 5.1 Cash Flow Statement for the Year Ended [end of financial period]

Cash flows from operating activities

Profit for the financial year
Adjustments for:
    Depreciation of property, plant and equipment
    Amortisation of intangible assets
    Profit on disposal of property, plant and equipment
    Interest paid
    Interest received
    Taxation
    Decrease/(increase) in trade and other receivables
    Decrease/(increase) in inventories
    Increase/(decrease) in trade payables
    <u>Transactions with members and former members*</u>

Cash from operations

Interest paid
Income taxes paid
<u>Members remuneration paid under an employment contract*</u>
<u>Other members remuneration for services provided*</u>
<u>Post retirement payments to former members*</u>

Net cash generated from operating activities

Cash flows from investing activities

Proceeds from sale of equipment
Purchases of property, plant and equipment
Purchases of intangible assets
Interest received

Net cash from investing activities

Cash flows from financing activities

~~Issue of ordinary share capital~~ <u>Capital introduced by members</u>
<u>Repayment of capital or debt to members</u>
<u>Payments to members that represent a return on amounts subscribed or otherwise contributed</u>
Repayment of borrowings
~~Dividends paid~~

Net cash used in financing activities

Net increase/(decrease) in cash and cash equivalents

Cash and cash equivalents at beginning of year

Example 5.1 (cont'd)

Cash and cash equivalents at end of year

* Paragraph 74B of the LLP SORP requires separate disclosure of transactions with members and former members. Where these have been included in arriving at profit for the year and adjustment will be required to remove them and they must then be presented separately.

Note – Components of cash and cash equivalents

Cash
Overdraft
Cash equivalents

Inserted text is underlined

For those small entities preparing accounts in accordance with the FRSSE, the FRSSE does not include a requirement for a cash flow statement. Nevertheless, the FRC 'strongly encourages', within a non-mandatory 'voluntary disclosures' section of the FRSSE, smaller entities to present a simplified cash flow statement using the indirect method.

The form of cash flow statement indicated as voluntary disclosure by the FRSSE is set out in **Table 5.2**. This example has been based on and adapted for LLPs from the example contained in the FRSSE (effective January 2015) (Appendix III).

Example 5.2 – Small LLP Cash Flow Statement for the Year Ended [end of financial period]

Cash generated from operations

Operating profit/(loss)
Reconciliation to cash generated from operations:

Depreciation
Increase in stocks
Decrease in trade debtors
Decrease in trade creditors
Increase in other creditors
Transactions with members and former members*

Cash from other sources

Interest received
~~Issues of shares for cash~~ Capital introduced by members
New long-term bank borrowings
Proceeds from sale of tangible fixed assets

Application of cash

Interest paid
Tax paid
Dividends paid
Purchase of fixed assets
Repayment of amounts borrowed
Repayment of capital or debt to members
Members remuneration paid under an employment contract*
Other members remuneration for services provided*
Post retirement payments to former members*

Example 5.2 (cont'd)

Net increase in cash

   Cash at bank and in hand less overdrafts at beginning of year

Cash at bank and in hand less overdrafts at end of year

   Consisting of:

Cash at bank and in hand
Overdrafts included in bank loans and overdrafts falling due within one year

* Paragraph 74B of the SORP requires separate disclosure of transactions with members and former members. Where these have been included in arriving at profit for the year an adjustment will be required to remove them and they must then be presented separately.

Inserted text is underlined

5.7   Other comprehensive income

Other comprehensive income (OCI) comprises certain gains and losses, as specifically permitted or required by law or accounting standards, which have been taken directly to reserves and not therefore included within the profit and loss account for the period. Examples of items which would be included in OCI are:

- revaluation surpluses and unrealised revaluation losses on tangible fixed assets, but not those on investment properties and most financial instruments;
- actuarial gains and losses on defined benefit pension schemes; and
- exchange gains and losses on retranslation of opening net assets of overseas subsidiaries.

FRS 102 has two alternatives for the presentation of OCI, it can either be presented as a separate statement (called a statement of comprehensive income) or shown at the end of a single statement combining the income statement and OCI (again, this is called a statement of comprehensive income).

Whichever option is chosen it should start from 'Profit for the year available for discretionary division among members', then show each element of OCI and total to 'Total comprehensive income for the year'.

Example 5.3 Statement of comprehensive income for the year/period ended 31 December 2015		
	2015	**2014**
	£	**£**
Profit for the financial year available for discretionary division among members		
Actuarial loss in respect of defined benefit pension scheme Revaluation surplus		
Total comprehensive income for the year		

For companies adopting the FRSSE the equivalent to OCI is a Statement of Total Recognised Gains and Losses (STRGL), which is required to be presented as a separate statement.

5.8   Notes to the accounts

The Regulations also require that an LLP must set out in the notes (if not given in the LLP's accounts) the following information (also see **Section 5.11** for disclosures required regarding the remuneration of auditors).

Table 5.4

Notes	Small LLPs regime SI 2008/1912	Other LLPs SI 2008/1913
Reserves		
Any amount set aside or proposed to be set aside to, or withdrawn or proposed to be withdrawn from, reserves must be stated.	*Sch 1.43*	*Sch 1.43*
Disclosure of accounting policies		
Policies in respect of items on the balance sheet and used in determining the profit or loss of the LLP	*Sch 1.44*	*Sch 1.44*
State whether the accounts have been prepared in accordance with the applicable accounting standards and particulars of and reason for any material departure	*n/a*	*Sch 1.45 (does not apply to medium-sized LLPs)*
Information supplementing the balance sheet:		
Loans and other debts due to members	*Sch 1.46*	*Sch 1.47*
– the aggregate amount of loans and other debts due to members as at the date of the beginning of the financial year, – the aggregate amounts contributed by members during the financial year, – the aggregate amounts transferred to or from the profit and loss account during that year, – the aggregate amounts withdrawn by members or applied on behalf of members during that year, – the aggregate amount of loans and other debts due to members as at the balance sheet date, and – the aggregate amount of loans and other debts due to members that fall due after one year. (for the format of members disclosure note given in the LLP SORP see Treatment of members transactions in **Chapter 8**.)		
Debentures		
The classes of debentures issued and for each class of debentures, the amount issued and the consideration received by the LLP. The nominal amount of the debentures held by a nominee of or trustee for the LLP and the amount at which they are stated in the accounting records.	*n/a*	*Sch 1.48*
Fixed assets		
Additions, disposals, revaluations, depreciation and other movements for each category of fixed assets. Details of land subject to freehold or leasehold tenure, including nature of the lease if applicable.	*Sch 1.47–48* *n/a*	*Sch 1.49–50* *Sch 1.51*

Table 5.4 (cont'd)

Investments

Listed investments; market valuation.	*Sch 1.49*	*Sch 1.52*

Fair value of assets and liabilities

Assumptions and techniques used; fair value and transfers to/ from reserves for each category of financial instruments; terms and details of each class of derivatives held at fair value.	*Sch 1.50–51*	*Sch 1.53–55*
Details of each class of derivatives not held at fair value.	*n/a*	*Sch 1.54*
Details of investment property and living animals and plants at fair value.	*Sch 1.52*	*Sch 1.56*

Reserves and provisions

Movements and transfers to/from reserves and provisions. Details of each 'other provisions' which is material.	*Sch 1.53*	*Sch 1.57*

Provision for taxation

The amount of any provision for deferred taxation must be stated separately from the amount of any provision for other taxation	*n/a*	*Sch 1.58*

Details of indebtedness

Creditors payable or repayable in more than five years; security	*sch 1.54*	*Sch 1.59*
Details of repayment and the rates of interest	*n/a*	*Sch 1.59*
Amount due within one year and in more than one year	*Sch 1.54*	*Sch 1.59*

Guarantees and other financial commitments

Particulars of charges on assets, contingent liabilities, capital commitments not provided for, pension commitments and other financial commitments.	*Sch 1.55*	*Sch 1.60*

Substituted price or cost of assets

Ascribed purchase price or production cost.	*Sch 1.56*	*Sch 1.61*

Information supplementing the profit and loss account:

Interest and similar charges

The amount of the interest on or any similar charges in respect of bank loans and overdrafts, and loans of any other kind made to the LLP.	*n/a*	*Sch 1.63*
(This does not apply to interest or charges on loans to the LLP from group undertakings, but, with that exception, it applies to interest or charges on all loans, whether made on the security of debentures or not.)		

Particulars of tax

Particulars must be given of any special circumstances which affect liability in respect of taxation of profits, income or capital gains for the financial year or liability in respect of taxation of profits, income or capital gains for succeeding financial years.	*n/a*	*Sch 1.64*

Table 5.4 (cont'd)

Turnover* (see note below)

Percentage attributable to geographical markets outside UK	*Sch 1.58*	*Sch 1.65 (more detailed requirements than for small entities)*

Particulars of members

The average number of members of the LLP in the financial year, which number is to be determined by dividing the relevant annual number by the number of months in the financial year. The relevant annual number is to be determined by ascertaining for each month in the financial year the number of members of the LLP for all or part of that month, and adding together all the monthly numbers.	*n/a*	*Sch 1.66*

Where the amount of the profit of the LLP for the financial year before members' remuneration and profit shares exceeds £200,000, there must be disclosed the amount of profit (including remuneration) which is attributable to the member with the largest entitlement to profit (including remuneration).

Miscellaneous*

Effect of prior year adjustments and exceptional transactions, and particulars of extraordinary charges or income.	*Sch 1.59*	*Sch 1.67*

* Not required for individual LLP where group accounts prepared as individual P&L not shown (CA 2006, s. 408)

Sums in foreign currencies

Basis of translation of foreign currencies	*Sch 1.60*	*Sch 1.68*

Dormant LLPs acting as agents

Where the members of an LLP take advantage of the exemption for dormant LLPs not to have an audit and the LLP has during the financial year in question acted as an agent for any person, the fact that it has so acted must be stated.	*Sch 1.61*	*Sch 1.69*

Related party transactions

Particulars may be given of transactions which the LLP has entered into with related parties, and must be given if such transactions are material and have not been concluded under normal market conditions (see reg. 4 for exemption for medium-sized LLPs).	*n/a*	*Sch 1.70*

The particulars of transactions required to be disclosed as noted above must include–
(a) the amount of such transactions,
(b) the nature of the related party relationship, and
(c) other information about the transactions necessary for an understanding of the financial position of the LLP.

Information about individual transactions may be aggregated according to their nature, except where separate information is necessary for an understanding of the effects of related party transactions on the financial position of the LLP.

Particulars need not be given of transactions entered into between two or more members of a group, provided that any subsidiary undertaking which is a party to the transaction is wholly owned by such a member.

Information about related undertakings (small groups):

Where the parent entity of a small group does not prepare group accounts, it must set out in the notes to the entity's accounts the information about related undertakings specified in SI 2008/1912, Sch. 2, para. 4.

5.9   Members' report

The sections within the CA 2006 which require a company to prepare a Directors' Report (and for certain larger companies, a Strategic Report) do not apply to LLPs.

The previous version of the LLP SORP required preparation of a Members' Report, containing certain information. The requirement to prepare a Members' Report has been dropped from the revised LLP SORP, however, paragraph 30 of the LLP SORP still requires that the following information previously contained in it is disclosed:

- the principal activities of the LLP and its subsidiary undertakings, indicating any significant changes during the year;
- an indication of the existence of any branches outside the UK;
- the identity of anyone who was a designated member during the year; and
- the policy of the LLP regarding members' drawings and the subscription and repayment of amounts subscribed or otherwise contributed by members.

The LLP SORP (para. 31) suggests that, although a Members' Report is no longer required, LLPs may wish to prepare one to present this information.

The policy relating to members' drawings should include an indication of the policy applicable where the cash requirements of the business compete with the need to allow cash drawings by members. Such disclosures should include any transfers of members' interests from equity to debt (and vice versa) during the year and up to the date the accounts are approved. The policy under which members contribute or subscribe amounts to the LLP by way of equity or debt and the policy under which their contributions and subscriptions are repayable by the LLP, should be disclosed.

FRS 102 (para. 3.24) also requires disclosure of the legal form of the entity, its country of incorporation and the address of its registered office (or principal place of business, if different from the registered office). This is required to be given in the notes to the accounts rather than the Members' Report.

Although the disclosure requirements contained in the CA 2006 requiring a strategic report for large and medium-sized companies do not apply to LLPs, many LLPs reflect this style of disclosure within the Members' Report.

Audited companies are required by s. 418 of CA 2006 to make a statement as to disclosure to auditors in the Directors' Report. This, like other requirements on companies relating to a Directors' Report, is not applied to LLPs.

5.10   Members' statements

An LLP which qualifies as a small LLP in relation to a financial year (other than a dormant LLP) and takes advantage of the provisions with respect to the preparation of annual accounts must include statements in its accounts, where appropriate, on the balance sheet confirming preparation in accordance with the small LLP provisions.

For small LLPs, every copy of any balance sheet that is published by or on behalf of the LLP must state the name of the person who signed it on behalf of the members of the LLP.   *s. 433*

5.10.1 Members' statement – small LLP accounts preparation: Section 414

If the accounts are prepared in accordance with the provisions applicable to LLPs subject to the small LLPs regime, the balance sheet must contain a statement to that effect in a prominent position above the signature.

s. 414(3)

The balance sheet therefore must contain (in a 'prominent position' above the signature of a member required by s. 433) a statement that the accounts have been prepared in accordance with the provisions applicable to LLPs subject to the small LLPs regime.

Where the designated members of an LLP subject to the small LLPs regime deliver to the Registrar of Companies IAS accounts, or non-IAS accounts that are not abbreviated accounts, but do not deliver a copy of the LLP's profit and loss account, the copy of the balance sheet delivered to the Registrar must contain in a prominent position a statement that the LLP's annual accounts have been delivered in accordance with the provisions applicable to LLPs subject to the small LLPs regime.

s. 444(5)

Reference to the FRSSE (effective January 2015) should also be made in the statement, but only if applicable, as indicated by the tinted text in **Example 5.5** below.

Example 5.5

Section 414 members' statement – balance sheet

These accounts have been prepared in accordance with the provisions applicable to LLPs subject to the small LLPs regime of CA 2006 (as applied by the *Limited Liability Partnerships (Accounts and Audit) (Application of Companies Act 2006) Regulations* 2008). *[and with the Financial Reporting Standard for Smaller Entities (effective January 2015)]*.

5.10.2 Members' statement – small LLP audit exemption entitlement: Section 475

A small LLP eligible for audit exemption (**Chapter 9**) is required to provide a statutory statement in accordance with s. 475(2) to appear in the balance sheet above the member's signature of approval.

Example 5.6

Section 475 Members' statement – entitlement to exemption from audit (Balance sheet)

For the financial year ended 30 June 2014 the LLP was entitled to exemption from audit under s. 477* of Companies Act 2006 (as applied by the *Limited Liability Partnerships (Accounts and Audit) (Application of Companies Act 2006) Regulations* 2008) relating to small LLPs.

The members acknowledge their responsibilities for complying with the requirements of the Act with respect to accounting records and the preparation of accounts.

These accounts have been prepared in accordance with the provisions applicable to LLPs subject to the small LLPs regime.

---

* s. 477 relates to the exemption for small companies, if the LLP is dormant replace "s. 477" with "s. 480".

5.10.3 Members' statement – members' responsibilities

Where an LLP is subject to audit, it is necessary (in order to accord with international standards on auditing) to prepare a more detailed statement. This is usually included within the members' report, but will be a separate statement if no members' report is produced.

The APB ISA (UK and Ireland) 700 (revised in September 2014), *The independent auditor's report on financial statements*, requires the auditor's report to include (a) a statement that those charged with governance are responsible for the preparation of the financial statements and (b) a statement that the responsibility of the auditor is to audit and express an opinion on the financial statements in accordance with applicable legal requirements and International Standards on Auditing (UK and Ireland).

APB Bulletin 2010/2 *Compendium of illustrative auditor's reports on United Kingdom private sector financial statements for periods ended on or after 15 December 2010*, envisages a Members' Responsibilities Statement within the financial statements or accompanying information to include an adequate statement of members' responsibilities. Specific reference is made to this statement in the Auditor's Report.

Example 5.7 provides an example members' responsibilities statement based on APB Bulletin 2010/2, which has been modified for LLPs (Bulletin 2010/2, Appendix 17).

An independent accountants' report on unaudited (audit-exempt) accounts, should, on the same basis, include a statement that the members are responsible for the preparation of the accounts.

Example 5.7

Example members' responsibilities statement

APB Bulletin 2010/2 *Appendix 17 (as modified for LLPs)*

Members' responsibilities statement

The members are responsible for preparing the financial statements in accordance with applicable law and regulations.

Company law as applied to *Limited Liability Partnerships by the Limited Liability Partnerships (Accounts and Audit) (Application of Companies Act 2006) Regulations* 2008 requires the members to prepare financial statements for each financial year. Under that law the members have elected to prepare the financial statements in accordance with United Kingdom Generally Accepted Accounting Practice (United Kingdom Accounting Standards and applicable law). Under company law as applied to Limited Liability Partnerships the members must not approve the financial statements unless they are satisfied that they give a true and fair view of the state of affairs of the LLP and of the profit or loss of the LLP for that period.

In preparing these financial statements, the members are required to:

- select suitable accounting policies and then apply them consistently;
- make judgments and estimates that are reasonable and prudent;
- state whether applicable UK Accounting Standards have been followed, subject to any material departures disclosed and explained in the financial statements *[Not applicable for LLPs subject to the small LLPs regime and medium-sized LLPs]*; and
- prepare the financial statements on the going concern basis unless it is inappropriate to presume that the LLP will continue in business. *[included where no separate statement on going concern is made by the members]*.

The members are responsible for keeping adequate accounting records that are sufficient to show and explain the LLP's transactions and disclose with reasonable accuracy at any time the financial position of the LLP and enable them to ensure that the financial statements comply with the *Companies Act* 2006 as modified by the *Limited Liability Partnerships (Accounts and Audit) (Application of Companies Act 2006) Regulations* 2008. They are also responsible for safeguarding the assets of the LLP and hence for taking reasonable steps for the prevention and detection of fraud and other irregularities.

[Where the financial statements are published on the internet: The members are responsible for the maintenance and integrity of the corporate and financial information included on the LLP's website. Legislation in the United Kingdom governing the preparation and dissemination of financial statements may differ from legislation in other jurisdictions] [Author's note – not illustrated in APB Bulletin 2010/2].

5.11 Disclosure of auditor's remuneration – audited LLPs

Requirements for the disclosure of auditors' remuneration are provided by SI 2008/489 (*Companies (Disclosure of Auditor Remuneration and Liability Limitation Agreements) Regulations* 2008) as amended by SI 2011/2198 the *Companies (Disclosure of Auditor Remuneration and Liability Limitation Agreements) (Amendment) Regulations* 2011. Parts 1 and 2 of these Regulations are also applicable for LLPs as amended by s. 494.

Remuneration receivable by a small or medium-sized LLP's auditor for auditing the accounts must be disclosed in a note to the annual accounts. Remuneration includes benefits in kind and the nature and estimated money-value of those benefits must also be disclosed.

SI 2008/489, reg. 4(1)–(3) Where more than one person has been appointed as an LLP's auditor in respect of any financial period, separate disclosure is required in respect of the remuneration of each person.

SI 2008/489, reg. 4(4) For a medium-sized LLP, disclosure of remuneration may be required in respect of assurance services (other than auditing), tax advisory services, and other services.

For other LLPs which are not small or medium-sized the following disclosure must also be given:

- Separate disclosure of the auditor's remuneration is required in respect of the auditing of the accounts and of each of the following types of service:
  1. the auditing of accounts of any associate of the LLP;
  2. audit-related assurance services;
  3. taxation compliance services;
  4. all taxation advisory services not falling within paragraph 3;
  5. internal audit services;
  6. all assurance services not falling within paragraphs 1 to 5;
  7. all services relating to corporate finance transactions entered into, or proposed to be entered into, by or on behalf of the LLP or any of its associates not falling within paragraphs 1 to 6;
  8. all non-audit services not falling within paragraphs 2 to 7.

- Separate disclosure is required in respect of services supplied to the LLP and its subsidiaries and to associated pension schemes.
- Any remuneration receivable in respect of the period to which the accounts relate by either the LLP's auditor or any person who was, at any time during the period to which the accounts relate, an associate of the LLP's auditor for the supply of other services to the LLP or any associate of the LLP. (Disclosure is not required of remuneration receivable for the supply of services falling within paragraph 8 above supplied by a distant associate of the LLP's auditor where the total remuneration receivable for all of those services supplied by that associate does not exceed either £10,000 or 1% of the total audit remuneration received by the LLP's auditor in the most recent financial year of the auditor which ended no later than the end of the financial year of the LLP to which the accounts relate).

SI 2008/489, reg. 6 A small eligible parent entity preparing audited group accounts must disclose consolidated auditor's remuneration information on the basis of SI 2008/489, reg. 6, in which case the parent entity's individual accounts need not disclose auditor's remuneration.

5.12 Dormant LLPs

s. 1169(1) As for companies, an LLP is 'dormant' during any period in which it has no significant accounting transaction ('significant accounting transaction' is explained below in **5.13**).

Dormant LLPs which are exempt from audit may file abbreviated accounts under the small LLPs regime (an abbreviated balance sheet and notes), without an Auditor's Rreport, provided the balance sheet contains a statement by the members in accordance with CA 2006, s. 475 (as applied by the *Limited Liability Partnerships (Accounts and Audit) (Application of Companies Act 2006) Regulations* 2008. (See Example accounts in **Chapter 10** and abbreviated accounts in **Chapter 6**.)

Conditions for audit exemption are subject to:

- the requirement for a statement to be contained in the balance sheet (see **5.16**); and
- LLPs excluded from dormant LLPs' exemption (see **5.15**).

Dormant subsidiary LLPs meeting certain requirements may be exempt from preparing and filing individual accounts (see **5.17**).

5.13   Definition of 'dormant LLP'

A dormant LLP is an LLP which (during any period) has no 'significant accounting transaction'.

A 'significant accounting transaction' means a transaction which is required by CA 2006, s. 386 to be entered in the LLP's accounting records, *other than* transactions consisting of penalties or payments to the Registrar of Companies for:

- change of name fee;
- penalty for failure to deliver accounts (*under* s. 453); or
- annual return filing fee.

5.14   Conditions for exemption from audit for dormant LLPs

A dormant LLP is exempt from the requirements for audit of its accounts in respect of a financial year if:

- it has been dormant since its formation; or
- it has been dormant since the end of the previous financial year.

s. 480

Further, to be exempt the LLP must also:

- be entitled to prepare its individual accounts in accordance with the small LLPs regime (see s. 381–384), or would be so entitled but for the fact that it is a member of an ineligible group; and
- not be required to prepare group accounts for that year.

There are circumstances where small LLPs which are part of a group are not entitled to the audit exemption. However, where an LLP is both a subsidiary undertaking and dormant throughout the whole of the period or periods during the financial year when it is a group entity, it is entitled to the audit exemption.

s. 479(3)

A dormant LLP is not entitled to audit exemption unless its balance sheet contains a statement or statements under *Companies Act* 2006, s. 475(2) as explained in **5.16** below.

A dormant LLP is not exempt from audit (and an audit of the accounts is, therefore, necessary) if there is a specific requirement in the LLP's membership agreement to appoint auditors.

5.15   LLPs excluded from dormant LLPs' exemption

An LLP is not entitled to the exemption from audit if:

(a)   it was at any time within the financial year one of the following:

- an authorised insurance LLP;
- a banking LLP;
- an e-money issuer;
- a MiFID investment firm; or
- a UCITS management firm.

SI 2007/2932
s. 481   (b)   the LLP carries on insurance market activity.

5.16   Members' statements – entitlement to exemption

A dormant LLP is not entitled to audit exemption unless its balance sheet contains a statement or
s. 480(3)   statements by the members to that effect that:

- the LLP is entitled to exemption from audit by virtue of *Companies Act* 2006, s. 480 (as applied by the *Limited Liability Partnerships (Accounts and Audit) Application of Companies Act 2006) Regulations* 2008; and
- the members acknowledge their responsibilities for complying with the requirements of the Act
s. 475(3)   with respect to accounting records and the preparation of accounts.

s. 475(2) and The statements required to entitle audit exemption as above must appear on the balance sheet
s. 475(4)   above the signature and printed name of the designated member.

5.17   Dormant subsidiary LLP exemption from preparing or filing accounts

The *Companies and Limited Liability Partnerships (Accounts and Audit Exemptions and Change of Accounting Framework) Regulations* 2012 (SI 2012/2301) have introduced CA 2006, s. 394A which is applied to LLPs by SI 2008/1911.

This section allows a dormant subsidiary LLP to be exempt from the requirement to prepare and file accounts if it fulfils the following conditions:

(a)   its parent undertaking is established under the law of an EEA state;
(b)   all of the members of the LLP agree to the exemption in respect of the financial year in question;
(c)   the parent gives a statutory guarantee of all the outstanding liabilities to which the subsidiary is subject at the end of the financial year in accordance with CA 2006, s. 394C;
(d)   the LLP is included in the consolidated accounts drawn up for that year or to an earlier date in that year by the parent undertaking, which must be prepared in accordance with Directive 83/349/EEC (the Seventh Company Law Directive) or International Accounting Standards;
(e)   the use of the exemption by the subsidiary must be disclosed in the notes in the consolidated accounts drawn up by the parent;
(f)   the following documents must be filed by the directors of the subsidiary at Companies House on or before the date that they were due to file the subsidiary's accounts:

   (i)   written notice of the agreement in (b);
   (ii)   a statement by the parent that it guarantees the subsidiary LLP under the particular section of the Act;
   (iii) a copy of the consolidated annual report and accounts referred to in (d) and the auditor's report on those accounts;

(g) the LLP is not an authorised insurance company, a banking LLP, an e-Money issuer, a MiFID investment firm or a UCITS management company, or carries on insurance market activity; and

(h) the LLP is not a trade union or an employer's association.

An annual return will still be required to be filed at Companies House.

Chapter 6 Abbreviated accounts

6.1 Abbreviated accounts

An LLP classified as small or medium-sized and preparing UK GAAP (but not IAS) accounts is permitted to deliver 'abbreviated accounts' in place of full statutory accounts ('individual accounts') to the Registrar of Companies. Accounts abbreviated in such a way are statutory accounts and are then filed as 'annual accounts' with the Registrar of Companies in accordance with s. 444 for small LLPs or s. 445 for medium-sized LLPs.

s. 441, s. 444 & s. 445

Abbreviated accounts are accounts prepared in accordance with:

Sch. 4

Small LLP

(a) SI 2008/1912, Sch. 3 (Part 1) – abbreviated balance sheet

(b) SI 2008/1912, Sch. 3 (Part 2) – notes to the accounts

Medium-sized LLP

SI 2008/1913, reg. 4 and Sch. 1 – there are minimal disclosure exemptions within the medium-sized LLP profit and loss account.

6.2 Contents of abbreviated accounts

Abbreviated accounts are not required to give a true and fair view; they are a form of accounts containing less information and disclosure than the full individual annual accounts for members and basically comprise:

Small LLP – 'an abbreviated balance sheet', being an abbreviated version of the full balance sheet, and certain notes.

Sch. 3

Medium-sized LLP – full statutory accounts (to accord with SI 2008/1913) except that the analysis of turnover set out in Sch. 1, para. 65 may be omitted and some items within the profit and loss account may be combined.

SI 2008/1913, reg. 4(3)

A summary of the options available for filing small LLP accounts with the Registrar of Companies is set out in **6.3**. Abbreviated accounts will usually comprise the elements shown in **Table 6.2.**

Abbreviated accounts for a small LLP, in practice, can be prepared on the basis of minimal or selective amendments to the full annual accounts prepared under SI 2008/1912, Sch. 1, remembering that abbreviated accounts must be copies of those elements of the LLP's (full members') annual accounts that are required under SI 2008/1912, Sch. 3 (see **6.3** below).

As the concessions for the abbreviated accounts of a medium-sized LLP are minimal there is no separate schedule in SI 2008/1913 regarding the format to be adopted.

6.3   Filing abbreviated accounts

The filing requirements for abbreviated accounts are set out in s. 444(3) (small LLPs) and s. 445(3) (medium-sized LLPs).

A small LLP (as defined) preparing non-IAS accounts is required to send a copy of its full annual accounts to its members. It must also deliver to the Registrar of Companies one of the following:

- full annual accounts – full individual or group annual accounts prepared in accordance with CA 2006 as applied to LLPs and SI 2008/1912, or full IAS accounts;
- abbreviated accounts – prepared in accordance with SI 2008/1912, reg. 5 and Sch. 3; or
- full accounts but excluding the profit and loss account.

There is no provision for 'abbreviated group accounts' within CA 2006 and therefore small or medium-sized groups are unable to file abbreviated accounts.

Eligible small LLPs that are subject to the small LLPs regime are able to choose whether or not to file a profit and loss account. **Table 6.1** below summarises the options available.

FILING OPTION	Full annual accounts	Full balance sheet only	Abbreviated accounts
	UK GAAP and IAS LLPs	UK GAAP and IAS LLPs	UK GAAP LLPs only
Copy full balance sheet	Yes	Yes	n/a
Balance sheet statement	Yes (s. 414)	Yes (s. 444(5))	Yes (SI 2008/1912, Sch. 3, para. 1(2))
Members' report	Not required by the Regulations	Not required by the Regulations	Not required by the Regulations
Copy full P&L account	Yes	No – n/a	Optional
Auditor's report (*if applicable*) – *under s. 495*	Yes – *if accounts audited*	Yes (full s. 495 auditor's report)* – *if full accounts audited*	No – n/a
Prescribed notes (*including accounting policies*)	Yes	Yes	Yes – Per SI 2008/1913 (*including Sch. 3*)
Special Auditor's report – *under s. 449*	n/a	n/a	Yes
Approval, signature and balance sheet statement – under s. 450 (*abbreviated accounts*)	No – n/a	No – n/a	Yes

Table 6.1   Filing accounts on public record – summary of options available for small LLPs

Where accounts delivered are audited but are neither abbreviated accounts nor full annual accounts, the auditor's report delivered with them is the full report under s. 495 notwithstanding that the accounts themselves may be restricted in content, for example to simply a balance sheet. (This is indicated in **Table 6.1** by*.) In these circumstances, APB in its Bulletin 2008/4 (April 2008) suggests (at Bulletin Paragraph 12) that the auditor's report should be accompanied by a textual explanation on the following lines (*author's amendments are shown in italics, deletions also highlighted*):

> Although the *LLP* is only required to file a balance sheet, CA 2006 *(as applied by Limited Liability Partnerships (Accounts and Audit) (Application of Companies Act 2006) Regulations 2008)* requires the accompanying auditor's report to be a copy of our report to the members on the *LLP's* full annual accounts ~~and directors' report~~. Readers are cautioned that the profit and loss account and certain other primary statements ~~and the directors' report~~, referred to in the copy of our auditor's report, are not required to be filed with the Registrar of Companies.

Table 6.2 sets out the normal contents of abbreviated accounts for small or medium-sized LLPs.

Table 6.2 **Abbreviated accounts**	*Small LLP* SI 2008/1912, Sch. 3	*Medium-sized LLP* SI 2008/1913, Sch. 1
Members' report	Not required by the Regulations and generally omitted as consistent with approach adopted by small companies	Not required by the Regulations but generally included as consistent with approach adopted by medium-sized companies
Profit and loss account	No profit and loss account	Profit and loss account must disclose 'turnover' but may combine certain items
Balance sheet	Abbreviated balance sheet – SI 2008/1913, Sch. 3 format	Full balance sheet – SI 2008/1913, Sch. 1 format
Cash flow and other primary statements	Not required	Full statements required
Notes	Limited information only SI 2008/1912, Sch. 3 disclosures	Full notes, including disclosure of turnover (but omitting turnover analysis) (SI 2008/1913, reg. 4(2))
	No information on members' transactions or employees' remuneration	
	No disclosure of auditors' remuneration	
Auditor's report	Special report (if applicable)	Special report

If abbreviated accounts are delivered to the Registrar, and the LLP is not exempt from audit (or the members have not taken advantage of any such exemption), the accounts must be delivered together with a copy of the special auditor's report required by s. 449.

The decision whether or not to take advantage of the exemptions to prepare abbreviated accounts will be a commercial one. Full statutory accounts have to be prepared in any case for members; in deciding whether to also prepare abbreviated accounts, the members of small or medium-sized LLPs will have regard to:

- the additional costs involved in the preparation of an additional set of accounts;
- the financial information omitted in abbreviated accounts; and
- the sensitivity or confidentiality of financial information required for public disclosure.

A decision can only be reached after a comparison is made of full and limited disclosure and after the relative costs and benefits have been considered. Many small LLPs choose to produce abbreviated accounts.

6.4   Abbreviated balance sheet (small LLPs only)

The balance sheet format and contents in abbreviated accounts of a small LLP are set out in regulations under SI 2008/1912, Sch. 3.

Sch 3.1(1)

A small LLP may deliver to the Registrar a copy of the balance sheet showing the items listed in either of the balance sheet formats set out in the Regulations, in the order and under the headings and sub-headings given in the format adopted, but in other respects corresponding to the full balance sheet of the LLP.

The abbreviated balance sheet formats provided by SI 2008/1912, Sch. 3 are set out in **Table 6.3**. Schedule 3 is reproduced in full in **Appendix C**.

Table 6.3   Form and content of abbreviated accounts of small LLPs delivered to the Registrar of Companies (SI 2008/1912, Sch. 3)

Balance sheet formats

Format 1	Format 2
	ASSETS
A. Fixed assets	A. Fixed assets
I Intangible assets	I Intangible assets
II Tangible assets	II Tangible assets
III Investments	III Investments
B. Current assets	B. Current assets
I Stocks	I Stocks
II Debtors	II Debtors
III Investments	III Investments
IV Cash at bank and in hand	IV Cash at bank and in hand
C. Prepayments and accrued income	C. Prepayments and accrued income
D. Creditors: amounts falling due within one year	LIABILITIES
E. Net current assets (liabilities)	A. Loans and other debts due to members
F. Total assets less current liabilities	B. Members' other interests
G. Creditors: amounts falling due after more than one year	I Members' capital
H. Provisions for liabilities	II Revaluation reserve
I. Accruals and deferred income	III Other reserves
J. Loans and other debts due to members	C. Provisions for liabilities
K. Members' other interests	D. Creditors
I Members' capital	E. Accruals and deferred income
II Revaluation reserve	
III Other reserves	

Debtors (both formats) – *the aggregate amount of debtors falling due after more than one year must be shown separately unless it is disclosed in the notes to the accounts.*

Creditors (format 2) – *the aggregate amount of creditors falling due after more than one year must be shown separately unless it is disclosed in the notes to the accounts.*

6.5 Notes to abbreviated accounts (small LLP only)

Any information required for the purposes of the abbreviated accounts of a small LLP must (if not given in the accounts themselves) be given by way of a note to the accounts.

Sch. 3.2

The information required to be given by way of a note is set out in **Table 6.4**.

SI 2008/1912, Sch. 3 is reproduced in **Appendix C**.

Table 6.4   Notes to abbreviated accounts of a small LLP

	SI 2008/1912 Sch. 3 paragraph:
Accounting policies	3
Fixed assets [for letter or Roman number format headings only]	4
Financial fixed assets in excess of fair value	5
Debtors: amounts falling due after more than one year (aggregate)	Refer Table 6.3
Creditors: amounts falling due within one year or after more than one year for each category of creditors (Format 2)	Refer Table 6.3
Particulars of creditors:	
Debts falling due after five years	6(1)
Secured debts	6(2)
Basis of translation of foreign currencies	7
	SI 2008/1912 Sch. 2 paragraph:
Subsidiary undertakings	1–3/9
Other significant (20% or more) undertakings	4–6/9
Parent undertakings and ultimate parent entity	7–9

Disclosures only required by accounting standards and the LLP SORP included in the accounts distributed to the members need not be given in the abbreviated accounts delivered to the Registrar. This would include, for example, the disclosure concerning the remuneration of members.

6.6 Approval and signing of abbreviated accounts

CA 2006, s. 450 sets out the provisions for the approval and signing of abbreviated accounts.

Abbreviated accounts must be approved by the members and signed on behalf of all of the members by a designated member. The signature must be on the balance sheet.

s. 450(1)–(2)

The balance sheet must contain in a prominent position above the signature, a statement to the effect that it is prepared in accordance with the provisions of the Companies Act as applied to LLPs relating (as the case may be) to LLPs subject to the small LLPs regime or to medium-sized LLPs.

s. 450(3)

The requirement can be illustrated as follows:

Small LLPs regime

'These [abbreviated] accounts have been prepared in accordance with the special provisions of section 444(3) Companies Act 2006 (as applied by Limited Liability Partnerships (Accounts and Audit) (Application of Companies Act 2006) Regulations 2008) applicable to LLPs subject to the small LLPs regime.'

Medium-sized LLPs

> 'These [abbreviated] accounts have been prepared in accordance with the special provisions of section 445(3) Companies Act 2006 (as applied by Limited Liability Partnerships (Accounts and Audit) (Application of Companies Act 2006) Regulations 2008) in regard to medium-sized LLPs.'

It is recommended that the Designated Member's signature should be in black ink and the name of the Designated Member who signs the balance sheet should be printed below or beside the signature.

s. 450(4)–(5) There are provisions dealing with penalties if abbreviated accounts are approved that do not comply with the statutory requirements of CA 2006.

Accounts that are subject to audit exemption are also required to have additional statements as explained in **Chapter 9** and illustrated in **Example 9.1**.

6.7 Parent entities

There is no statutory provision to file abbreviated group accounts. A parent entity which files its own abbreviated individual accounts includes within those accounts considerable disclosure relating to subsidiaries and other significant holdings in undertakings (see **Chapter 7** and **Appendix A** at **6 Alternative bases of accounting**).

A parent entity wishing to produce group accounts will need to prepare these as non-statutory accounts in addition to its own statutory individual abbreviated accounts.

6.8 Special auditor's report (s. 449)

Abbreviated accounts prepared by an audit-exempt LLP are not required to contain an auditor's report (but see the requirement for a statement from the designated members in **6.6**).

Where the members of an LLP deliver abbreviated accounts to the Registrar and the LLP is not exempt from audit (or the members have not taken advantage of any such exemption), they must also deliver to the Registrar a copy of a special report of the LLP's auditor.

APB guidance on the format of the auditor's report has been provided in APB Bulletin 2008/4 *The special auditor's report on abbreviated accounts in the United Kingdom* (April 2008) and is reflected in the example reports on abbreviated accounts in **Chapter 11**.

In Bulletin 2008/4, the APB recommends, where the auditor's report on the full accounts is unqualified but has been modified to include an explanatory paragraph regarding a fundamental uncertainty (for example, concerning the going concern basis), the special auditor's report should also include the explanatory paragraph, within a section entitled 'Other information'. The auditor should include whatever information is considered important for a proper understanding of the report.

The legislation does not envisage a qualified opinion; if the auditor cannot give the positive statements of opinion on the abbreviated accounts, the members are not entitled to deliver abbreviated accounts.

6.9 Medium-sized LLPs

6.9.1 Annual accounts – medium-sized LLPs

The members of an LLP that *qualifies* as a medium-sized LLP in relation to a financial year *must* deliver to the registrar a copy of:

- the LLP's annual accounts; and
- the auditor's report on the accounts.

6.9.2 Medium-sized LLP abbreviated accounts

Where a medium-sized LLP prepares non–IAS accounts, the members *may* deliver to the registrar 'abbreviated accounts', these being a copy of the LLP's annual accounts for the financial year that includes a profit and loss account in which items are combined in accordance with regulations under SI 2008/1913 *Large and Medium-sized Limited Liability Partnerships (Accounts) Regulations* 2008, and where any items whose omission is authorised by the Regulations are omitted.

Where the LLP chooses to submit abbreviated accounts to the Registrar, the LLP must submit:

- a copy of the abbreviated accounts drawn up in accordance with the SI 2008/1913 Regulations; and
- a Special auditor's report required by CA 2006, s. 449.

As the Members' Report is a requirement of the LLP SORP rather than the Regulations, the Registrar does not require the Members' Report to be submitted with the abbreviated accounts of a medium-sized LLP. However, standard practice is that the Members' Report is submitted with the abbreviated accounts of a medium-sized LLP.

6.9.3 Medium-sized LLP – abbreviated profit and loss account

A medium-sized LLP may prepare abbreviated accounts in which the profit and loss account includes items that are combined. The items which can be combined in each format of the profit and loss account are set out in **Table 6.5.**

SI 2008/1913, reg.4(3)

Table 6.5 Profit and loss account items which can be combined (SI 2008/1913, reg. 4(3))	
Format 1	Format 2
2 Cost of sales	
	2 Change in stocks of finished goods and work-in-progress
3 Gross profit or loss	
	3 Own work capitalised
6 Other operating income	4 Other operating income
	5 (a) Raw materials and consumables
	(b) Other external charges
*References are to item numbers in the statutory formats of **SI 2008/1913, Sch. 1***	

6.10 Small LLP abbreviated accounts checklist

As small LLPs more frequently produce abbreviated accounts than medium-sized LLPs, this checklist provides a guide to the appropriate disclosure requirements in producing 'abbreviated accounts' for delivery to the Registrar of Companies. This applies where the LLP prepares UK GAAP accounts. Abbreviated accounts are not available for filing where IAS accounts are prepared.

s. 444(3)

This checklist does not purport to be a complete checklist, detailing the disclosure requirements applicable where individual full accounts are prepared. For this purpose one of the accounts checklists suggested in **Appendix H** should be used.

Special provisions may additionally apply where an LLP is a 'dormant LLP' under CA 2006, s. 480 as applied to LLPs by the *Limited Liability Partnerships (Accounts and Audit) (Application of Companies Act 2006) Regulations* 2008 (see also Chapter 5).

References in this checklist to 'full accounts' include 'small LLP individual accounts' (in accordance with SI 2008/1912 (*Small Limited Liability Partnerships (Accounts) Regulations* 2008) – see **5.1**).

Where the small LLP is audit-exempt, there is no requirement for a special auditor's report (see 7 in the checklist below).

Table 6.6 Checklist for the preparation of abbreviated accounts

An LLP which qualifies as small is entitled to deliver abbreviated accounts to the Registrar of Companies (CA 2006, s. 444).

1. Complete the following information:			
Turnover	20xx £	20xx–1 £	20xx–2 £
Balance sheet total	£	£	£
Employees			
Dormant?	Yes/No	Yes/No	Yes/No

s.1169 (against the Dormant? row)

Refer to **Chapter 4** to determine the size of the LLP
Refer to **Chapter 5** for definition of a dormant LLP

Are abbreviated accounts appropriate?	tick or N/A

2. Based on the above information
(a) The LLP qualifies as:
   (i) small (if so, answer **3** to **11**)   } abbreviated accounts
   (ii) dormant (if so, answer **5, 6** and **8** to **12**) } may be prepared
 	
(b) The LLP is
   (i) ineligible   } if so, abbreviated or
   (ii) other (i.e. neither 'small' nor 'medium-sized') } accounts *not* appropriate	

Members' statements and signature	
3. Members are required to state in a prominent position above the approval signature on the balance sheet that the accounts are prepared and delivered in accordance with the special provisions of CA 2006 (as applied by the *Limited Liability Partnerships (Accounts and Audit) (Application of the Companies Act 2006) Regulations* 2008) applicable to LLPs subject to the small LLPs regime.	
4. Where advantage is taken of audit exemption, the members are required to confirm or acknowledge: (a) LLP's entitlement to audit exemption	

s. 450(3) (against item 3)
s. 477 (against item 4)

(b) duty to keep accounting records (s. 386)	
(c) duty to prepare true and fair view accounts (s. 393–394)	
5. If the LLP is dormant and is exempt from the provisions relating to the audit of accounts, a statement is required as in 4 above.	*s. 475(2)*
6. Abbreviated balance sheet must be signed by a Designated Member (in accordance with CA 2006, s. 450 as applied to LLPs).	*s. 450*

Special auditor's report

(Not applicable where 'dormant LLP' under CA 2006, s. 480 or advantage taken of small LLP audit exemption)   *s. 449(1)*

7.   Where abbreviated accounts are filed, the special auditor's report is required to state that in the auditor's opinion: *s. 449(2)*

(a)   the small LLP is entitled to deliver abbreviated accounts prepared in accordance with the relevant provision   *s. 444(1)–(3)*

(b)   the accounts are properly prepared in accordance with that relevant provision.

If the auditor's report on the full annual accounts was qualified, the special report must reproduce the text in full (with further material necessary to understand a qualification).   *s. 449(3)*

The special auditor's report must also reproduce any statement contained in the full auditor's report under s. 498(2) or (3) (proper accounting records or failure to obtain necessary information, etc.).   *s. 449(3)*

8.   No members' report

9.   No profit and loss account.   *s. 444(3)*

10.   Balance sheet – abbreviated version

    (a) Only format headings with letter or Roman numeral need be shown (in the order and presentation of SI 2008/1912 Sch 3)

    (b) For debtors *and* creditors, show aggregate amounts falling due: *Sch 3.1*
        (i)   within one year,
        (ii)   after more than one year,
        (unless shown in notes).

    (c) The name and signature of a Designated Member (see 6 above).   *s. 444(6)*

11.   Notes – show only: *Sch. 3*

(a)   Accounting policies adopted – including: *Sch 3.3*

    • depreciation and diminution in value of assets, and

    • statement of preparation in accordance with the FRSSE (if applicable).

(b)   Fixed assets –

    • movements – only format headings with letter or Roman number (i.e. movements in tangible fixed assets, intangible fixed assets, and fixed asset investments for the categories in total) need be shown, including cost or valuation and accumulated depreciation at beginning and end of year; additions, disposals, revaluations, and depreciation provisions,   *Sch 3.4*

    • fair value disclosure of financial fixed assets, if applicable.   *Sch 3.5*

(c)   Creditors and indebtedness

    (i)   liabilities repayable in more than five years   *Sch 3.6(1)*

        (1)   amount due for repayment, other than by instalments, after more than five years from the balance sheet date;

        (2)   amount repayable by instalments, after more than five years;

    (ii)   aggregate amount of *secured* liabilities.   *Sch 3.6(2)*

(d)   Foreign currencies – basis for translating sums denominated in foreign currencies.   *Sch 3.7*

(e)   Comparative figures (in accordance with accounting standards). Where corresponding amounts are not comparable, adjust and give particulars of and reasons for adjustment.

(f)   Particulars of subsidiary undertakings.   *Sch 2.1*

For disclosure details see **Appendix A**.	
(g) Particulars of holdings in undertakings (other than subsidiary undertakings) where holdings exceed 20% ('significant holdings').	
For disclosure details see **Appendix A**.	
(h) Parent undertakings (name and country of incorporation or principal business address if unincorporated).	
(i) Ultimate parent company.	
Dormant LLP – acting as agent	
12. Where an audit-exempt dormant LLP (under s. 480) has acted as agent for any person during the financial year, that fact must be disclosed in the notes to the accounts.	

Sch 2.4 (row g)
Sch 2.7 (row h)
Sch 2.8 (row i)
Sch 3.8 (row 12)

6.11 Future developments

For periods commencing on or after 1 January 2016, companies are no longer able to file abbreviated accounts, however, the disclosures required in their full accounts have been reduced. The Government has announced that it intends to extend this change to LLPs (see **Chapter 13** for further details).

Chapter 7 Requirement to prepare group accounts

7.1 Small LLPs – option to prepare group accounts

If at the end of a financial year an LLP subject to the small LLPs regime is a parent entity the members, as well as preparing individual accounts for the year, *may* prepare group accounts for the year. On this basis, a small parent LLP (as defined) is not, therefore, required to prepare group accounts.

All other parent LLPs (being LLPs that are ineligible or excluded from the small LLPs regime under CA 2006, s. 384) *must* prepare group accounts for the year *unless* the LLP is otherwise exempt from that requirement under exemptions set out in CA 2006, s. 399(3).

Notwithstanding the above, a small parent LLP may prepare group accounts for its own management accounting purposes and not submit them to the Registrar of Companies but file instead its own individual statutory accounts with appropriate disclosures. If group accounts are not prepared because of the group accounts exemption entitlement, the LLP may, if it wishes, file abbreviated accounts provided it qualifies as a small (or medium-sized) LLP.

A medium-sized parent LLP is not exempt from the requirement to prepare group accounts.

There is no statutory provision to prepare and submit abbreviated group accounts.

7.2 Qualifying conditions – group accounts exemptions

CA 2006, s. 383(4) and 466(4) as applied to LLPs set out the conditions to be met by a group for the parent LLP to qualify as 'small' or 'medium-sized' as appropriate.

A parent LLP qualifies as a small LLP in relation to a financial year only if the group headed by it qualifies as a small group. *s. 383(1)*

The size classification of a parent LLP is determined with regard to the aggregate qualifying criteria of the group taken as a whole (parent LLP and subsidiary undertakings), irrespective of the actual size qualification of the parent LLP itself.

A group qualifies as small in relation to the parent LLP's first financial year if the qualifying conditions are met in that year. In subsequent years, a group qualifies as small if the qualifying conditions:

* are met in that year and the preceding financial year;
* are met in that year and the group qualified as small in relation to the preceding financial year; or
* were met in the preceding financial year and the group qualified as small in relation to that year. *s. 383(2)-(3)*

A group meets the qualifying conditions (and is, therefore, exempt from producing group (consolidated) accounts) if it does not exceed more than one of the following criteria on one or other of the following two bases: *s. 383(4)-(7)*

Criteria	(The bases may be mixed)	
	Net basis	*Gross basis*
Small group (CA 2006, s. 383(4))		
Turnover	£6.5m	£7.8m
Balance sheet total	£3.26m	£3.9m
Average number of employees (on a monthly basis)	50	50

Similarly a group meets the qualifying conditions for a medium-sized group if it does not exceed more than one of the following criteria on one or other of the following gross and net bases.

Criteria	(The bases may be mixed)	
	Net basis	*Gross basis*
Medium-sized group (CA 2006, s. 466(4))		
Turnover	£25.9m	£31.1m
Balance sheet total	£12.9m	£15.5m
Average number of employees (on a monthly basis)	250	250

e.g. if a group has turnover of £8m (gross) and £6m (net), a balance sheet total of £3.8m (gross) and £3.5m (net) and 60 employees, on the size criteria the group would qualify as a small group. Although it exceeds the employee number threshold it does not exceed the net turnover threshold or gross balance sheet threshold.

The aggregate figures are ascertained by aggregating the relevant figures from individual statutory accounts (determined in accordance with CA 2006, s. 382) for each member of the group.

The alternative bases for turnover and balance sheet totals (as qualifying conditions for exemption) are:

- *'Net' basis* – Aggregate figures for turnover and balance sheet totals after any set-offs and consolidation adjustments made for the elimination of group transactions in accordance with SI 2008/1912, Sch. 4 (small LLPs) or SI 2008/1913, Sch. 3 (medium-sized and large LLPs) for non IAS group accounts or international accounting standards for IAS group accounts; and
- *'Gross' basis* – Aggregate figures for turnover and balance sheet totals without such set-offs and consolidation adjustments.

In both SI 2008/1912, Sch. 4 and SI 2008/1913, Sch. 3 consolidation adjustments include:

- elimination of intra-group transactions and assets and liabilities;
- elimination of intra-group unrealised profits or losses; and
- adjustments to effect uniform accounting policies within the group.

Because the gross thresholds are higher than the individual thresholds, it is possible for a group containing a medium-sized company to be a small group, for example in the following circumstances:

Holding LLP owns 100% of its subsidiary, Subsidiary Limited (assume circumstances do not change year on year):

	Holding LLP	Subsidiary Limited
Turnover	£0	£7.5m
Balance sheet total	£250,000	£3.5m
Average number of employees	0	40
Ineligible?	No	No

On its own, Subsidiary Limited is a medium-sized company as it breaches two out of three of the size criteria defining a small company for two years in a row. However the group headed by Holding LLP is small, as the total turnover and total assets are both below the gross thresholds.

The Government has announced that it intends to increase the size criteria (see **Chapter 13**).

7.3   Exempt small groups – related undertakings disclosures

The information to be given in notes to a small LLP's annual accounts in relation to related undertakings where group accounts are not required are provided by SI 2008/1912, Sch. 2, Pt. 1 (*Small Limited Liability Partnerships (Accounts) Regulations* 2008) 'Information about related undertakings where LLP not preparing Group accounts (Companies Act or IAS individual accounts)').

Details of required disclosures are set out in **Appendix A**. SI 2008/1912, Sch. 2 is reproduced in full in **Appendix C**.

7.4   Disclosure requirements for small group accounts

7.4.1   Non-IAS small group accounts

Where the members of a parent entity which is subject to the small LLPs regime and has prepared Companies Act individual accounts choose to prepare Companies Act group accounts under CA 2006, s. 398 (Option to prepare group accounts), those group accounts must comply with the provisions of:

- SI 2008/1912,Sch. 4 (Pt. 1) – Form and content of non-IAS group accounts (consolidated balance sheet and consolidated profit and loss account, and additional information to be provided by way of notes to the accounts).
- SI 2008/1912, Sch. 4 (Pt. 2) – Information about related undertakings where LLP preparing group's accounts.

Information about related undertakings may be omitted from the notes to the accounts in certain circumstances where the undertaking (e.g. a subsidiary within the group) is established under the law of a country outside the United Kingdom, or carries on business outside the United Kingdom.

SI 2008/1912 reg. 7(1)

The group accounts of a small LLP are treated as having complied with any provision of SI 2008/1912, Sch. 4 (Pt. 1) (Form and content of non-IAS group accounts) if they comply instead with the corresponding provisions of SI 2008/1913, Sch. 3 (*Large and Medium-Sized Limited Liability Partnership (Accounts) Regulations* 2008).

7.4.2   Small groups and the FRSSE

A small group voluntarily preparing group accounts may take advantage of the provisions and exemptions afforded by the FRSSE (effective January 2015) (see **Chapter 3**) but must have regard to the legal requirements reflected in the FRSSE and SI 2008/1912, Sch. 4 (see **7.4.1** above). When considering SI 2008/1912, Sch. 4, any references in that Schedule to compliance with the provisions of 'Part 1 of Schedule 4' are to be construed as references to the legal requirements reflected in the FRSSE.

The FRSSE does not contain detailed requirements on how to prepare group accounts. Instead, it says that small entities should have regard to the requirements of FRS 102 in developing their accounting policies, not as a mandatory document, but as a means of establishing current practice.

Sections 9 (*Consolidated and Separate Financial Statements*), 14 (*Investments in Associates*), 15 (*Investments in Joint Ventures*) and 19 (*Business Combinations and Goodwill*) should be considered, but only to the extent that they relate to the preparation of consolidated accounts.

Where group accounts are prepared, the balance sheet should contain in a prominent position on the balance sheet, above the member's approval signature, that they are prepared in accordance with the provisions in Pt. 15 of CA 2006 relating to small companies as applied to LLPs (see **Chapter 5** at **5.10**).

7.4.3 Small group accounts – balance sheet format heading ('Investments')

SI 2008/1912, Sch. 4.1(2)

Where small group accounts are prepared, SI 2008/1912, Sch. 4 ('Group Accounts') amends the balance sheet format headings for 'Investments'.

For item B.III in each of the balance sheet formats, the sub-headings of 'Investments' are modified to be as follows:

'B. III. Investments

1. Shares in group undertakings
2. Interests in associated undertakings
3. Other participating interests
4. Loans to group undertakings and undertakings in which a participating interest is held
5. Other investments other than loans
6. Others.'

7.5 Medium-sized LLP – group accounts

A medium-sized parent LLP (being an LLP that is ineligible or excluded from the small LLPs regime under CA 2006, s. 384) *must* prepare group accounts for the year *unless* the LLP is otherwise exempt from that requirement under exemptions set out in CA 2006, s. 399(3).

The exemptions available are under:

- CA 2006, s. 400 (LLP included in EEA accounts of larger group);
- CA 2006, s. 401 (LLP included in non-EEA accounts of larger group); and
- CA 2006, s. 402 (LLP where no subsidiary undertakings need be included in the consolidation).

A medium-sized parent LLP to which these exemptions apply may nevertheless prepare group accounts (CA 2006, s. 399(4)).

7.6 Entitlement to group exemption – auditor's report

s. 498(5)

If the members of an LLP have prepared accounts in accordance with the small LLPs regime and in the auditor's opinion they were not entitled to do so, the auditor must state that fact in the auditor's report.

7.7 Group LLP – availability of small audit exemption

An LLP is exempt from the requirements for the audit of its accounts in respect of a financial year if it meets the conditions set out in CA 2006, s. 477 (see **9.3**). Whether a group qualifies as small is determined in accordance with CA 2006, s. 383 (LLP qualifying as small: parent entities) (see **7.2**).

An LLP which is a group entity (being a parent LLP or a subsidiary undertaking) is only entitled to audit exemption if the following conditions are met:

- the group qualifies as a small group in relation to the financial year; and
- the group was not at any time in the year an 'ineligible' group.

Audit exemption, including the availability of the small LLP audit exemption for group entities, is covered in **Chapter 9**.

Chapter 8 Specific LLP accounting requirements

8.1 Introduction

This chapter aims to highlight the specific accounting issues which are addressed in the LLP SORP with reference to new UK GAAP (specifically FRS 102). It also gives some example accounting policies and notes.

This chapter does not purport to be a complete accounting guide for LLPs and underlying accounting standards should be referred to for the treatment of general transactions.

8.2 Transactions with members

8.2.1 Members' participation rights

One of the fundamental questions to resolve when preparing the accounts of an LLP is whether the participation rights of the members give rise to a financial liability or equity or both, in accordance with section 22 of FRS 102. The treatment will depend upon the terms of the membership agreement for each LLP and therefore the treatment can vary significantly between different LLPs as compared to the memorandum and articles for limited companies; LLPs have considerable flexibility over how that agreement is drafted, and there is wide diversity in practice. The absence of standard arrangements makes it necessary to analyse each members' agreement with care so that members' equity and liability interests are properly reflected in financial statements.

A key element of determining whether the members' participation rights should be treated as a financial liability rather than an equity instrument is the consideration of whether the LLP has a contractual obligation to deliver either cash (or another financial asset) to the member.

Generally, a member's participation right will result in a liability unless either the LLP has an unconditional right to avoid delivering cash or other assets to the member (i.e. the right to any payment or repayment is discretionary on the part of the LLP) or certain conditions are met for puttable instruments or amounts payable on liquidation (see **Appendix A 4.15** for the definition of a puttable instrument from section 22 of FRS 102 which requires such instruments to be classified as equity in some circumstances).

Participation rights in respect of amounts subscribed or otherwise contributed by members to an LLP should be analysed separately from participation rights in respect of remuneration (which may include, for example, salary, interest, bonus, risk premium and allocated share of profits), except where the remuneration, or part thereof, is clearly identifiable as a return on amounts subscribed or otherwise contributed. Therefore, where the remuneration cannot be clearly identified as a return on amounts subscribed, it should be analysed separately (e.g. profit share payable at the discretion of the LLP would be accounted for as an equity interest, even if the member's capital is treated as a liability).

Where remuneration, or part thereof, is clearly identifiable as a return on the amounts subscribed by the members to the LLP (e.g. non-discretionary interest payments), rather than a return for the services provided by the members, then the amounts subscribed and that part of the remuneration that is clearly identifiable as a return on the amounts subscribed should be analysed together for accounting purposes.

The table below gives some examples of how the participation rights in respect of amounts contributed and returns thereon will be classified in the financial statements of the LLP.

As debt	As equity
If in accordance with the membership agreement all profits are automatically divided between the members and if members have a right to demand payment of amounts subscribed or otherwise contributed.	If the LLP has an unconditional right to refuse repayment to members of amounts subscribed or otherwise contributed by them then, providing there is no obligation to pay a return on those amounts, this will be classified as equity.
The ability of a member to exercise a contractual right may be conditional on a future event (e.g. a member may only be able to demand amounts subscribed or otherwise contributed on retirement). Despite the fact that the member's right is conditional on a future event, the LLP does not have an unconditional right to avoid making the payment, so, unless the conditions for puttable instruments are met, a financial liability exists.	
Even if the LLP has an unconditional right to refuse repayment of members' capital, but interest is mandatorily payable on members' capital, then because the interest would be a clearly identifiable return on that capital a liability will be recognised on subscription reflecting the present value of minimum non-discretionary outflows (where the interest is at a market rate, in many cases this will result in all of the relevant capital being classified as a liability). This does not qualify as equity because of the contractual obligation to pay interest.	

8.2.1.1 Treatment of the division of profits

The treatment of members' remuneration in the profit and loss account is summarised in the following table.

Nature of element of a member's remuneration:	Treat as:
Remuneration that is paid under an employment contract **(1)**	Expense, described as 'Members' remuneration charge as an expense', and deducted after arriving at 'Profit for the financial year before members' remuneration and profit shares'
Other payments, arising from components of members' participation rights in the profits for the year that give rise to liabilities in accordance with section 22 of FRS 102, such as mandatory interest payments **(2)**	
Automatic division of profits **(3)**	
Any share of profits arising from a division of profits that is discretionary on the part of the LLP (i.e. where the decision to divide the profits is taken after the profits have been made) **(4)**	Allocation of profit

1. Any remuneration paid under an employment contract – this will be treated as an expense in the profit and loss account and a liability in the balance sheet to the extent that it is unpaid.

2. No equity participation rights – where there are no equity participation rights in the profits for the year, it follows that all amounts becoming due to members in respect of those profits will be presented within 'members' remuneration charged as an expense' (i.e. it will be treated as a charge against profits and not an allocation of profits). The presentation to be adopted in the profit and loss account, as set out in the Regulations and the LLP SORP is shown in **Chapter 5** (see **5.5**).

3. Profits automatically divided – where profits are automatically divided as they arise or are determined, so that the LLP does not have an unconditional right to refuse payment, the amounts arising that are due to members are in the nature of liabilities. They should therefore be treated as an expense in the profit and loss account in the relevant year and, to the extent they remain unpaid at the year end, they should be shown as liabilities in the balance sheet.

4. No automatic division of profits – where there is no automatic division of profits, the LLP has an unconditional right to refuse payment of the profits of a particular year unless and until those profits are divided by a decision taken by the members (or a committee of the members to which the authority to divide profits has been delegated); and accordingly, following such a division, those profits are classed as an appropriation of equity rather than as an expense. They are therefore shown as a residual amount available for appropriation in the profit and loss account. Once profits are divided, the amount of the divided profits is treated as an appropriation which is deducted from equity and should not be presented as an expense within the profit and loss account. To the extent that any divided profits remain unpaid at the year end, the amount unpaid will be recorded as a liability.

Combination of 3 and 4 – it is possible that a combination of these circumstances may arise, for example if 75% of profits are automatically divided, but the remaining profits are only divided at the discretion of the LLP, then the 75% will be treated as an expense in the profit and loss account and a liability in the balance sheet and the remainder when divided will be treated as an appropriation in the profit and loss account.

8.2.2   Members' interests – presentation and disclosure

Balance sheet presentation – All amounts due to members that are classified as liabilities (see **8.2.1**) should be presented within 'Loans and other debts due to members' on the balance sheet. This heading will include any unpaid element of 'Members' remuneration charged as an expense' together with any unpaid allocated profits arising from a discretionary division of profits made during the year. It will also include members' capital classified as a liability. The Regulations require disclosure of the amount of loans and other debts due to members falling due after more than one year.

The members' other interests (i.e. the elements which constitute the equity of the LLP (such as Members' capital (classified as equity), the revaluation reserve and other reserves) are classified separately on the balance sheet as 'Members' Other Interests', with the three main elements shown separately on the face of the balance sheet (see **Chapter 5** for format of the balance sheet).

The Regulations also specifically note that the revaluation reserve must be shown on the LLP's balance sheet. The treatment for taxation purposes of amounts credited or debited to the revaluation reserve must be disclosed in the note to the accounts.

FRS 102 requires inclusion of a statement of changes in equity as a primary financial statement and the LLP SORP requires inclusion of a reconciliation of all elements of members' interests (debt and equity).

As these requirements overlap, the LLP SORP (para. 60A) allows the reconciliation of all elements of members' interests to be presented as a primary statement instead of the statement of changes in equity. Where this option is taken, this statement must include a full table for the comparative period, however, if the primary statement only includes the equity components of members' interests and the reconciliation of all elements is included in the notes, the reconciliation in the notes need only show comparatives in total.

Table 8.1 shows the example note or primary statement set out in the LLP SORP. In reality the note often looks simpler as not all of the rows or columns will be applicable. If it aids clarity the 'Other reserves' column can be analysed further within the note. Any unallocated profits (i.e. amounts retained in the business) should be disclosed as 'Other reserves'.

Table 8.1 Reconciliation of members' interests	EQUITY Members' Other Interests				DEBT Loans and other debts due to members less any amounts due from members in debtors			TOTAL MEMBERS' INTERESTS
	Members' Capital (Classified as equity)	Revaluation Reserve	Other Reserves	Total	Members' Capital (Classified as debt)	Other amounts	Total	**Total 20X1**
Amounts due to members						X	X	
Amounts due from members						(X)	(X)	
Balance at [start of the period]	X	X	X	X	X	X	X	X
Members' remuneration charged as an expense, including employment and retirement benefit costs						X	X	X
Profit/(loss) for the financial year available for discretionary division among members			X	X				X
Members' interests after profit/(loss) for the year	X	X	X	X	X	X	X	X
Other divisions of profits			(X)	(X)		X	X	–
Surplus arising on revaluation of fixed assets		X		X				X
Introduced by members	X			X	X		X	X
Repayments of capital	(X)			(X)	(X)		(X)	(X)
Repayments of debt (including members' capital classified as a liability)					(X)		(X)	(X)
Drawings						(X)	(X)	(X)
Other movements	X	X	X	X	X	X	X	X
Amounts due to members						X	X	
Amounts due from members						(X)	(X)	
Balance at [end of the period]	X	X	X	X	X	X	X	X

Note 1 – In the table above, the amounts owing to and from members should not be offset in the accounts, except where they are in respect of the same member and the conditions set out in paragraph 11.38A of FRS 102 are met. This states that:

'A financial asset and a financial liability shall be offset and the net amount presented in the balance sheet when, and only when, an entity:

(a) currently has a legally enforceable right to set off the recognised amounts; and
(b) intends either to settle on a net basis, or to realise the asset and settle the liability simultaneously.

Debits on members' balances (where, for example, drawings were made during the year in anticipation of profits) should be reviewed for recoverability and shown separately in debtors.

Often the 'Reconciliation of members' interests' can be more straightforward as many of the possible transactions have not occurred in the year; the following is an example for an LLP in its first year of operation.

Example 8.1	EQUITY			DEBT	TOTAL MEMBERS' INTERESTS
	Members' Other Interests			Loans and other debts due to members less any amounts due from members in debtors	
	Members' capital (classified as equity) £	Other reserves £	Total £	Other amounts £	Total 20X3 £
Balance at 1 July 20X3	–	–	–	–	–
Members' remuneration charged as an expense	–	–	–	130,000	130,000
Loss for the financial period available for discretionary division among members	–	(262,202)	(262,202)	–	(262,202)
Members' interests after loss for the period	–	(262,202)	(262,202)	130,000	(132,202)
Introduced by members	750,000	–	750,000	–	750,000
Drawings	–	–	–	(120,000)	(120,000)
Amounts due to members				10,000	
Amounts due from members				–	
Balance at 30 June 20X4	750,000	(262,202)	487,798	100,000	497,798

The notes to the accounts should also explain where amounts in 'loans and other debts due to members' would rank in relation to other creditors in the event of a winding up.

Details of any protection afforded to creditors in such an event which is legally enforceable and cannot be revoked at will by the members should be included in a note to the accounts.

The notes should also disclose what restrictions or limitations exist on the ability of the members to reduce the amount of 'Members' other interests' or state that there are no such restrictions. (**Example 8.2**)

In the absence of agreement to the contrary, unsecured debts due to members will rank equally with debts due to other unsecured creditors in a winding up.

Example 8.2

'In the event of a winding up, members' other reserves rank after unsecured creditors. Loans and other debts due to members rank pari passu with unsecured creditors in the event of a winding up. There is no formal restriction on the ability of the LLP to reduce the amount of members' other interests.'

The Regulations also require separate disclosure of the aggregate amount of money advanced by members by way of loan, the aggregate amount of money owed to members in respect of profits and any other amounts owed to members (see **Chapter 5 Table 5.2**).

8.2.3   Treatment of losses

Where a loss is incurred by an LLP, the loss should be allocated to 'Other reserves' unless there is a specific requirement set out in the membership agreement.

8.2.4   Disclosure of policy in relation to drawings

As set out in **5.9**, LLPs should disclose the overall policy followed in relation to members' drawings, including an indication of the policy applicable where the cash requirements of the business compete with the need to allow cash drawings by members. This disclosure is usually given in a Members' Report.

Such disclosures should include any transfers of members' interests from equity to debt (and vice versa) during the year and up to the date the accounts are approved. The policy under which the members contribute or subscribe amounts to the LLP by way of equity or debt and the policy under which their contributions and subscriptions are repayable by the LLP should also be disclosed.

Set out below are some examples of the statements.

Example 8.3

'Profits are allocated between members on a fixed amount plus a share of the remaining profit according to their investment. The fixed amounts allocated to members are paid in full each month throughout the year, with further profit only being distributed once this has been made on the basis of quarterly management accounts and when funds are available.

Fixed capital is maintained which members contribute to in proportion to their investment. Capital can only be withdrawn with a reduction in investment or upon ceasing to be a member except where there is a return of capital to all members in proportion to their investment in the LLP. There is no opportunity for appreciation of the capital contribution.'

Example 8.4

'The partnership operates a drawings policy which has regard to a cautious estimate of budgeted profits. Drawings are restricted to prudent levels, taking into account working capital performance, until the results for the year and individual members' allocations have been determined. In addition, the Membership Agreement provides a framework for further restriction of drawings under circumstances where the cash requirements of the business need to take priority over the cash needs of the members.

Members' capital requirements are determined from time to time by the Managing Partner having regard to the short, medium and long-term needs of the partnership. The amount of capital required to be contributed increases depending on the amount of fixed profit share or number of sharing units a member has. Members may opt to contribute up to the highest required level. Whilst the Membership Agreement provides power to the Managing Partner to repay a member's capital before retirement, such discretion is only exercised in exceptional cases.'

Example 8.5

'During the period, new members contributed capital totalling £450,000 on becoming members of the LLP. Members may contribute further capital, with the agreement of the founding members. No member is entitled to interest on his capital contribution. No member may be required to contribute any further capital on the insolvency of the LLP.

No member has the right to withdraw or receive back any part of the amount standing to the credit of his capital account. No member shall have any obligations to make any payment to the LLP in respect of losses.

Profit shall be divided between the members as per the LLP agreement.

Each founding member shall be paid a fixed amount for each financial period that he is actively involved with the LLP, irrespective of the LLP's profit level. No member's Fixed Amount Account may have a credit balance and no member shall have any obligation to make any payment to reduce any debit balance on his Fixed Amount Account.'

8.2.5 Presentation in the Statement of cash flows

The format of the statement of cash flows set out in section 7 of FRS 102 should be used when preparing the accounts of an LLP. The LLP SORP sets out how to amend some of the standard headings within a statement of cash flows so that the format is applicable for LLPs.

The adaptations required by the LLP SORP are shown in **5.6**. Within the statement of cash flows various headings are added by the LLP SORP relating to payments to members. These relate to payments made to members in respect of their role as a member. Where there are payments made to a member for transactions which are part of the normal business activities of the LLP (e.g. rent payments made to a corporate member) rather than payments made in relation to their role as a member, these transactions should not be included within these headings.

8.3 Retirement benefits

8.3.1 Retirement benefits of employees and members

The treatment of retirement benefits provided for employees should be accounted for in accordance with section 28 of FRS 102 *Employee Benefits* (i.e. consideration is given as to whether the pension arrangements are of a defined benefit or defined contribution nature and treatment of transactions and disclosures are given as appropriate).

Where retirement benefits payable to a member of an LLP are based on a salary received by the member under an employment contract then section 28 should also be followed for these transactions.

8.3.2 Other post-retirement payments to members

In relation to other post-retirement payments to members, consideration should be given to:

- which accounting standard should be used for the recognition and measurement of the transactions;
- how the transactions should be presented within the accounts; and
- what disclosure is required.

8.3.2.1 *Other post-retirement payments to members – recognition and measurement*

The payments made by an LLP to members after they have retired, which are often referred to as annuities, can take many different forms. When determining how to treat these post-retirement payments, the LLP should analyse contractual or constructive obligations to make payments to members at and/or after the point of their ceasing to be members between those which give rise to financial liabilities falling within the scope of sections 11 and 12 of FRS 102 *Basic Financial Instruments* and *Other Financial Instruments*, those that give rise to liabilities of uncertain timing and amount which fall within the scope of section 21 of FRS 102 *Provisions and contingencies* and those which meet the definition of an insurance contract and therefore fall within the scope of FRS 103 *Insurance Contracts*.

A contractual liability to deliver cash or other financial assets will give rise to a financial liability under section 11 or 12 of FRS 102 (unless outside the scope of those sections).

A constructive obligation of uncertain timing or amount or a contractual obligation which is conditional on further service will fall within the scope of section 21 of FRS 102 (e.g. where post-retirement payments have been offered consistently to previous members at the point of, but not prior to, retirement, a constructive obligation may arise as it could be argued that the past practice would build an expectation and, hence, a constructive obligation that all members would be offered this benefit on retirement. If so, then the point of recognition of the liability would be earlier than retirement).

A constructive obligation of certain timing and amount is accounted for as a liability. Whilst these do not meet the definition of financial liabilities, as there is no contract, the measurement basis will be the same as that for a similar contractual obligation.

An unconditional contractual obligation that meets the definition of an insurance contract (in which the LLP accepts significant insurance risk (typically mortality risk)) will fall within the scope of FRS 103, unless it is conditional on future service (in which case section 21 of FRS 102 applies). This will be the case where, for example, the total amount payable by the LLP may be significantly affected by how long the former member lives.

Annuity payments can generally be classified as either 'pre-determined' or 'profit-dependent'.

Pre-determined annuity payments are amounts payable that are fixed at the time of retirement; for example, by reference to historical earnings (such as a percentage of the final year's profit share) or fixed at an amount, which may be index-linked or linked to a measure independent of the LLP's future profit. The period for which they are payable may or may not be pre-determined. The payment of the retirement benefit is thus not dependent on the LLP earning profits in the post-retirement period and, if there is no significant mortality risk, will generally give rise to a basic financial liability which is accounted for under section 11 of FRS 102. For example, as set out in the LLP SORP, where a former member is to be paid a fixed annual amount for a fixed term beginning on the first anniversary of his retirement and, if he were to die, an amount representing the present value of the future payments would be paid, to his estate, this would fall within the scope of section 11.

Profit-dependent annuity payments are amounts payable to former members that are, in effect, a share of the LLP's ongoing profits, by way of a preferential first share, profit-points, profit-dependent bonus or some other mechanism. Many different arrangements exist, and there may be no amount payable in a year in which no or insufficient profits are earned. Although there is uncertainty over the timing or the amount to be paid, the obligation arises from a contract which is not conditional on further service, so profit-dependent annuity payments are accounted for as financial liabilities. However, they do not meet the definition of basic financial liabilities and are therefore accounted for at their fair value in accordance with section 12 of FRS 102.

Annuities are likely in many cases to be subject to uncertainties. This will be the case, for example, where the member has a choice of retirement dates, the payments are dependent on future profits or there is significant mortality risk.

Recognition of the liability – A liability in respect of an annuity is recognised when a member obtains an actual or constructive right to the annuity, which the LLP has no discretion to withhold. If the rights to an annuity are earned over a period, then costs should be recognised over that period. This treatment applies whether the liability is measured in accordance with section 11, section 12 or section 21 of FRS 102.

The flowchart below (from the LLP SORP) summarises how to determine which guidance applies to a particular obligation:

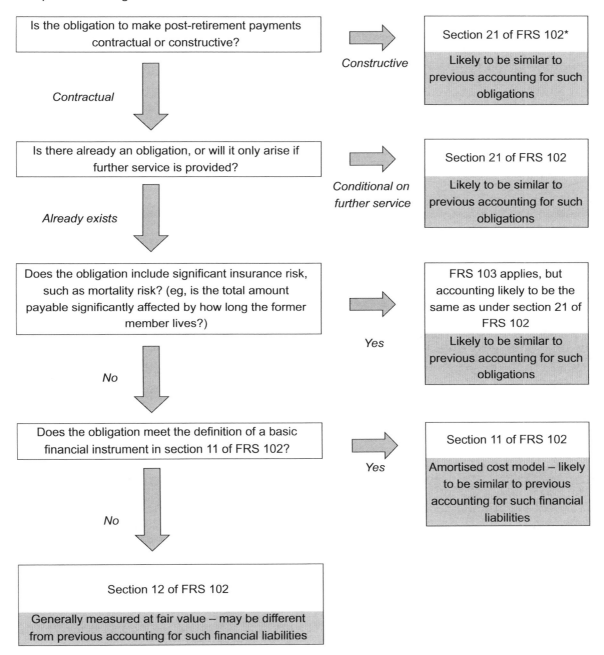

Accounting for annuities which meet the definition of an insurance contract – An annuity which meets the definition of an insurance contract is accounted for under FRS 103. However, FRS 103 permits the LLP to continue to use the accounting policies which it previously used for such contracts. As the previous LLP SORP required LLPs to account for such contracts in accordance with FRS 12 *Provisions, Contingent Liabilities and Contingent Assets* and as the requirements of that standard have been carried forward into section 21 of FRS 102, this will effectively require LLPs to account for such annuities in the same way as those classified as provisions.

The LLP still needs to consider whether it needs to provide any additional disclosure in order to meet the requirements of FRS 103 (LLP SORP para. 80B).

When should the liability be recognised if absolute entitlement is only reached at a specific milestone (e.g. reaching a particular age or number of years of service)? Even if the member will not be entitled to the annuity if they choose to leave before reaching the specified milestone, unless the LLP has the right to terminate the membership without compensation for the loss of annuity rights (which is unlikely), the LLP cannot avoid the liability that is accruing through the service period. In these circumstances, therefore, a liability should be built up over the period of service rather than just recognised at the date on which the milestone is reached.

Consideration of the probable transfer of economic benefits – If the liability falls within the scope of section 21 of FRS 102, the LLP should assess the probability of a future cash outflow. Any liability for post-retirement payments to members earned to date and therefore recognised in the accounts should reflect the latest expectations in respect of the likely date of ceasing to be a member; and the amounts likely to be payable from that date.

The value of the liability should be based on the best estimate of the current value of future cash flows. In practice, it will often be appropriate to value the liability on an actuarial basis, consistent with the principles of section 28 of FRS 102 *Employee Benefits* for the measurement of pension liabilities. Where, because of their nature and/or complexity, the arrangements are such that it is appropriate to apply the guidance in section 28, then that guidance should be applied in arriving at the measurement of the liability. In the case of profit-dependent payments, it will be necessary for the LLP to make a best estimate of the level of future profits of the LLP. Only in extremely rare cases will no reliable estimate be capable of being made. In these extremely rare cases, if accounting for the liability under section 21, then a liability exists that cannot be recognised. This must then be disclosed as a contingent liability. The liability should be recalculated annually to take account of changes in membership, eligibility for post-retirement payments, financial estimates and actuarial assumptions.

8.3.2.2 Other post-retirement payments to members – presentation

Profit and loss account – Within the profit and loss account amounts recognised in respect of current members, including any change in the liability, should be included within 'Members' remuneration charged as an expense'. For former members any change in the liability should not be included as part of Members' remuneration but should be charged to another relevant expense item in the profit and loss account, generally charged to administrative expenses or other operating charges.

Where the liability has been discounted (for example as required by section 21 of FRS 102 where the effect is material), the unwinding of the discount for current members should be including within 'Members' remuneration charged as an expense'. For former members the unwinding of the discount should be presented next to the interest cost line in the profit and loss account.

If additional annuities are granted to former members (i.e. after the date of a member's retirement), the full value of the annuity should be included within operating profit (generally within administrative expenses or other operating charges) as soon as the award is granted.

Balance sheet – Within the balance sheet, the liability for post-retirement payments should be shown separately. For current members the liability, if material, should be shown as a separate component of 'Loans and other debts due to members' on the balance sheet.

For former members, the liability should be shown separately as 'Post-retirement payments to former members' under 'Provisions for liabilities' or 'Creditors' as appropriate. In the year that the member retires a transfer should be made between the balance shown for current members and the balance shown for former members.

8.3.2.3   Other post-retirement payments to members – disclosure

The note of principal accounting policies should disclose the LLP's policy in respect of post-retirement payments to members.

8.4   Taxation

Where tax (both current and deferred) in respect of members' remuneration is a personal liability of the members, it is dealt with under 'Members' interests' on the balance sheet and should not appear in the profit and loss account.

Amounts retained by an LLP in respect of members' tax liabilities do not require separate disclosure and should be included in 'Loans and other amounts due to members'. Amounts in respect of tax liabilities withheld from members who subsequently retire from membership should be dealt with as any other balance due to former members.

Where an LLP is subject to tax in a jurisdiction where LLPs are taxed as corporate entities, the LLP should report such taxes in their accounts as required by section 29 of FRS 102.

In the group accounts of an LLP which include entities that are not partnerships or LLPs (e.g. subsidiary companies), the tax liabilities of those entities should be recorded in the profit and loss account under the relevant heading and any related liability carried as a creditor in the balance sheet.

8.5   Business combinations and group accounts

8.5.1   Group accounts

An LLP should follow the rules on the requirement to prepare group accounts (and the exemptions therefrom) and the contents of the group accounts (and on inclusion and exclusion of subsidiaries) set out in section 9 of FRS 102 *Consolidated and Separate Financial Statements*, modified where necessary to comply with the Regulations. See **Chapter 7** for details of when group accounts are required and when exemptions can be taken.

8.5.2   Business combinations

The accounting treatment for business combinations which include one or more LLPs should have regard to the substance of the combination. The application of accounting standards with respect to business combinations should be considered in the context of both the group accounts and the entity accounts of the LLP. The circumstances of business combinations will vary greatly.

FRS 102 removes the concept of a merger from UK GAAP so all business combinations other than group reconstructions are now accounted for using the purchase method. However, FRS 102 does not require LLPs to restate any business combinations which took place before the transition date that have previously been accounted for as mergers (FRS 102 para 35.10(a))

8.5.2.1 The purchase method

The purchase method is required when the conditions set out in paragraph 19.27 of FRS 102 (see **8.5.2.2**) to treat the business combination as a group reconstruction are not met. The steps to be followed in applying the purchase method are set out in section 19 of FRS 102 *Business Combinations and Goodwill*.

When a business combination occurs, the identifiable assets and liabilities of the acquired entity should be included in the consolidated financial statements of the acquiring LLP at their fair values at the date of acquisition. The difference between these and the cost of acquisition is recognised as goodwill or negative goodwill. The results of the acquired entity are included in the profit and loss account of the acquiring group from the date of acquisition.

FRS 102 requires intangible assets to be included within the identifiable assets and liabilities of the acquired entity where they are separable (i.e. could be sold without selling the entity) or arise from legal rights and their fair value can be measured reliably. This is wider than under previous UK GAAP and is likely to lead to more intangible fixed assets being separately identified and consequently lower goodwill.

When an acquiring LLP is determining the value of goodwill, particular attention should be paid to the following areas:

- The profit share promised to the new members in the enlarged LLP should be assessed to determine whether any portion of that remuneration represents consideration for the business acquired rather than future members' remuneration. For example, if members of the purchased entity were awarded an increased profit share for a limited period of time after the acquisition, falling back to 'normal' remuneration levels thereafter, this could indicate that the short-term excess amounts were part of the purchase consideration.
- If it is not possible to value the consideration given in accordance with the requirements of paragraph 19.11 of FRS 102, the best estimate of its value may be obtained by valuing the entity acquired.

8.5.2.2 Merger accounting

If the following conditions are met, a group reconstruction may be accounted for using the merger accounting method:

- the use of the merger accounting method is not prohibited by company law or other relevant legislation;
- the ultimate equity holders remain the same, and the rights of each equity holder, relative to the others, are unchanged; and
- no non-controlling interest in the net assets of the group is altered by the transfer.

The most common example of this for LLPs is the transfer of the business of an existing undertaking (usually a general partnership) to an LLP, which the LLP SORP requires to be accounted for using the merger method (see **8.5.3**).

Under the merger method, the results and cash flows of the combining entities are brought into the accounts of the combined entity from the beginning of the financial year in which the combination occurred and the comparative information includes the amounts for all of the combining entities for that period, in each case adjusted so as to achieve uniformity of accounting policies. The assets and liabilities of the combining entities are not restated to fair values and no goodwill arises.

8.5.3 Transition from an existing partnership

Where existing undertakings, including partnerships, are transferred into an LLP the LLP SORP recommends (para. 112) that the transfer be accounted for as a group reconstruction where the conditions of paragraph 19.27 of FRS 102 are met.

Where a single entity LLP is formed by the transfer or incorporation of existing undertakings, including a partnership, which meet the requirements of FRS 102 to use merger accounting for the initial transfer of business, the initial transfer should be reflected at book value at the date of transfer and the financial statements for the first period after incorporation should disclose comparative *pro forma* amounts. Such comparative amounts should be stated on the basis of the accounting policies adopted by the LLP.

Where an existing undertaking is transferred some time after the incorporation of the LLP and the transfer meets the merger accounting requirements of FRS 102, the principles of merger accounting should be used and the transfer reflected at book value at the date of transfer with profits recognised from the transfer to the accounting period end. A *pro forma* profit and loss account, including comparative amounts, should be given for the whole of the original entity's accounting period spanning the transfer.

A difference in the total interests of partners in the predecessor firm shown in its final balance sheet and the members' interests in the opening balance caused by the restatement of comparatives to be consistent with ongoing accounting policies should not be dealt with in the accounts of the LLP.

Where a new LLP is put at the top of an existing group (whether as part of a reconstruction or in order to convert to an LLP) and the group uses merger accounting, the accounts of the group for the period of the merger should present corresponding amounts as required by section 19 of FRS 102.

Example 8.6 – accounting policy relating to transition (in first year – 30 September 20x2)

The transfer of the business previously carried on by XYZ Partnership has been accounted for in accordance with the principles of merger accounting because the members of XYZ Partnership LLP were the same as the former partners of XYZ Partnership and their rights relative to one another are unchanged. Therefore, the members had a continuing interest in the business, both before and after the transfer to XYZ Partnership LLP and the financial statements have been prepared as if XYZ Partnership LLP had been in existence for both the current year and the previous year.

In accordance with the principles of merger accounting, the assets and liabilities of XYZ Partnership have been brought in at their book values under the accounting policies of XYZ Partnership LLP. Also, using these accounting policies, the income and expenditure and cash flows of XYZ Partnership have been brought in as *pro forma* comparatives for the year ended 30 September 20x1. The balance sheet of XYZ Partnership as at 30 September 20x1 is presented as a *pro forma* comparative.

8.6 Revenue recognition

8.6.1 Basic principles of revenue recognition

The LLP SORP (para. 100–101) states that in respect of stock, including work in progress, the costs of members' time and related overheads should be accounted for in accordance with section 13 of FRS 102 *Inventories*. When calculating the value of stock, including work in progress, it is only those elements of members' time which would be expensed to the profit and loss account within 'Members' remuneration charged as an expense' which should be considered and included as necessary. However, regardless of whether the time input by a member is a cost to be included in the value of stock, any overhead related to that time should be included in the cost of stock or work in progress.

Contracts should be accounted for in accordance with section 23 of FRS 102 *Revenue*, which provides guidance on the principles of revenue recognition and the treatment of turnover. This section codifies existing practice and sets out a consistent treatment of revenue transactions ('exchange transactions' between seller and customer). The section, together with an appendix showing various examples, explains how, when and whether to recognise revenue, in a variety of circumstances.

Turnover (or 'sales') is the revenue resulting from exchange transactions under which a seller supplies to customers the goods and services that it is in business to provide, as part of its 'operating activities'. Sales of fixed assets are not normally revenue transactions giving rise to 'turnover'.

In essence, revenue is recognised on the performance of a transaction when a seller:

* fulfils its contractual obligation to a customer through the supply of goods and services; and
* obtains the right to consideration (payment) in exchange for performance of the transaction.

This means that revenue must be accounted for generally at the point of delivery ('fulfilling a contractual obligation') rather than, for example, when an order is taken or agreement to provide a service is made.

Payments in advance from a client or customer give rise to a liability (rather than revenue) until such time as the service is provided or the transaction is completed ('performed'), with the seller fulfilling their contractual obligation. In the case of partial performance of an obligation, revenue is recognised to the appropriate extent of such partial performance. Stage payments may, or may not, represent 'partial performance' under a contractual arrangement and will only equate to partial performance where the timing of payments coincide with the extent of partial performance.

Revenue is measured at 'fair value' of the right to consideration (amount receivable), which is normally the price specified in the contractual arrangement net of discounts, value added tax and similar sales taxes. Occasionally, the fair value at the time of the transaction may also reflect the time value of money (for example, an interest free period) or allow for possible debtor default (credit risk), but any such adjustments made subsequently should not be included in revenue but expensed within costs and overheads.

'Fair value' is defined in FRS 102 as 'the amount for which an asset could be exchanged, a liability settled, or an equity instrument granted could be exchanged, between knowledgeable, willing parties in an arm's length transaction.'.

8.6.2 *Revenue recognition: areas of specific guidance*

Revenue recognition is generally straightforward. However, for a number of instances where there has been inappropriate or inconsistent accounting treatment, FRS 102 provides specific guidance and examples. Revenue from rendering services and under construction contracts, is recognised by the seller as contract activity progresses, to the extent that the contract can be assessed reliably. Recognition is determined by, and in accordance with, the stage of completion of the contractual obligations; proportion of costs incurred should be a determining factor of recognition only where the costs provide evidence of the extent of the seller's performance.

Separation and linking should reflect the commercial substance of an arrangement. The accounting treatment of such arrangements invariably depends upon the contractual detail and whether component parts of the arrangement can be separately and independently identified (for example, the sale of some packaged software and a subsequent support service).

Turnover is generally assumed to be sales on the seller's own account. Where there is no disclosure of acting as 'Agent', there is a rebuttable presumption that the seller is acting as 'Principal'. Turnover should accordingly be reported as follows:

- as principal – gross amount received or receivable; and
- as agent – commission or such other income (excluding amounts payable to the Principal).

8.6.3 *Revenue recognition: contracts for services*

Revenue on service contracts should be accrued as service activity takes place (to reflect the seller's partial performance of its contractual obligations). Revenue should reflect the accrual of the right to consideration as contract activity progresses by reference to value of the work performed. Distinguishable phases of a single contract may be accounted for as two or more separate transactions, provided the value of each phase can be reliably estimated.

However, revenue is only recognised where the outcome of the transaction can be estimated reliably. This means that the revenue, the costs to date under the transaction, the costs to complete it and its stage of completion can all be measured reliably and it is probable that the economic benefits associated with the transaction will flow to the LLP. Where this is not the case, revenue should only be recognised to the extent of any expenses recognised which are recoverable.

In addition, where a specific act is much more significant than any other act, revenue should not be recognised until this significant act is carried out.

Under previous GAAP, UITF 40 required that where the substance of a contract was that a right to consideration did not arise until the occurrence of a specified future event or outcome outside the control of the service provider (a 'critical event'), revenue was not recognised until that event occurred. This requirement has not been carried forward under FRS 102, so such revenue should be recognised unless it is not probable or a significant act has not yet been executed. A significant act is something that the LLP must do itself. Where the contract contains a significant act, the LLP does not recognise the revenue under the contract until the specific act is performed. This is different from a contingent contract where receipt of the consideration under the contract could be determined by events outside the LLP's control. Where the LLP has performed under the contract but the revenue is contingent, revenue is recognised to the extent that the LLP can determine that an inflow of economic benefit is probable and can be measured reliably.

The FRSSE incorporates the essential principles of revenue recognition promoted by section 23 of FRS 102.

Examples of revenue recognition accounting policies are:

Example 8.7

'Fee income represents the amounts including recoverable expenses receivable for services rendered during the year, net of value added tax.

Fees are recognised when the right to consideration has arisen through performance under each assignment undertaken. Consideration accrues as the assignment progresses by reference to the value of the work performed. Fees are not recognised where the right to receive payment is contingent on events outside the control of the entity unless it is assessed that it is probable that we will receive the amounts and that the amounts can be measured reliably.

To the extent that revenue is recognised on assignments for which an invoice has not yet been raised, it is included in debtors as 'Amounts recoverable on contracts'. To the extent that amounts billed on account of assignments exceeds work in progress it is included in creditors as 'Payments on account'.

Example 8.8

'Turnover is the revenue arising from the sales of services. It is stated at the fair value of consideration receivable net of Value Added Tax. Revenue is recognised when the LLP has performed its obligations and, in exchange, obtained the right to consideration.'

8.7 Related parties

The disclosure requirements of section 33 of FRS 102 *Related Party Disclosures* are applicable to LLPs.

8.7.1 Who are related parties?

The definition of a related party provided by FRS 102 is as follows:

'A related party is a person or entity that is related to the entity that is preparing its financial statements (the 'reporting entity').

(a) A person or a close member of that person's family is related to a reporting entity if that person:
   (i) has control or joint control over the reporting entity;
   (ii) has significant influence over the reporting entity; or
   (iii) is a member of the key management personnel of the reporting entity or of a parent of the reporting entity.

(b) An entity is related to a reporting entity if any of the following conditions applies:
   (i) The entity and the reporting entity are members of the same group (which means that each parent, subsidiary and fellow subsidiary is related to the others).
   (ii) One entity is an associate or joint venture of the other entity (or an associate or joint venture of a member of a group of which the other entity is a member).
   (iii) Both entities are joint ventures of the same third party.
   (iv) One entity is a joint venture of a third entity and the other entity is an associate of the third entity.
   (v) The entity is a post-employment benefit plan for the benefit of employees of either the reporting entity or an entity related to the reporting entity. If the reporting entity is itself such a plan, the sponsoring employers are also related to the reporting entity.
   (vi) The entity is controlled or jointly controlled by a person identified in (a).
   (vii) A person identified in (a)(i) has significant influence over the entity or is a member of the key management personnel of the entity (or of a parent of the entity).'

For accounting periods commencing on or after 1 January 2016, a further type of related party is added to the definition, as follows:

   '(viii) The entity, or any member of a group of which it is a part, provides key management personnel services to the reporting entity or to the parent of the reporting entity.'

In considering each possible related party relationship, attention is directed to the substance of the relationship and not merely the legal form.

Close members of the family of a person are defined as those family members who may be expected to influence, or be influenced by, that person in their dealings with the entity and include:

(a) that person's children and spouse or domestic partner;
(b) children of that person's spouse or domestic partner; and
(c) dependants of that person or that person's spouse or domestic partner.

Based on the definition above, an LLP which is under the control of another LLP, partnership, company or other entity will be a related party of that other entity. The fact that some members of an LLP are members of another LLP or another partnership does not in itself make the two businesses related parties. It is the extent of common control and/or influence which determines this. Predecessor partnerships of an LLP should be treated as related parties of the LLP.

Unlike a company where all the directors and key management personnel are assumed to be related parties of the entity, for an LLP the nature and extent of the members' involvement in the management of the LLP should be considered when determining which of the members are related parties of the LLP.

As stated in the LLP SORP, in the case of smaller LLPs, where all members play a part in the management of the entity, it will frequently be the case that all of the members are related parties. However, for larger LLPs it cannot be assumed that this will be the case. Key management personnel of an LLP are those persons having authority and responsibility for planning, directing and controlling the activities of the LLP directly or indirectly.

Where an LLP has a corporate member it is likely that the corporate member will be a related party.

8.7.2 Disclosure of related party transactions

As set out in FRS 102 paragraph 33.9:

'If an entity has related party transactions, it shall disclose the nature of the related party relationship as well as information about the transactions, outstanding balances and commitments necessary for an understanding of the potential effect of the relationship on the financial statements. ... At a minimum, disclosures shall include:

(a) The amount of the transactions.
(b) The amount of outstanding balances and:
  (i) their terms and conditions, including whether they are secured, and the nature of the consideration to be provided in settlement; and
  (ii) details of any guarantees given or received.
(c) Provisions for uncollectible receivables related to the amount of outstanding balances.
(d) The expense recognised during the period in respect of bad or doubtful debts due from related parties.'

Where an LLP has created a provision as a result of an undertaking to repay a loan of a member who is considered a related party (a provision will be necessary where the LLP has a legal or constructive obligation to ensure that the full liability to the lender is settled and it is more likely than not that the guarantee will be called upon), details of this transaction should be given as part of the related party disclosures within the notes to the financial statements.

Transactions with related parties may be disclosed on an aggregated basis (aggregation of similar transactions by type of related party) unless disclosure of an individual transaction, or connected transactions, is necessary for an understanding of the impact of the transactions on the financial statements of the reporting entity or is required by law.

As a minimum, related party disclosures must be made separately for each of the following categories:

- entities with control, joint control or significant influence over the entity;
- entities over which the entity has control, joint control or significant influence;
- key management personnel of the entity or its parent (in the aggregate); and
- other related parties.

Transactions are material when their disclosure might reasonably be expected to influence decisions made by the users of the accounts of the LLP. The materiality of related party transactions is to be judged, not only in terms of their significance to the LLP, but also in relation to the other related party. However, if the accounts are prepared in accordance with the FRSSE, it is only transactions which are material to the LLP which should be disclosed as related party transactions.

Example 8.9

Below is an example of a related party note from a set of LLP accounts.

'During the period, £36,500 of administrative expenses were paid by the LLP on behalf of a company under common control and £12,400 of administrative expenses were paid by them on behalf of the LLP. At the period end, £24,100 is owed by them to the LLP.

During the period £8,050 of administrative expenses were paid by the LLP on behalf of an associated company and £12,000 of administrative expenses were paid by them on behalf of the LLP. £7,200 is owed to the LLP in relation to accrued rent. At the period end, £3,250 is owed by them to the LLP.

8.7.3 Controlling or ultimate controlling party

In accordance with FRS 102 paragraph 33.5, if a controlling or ultimate controlling party exists this fact should be disclosed in the notes to the accounts. This disclosure is required regardless of whether there are any transactions with the controlling or ultimate control party.

An individual or entity which has the ability to direct the financial and operating policies of an LLP would be considered to be the controlling or ultimate controlling party even though that party may not be entitled to the majority of profits or have invested the majority of capital represented by equity or debt. In considering each possible related party relationship, attention is directed to the substance of the relationship and not merely the legal form.

8.7.4 Key management personnel compensation

Paragraph 33.7 of FRS 102 requires disclosure of key management personnel compensation in total.

For an LLP, key management personnel are those persons, whether designated members, members or employees, having authority and responsibility for planning, directing and controlling the activities of the LLP directly or indirectly. Therefore, key management personnel compensation may comprise elements of employee remuneration and profit attributable to members.

Appendix G contains an LLP SORP disclosure checklist.

Chapter 9 Determining LLP audit exemption

There are three main categories of LLP for which exemption from statutory audit is available under the CA 2006 as applied to LLPs:

- small LLPs (s. 477);
- subsidiary LLPs (s. 479A); and
- dormant LLPs (s. 480);

The *Companies and Limited Liability Partnerships (Accounts and Audit Exemptions and Change of Accounting Framework) Regulations* 2012 (SI 2012/2301) amended CA 2006 as applied to LLPs, to align small LLP audit thresholds with accounting thresholds. They also exempt certain subsidiaries from audit. This revised legislation applies to accounting periods ended on or after 1 October 2012.

The audit exemption available for small LLPs under s. 477 is not available if the LLP is part of a non-small group. There are also a number of other restrictions and requirements for each exemption as set out in detail below.

In considering if the LLP is to take advantage of these exemptions, the members and directors should also consider if an audit is beneficial or required for other reasons, such as providing peace of mind, to assist in obtaining financing, to meet banking terms or as a requirement of the LLP's membership agreement.

The audit exemption thresholds and conditions for periods commencing on or after 1 January 2016 are to be increased (see **Chapter 13**).

9.1 Small LLPs – conditions for exemption from audit

An LLP is exempt from the requirements for the audit of its accounts in respect of a financial year if it qualifies as a small LLP. However, if the LLP is a member of a group, then further conditions apply (see **9.3**).

Whether an LLP qualifies as a small LLP is determined in accordance with CA 2006, s. 382(1)–(6), as set out in **Chapter 4** at **4.2**.

Once it is established that the LLP is small, the LLP must also:

- if a member of a group, consider the group requirements (see **9.3** below);
- provide within its balance sheet a members' statement (s. 475(2)–(4));
- not be precluded by the members' agreement; and
- not be one of the categories of LLPs excluded from small LLP exemption (s. 478) (see **9.2** below).

9.2 LLPs excluded from the small LLP audit exemption

An LLP is not entitled to the small LLP audit exemption conferred by CA 2006, s. 477 if it was at any time within the financial year in question:

- an LLP whose securities are admitted to trading on a regulated Market in an EEA State;

- an LLP that is an authorised insurance company, a banking LLP, an e-money issuer, a MiFID investment firm or a UCITS management company, or carries on insurance market activity; or
- an employers' association (as defined in the *Trade Union and Labour Relations (Consolidation) Act* 1992, s. 122) or the *Industrial Relations (Northern Ireland) Order 1992, art. 4*).

s. 478

9.3 Groups – availability of small audit exemption

Whether a group qualifies as small is determined in accordance with CA 2006, s. 383 (companies qualifying as small: parent LLP) (see **Chapter 7** at **7.2**).

In accordance with CA 2006, s. 479(2) an LLP which is a group entity (being a parent LLP or a subsidiary undertaking) is only entitled to audit exemption if the following conditions are met:

- the group it is a member of qualifies as a small group in relation to the financial year (during any part of which it was a group entity); and
- the group was not at any time in the year an 'ineligible' group (as defined by CA 2006, s. 384(2), (3)).

A group is 'ineligible' if any of its members is:

(a) a public company;
(b) a body corporate (other than a company) whose shares are admitted to trading on a regulated market in an EEA State;
(c) a person (other than a small company) who has permission under the *Financial Services and Markets Act* 2000, Pt. 4A (c. 8) to carry on a regulated activity;
(ca) an e-money issuer;
(d) a small company that is an authorised insurance company, a banking company, a MiFID investment firm or a UCITS management company; or
(e) a person who carries on insurance market activity.

A dormant subsidiary undertaking being a group entity and dormant during the financial year for the whole period it was a group entity is also entitled to audit exemption. (This exemption applies to all sizes of groups with dormant subsidiaries).

s. 479(3)

CA 2006, s. 479(4) defines a 'group', in relation to a group LLP, as that LLP together with all its associated undertakings.

s. 479(4)

9.4 Subsidiaries audit exemption for LLPs

In accordance with CA 2006, s. 479A, as applied to LLPs, a subsidiary LLP (irrespective of its size) is exempt from audit if it fulfils all of the following conditions:

(a) its parent undertaking is established under the law of an EEA state;
(b) all of the subsidiary LLP's members agree the exemption in respect of the financial year in question;
(c) the parent gives a guarantee (under s. 479C) of all the outstanding liabilities to which the subsidiary LLP is subject at the end of the financial year until they are satisfied in full;
(d) the LLP is included in the consolidated accounts drawn up by the parent undertaking. These accounts must be prepared in accordance with Directive 83/349/EEC (the Seventh Company Law Directive) or International Accounting Standards;
(e) the consolidated accounts drawn up by the parent must disclose the use of the exemption by the subsidiary LLP;
(f) the Designated Members of the subsidiary LLP must file the following documents at Companies House on or before the date that they file the subsidiary's accounts:
(i) written notice of the agreement in (b);
(ii) a written statement by the parent of the guarantee in (c); and

(iii) a copy of the consolidated annual report and accounts referred to in (d) and the auditor's report on those accounts;

(g) the LLP is not quoted (as defined by s. 385);

(h) the LLP is not an authorised insurance company, a banking company, an e-money issuer, a MiFID investment firm or a UCITS management company, or carries on insurance market activity; and

(i) the LLP is not a special register body (as defined under the *Trade Union and Labour Relations (Consolidation) Act* 1992) or an employers' association (as defined under the *Industrial Relations (Northern Ireland) Order* 1992).

The members of the subsidiary LLP must make the statements required by CA 2006, s. 475(2) and (3) as applied to LLPs before the signature on the balance sheet, as set out in **9.5**.

A list of EEA states is available on the Government website at www.gov.uk/eu-eea.

In making the decision as to whether the parent entity will provide the guarantee referred to in (c) above, the directors of the parent entity must consider if the guarantee provided exposes the parent entity to significant liabilities (actual and contingent).

If the LLP is a subsidiary of an entity which prepares a consolidated annual report and accounts in a language other than English, the group accounts will need to be translated into English and filed at Companies House together with form VT01 'Certified voluntary translation of an original document that is or has been delivered to the Registrar of Companies'.

Often the purpose of the subsidiary/LLP structure is to limit the liability of the parent. If the subsidiary has minority members, or may be sold in the future, this may complicate matters further. In many cases legal advice should be obtained before the parent enters into any such guarantee.

Furthermore, the parent should consider if there is a significant cost saving in taking advantage of the exemption as the figures included in the LLP's accounts may have to be audited in any case as part of the group's audit.

There is no legal provision that the LLP's members may require the LLP to have an audit. The LLP's members' agreement, however, could include this type of provision optionally.

9.5 Audit exemption – Members' statement

An LLP's annual accounts for a financial year must be audited unless the LLP is exempt from audit under CA 2006, s. 477 (small LLPs), 479A (subsidiary LLPs), or 480 (dormant LLPs).

s. 475

However, to take advantage of audit exemption, the balance sheet of the LLP must contain a statement by the members to the effect that:

- the LLP is exempt from audit under CA 2006, s. 477 (small LLP), 479A (subsidiary LLP), or 480 (dormant LLP); and
- the members acknowledge their responsibilities for complying with the requirements of CA 2006 with respect to accounting records and the preparation of accounts.

s. 475(2)–(3)

The members' statement required by CA 2006, s. 475 must appear on the balance sheet above the signature required by CA 2006, s. 414.

Examples of a form of members' statement covering the above requirements are illustrated in **Example 9.1**.

s. 475

83

Example 9.1   Small LLP audit exemption members' statements: balance sheet

For the financial year ended [30 June 2016], the LLP was entitled to exemption from audit   *[Note 1]*
under [s. 477 (*small LLP exemption*), 479A (*subsidiary LLP exemption*), or 480 (*dormant LLP
exemption*)] [*as the case may be*] *Companies Act* 2006 (as applied by the *Limited Liability
Partnerships (Accounts and Audit) (Application of the Companies Act 2006) Regulations*
2008) relating to LLPs.

The members acknowledge their responsibilities for complying with the requirements of the
Act with respect to accounting records and the preparation of accounts.

These accounts have been prepared in accordance with the provisions applicable to LLPs   [Note 2]
subject to the small LLPs regime.

Note: [Words in italics are explanatory only]

The above statements are applicable as follows:

(1) *applicable, where audit exemption applies, in*
   (a) *small LLP (SI 2008/1912) balance sheets (individual and group);*
   (b) *abbreviated balance sheets.*
(2) *applicable where the LLP's annual accounts have been delivered in accordance with the provisions
applicable to LLPs subject to the small LLPs regime and where small LLP accounts (on the basis of
Sch. 4 (SI 2008/1912)) are adopted, for both audited or audit-exempt accounts; also applicable where
abbreviated accounts are prepared, for both audited or audit-exempt accounts.*

Chapter 10 Example accounts

The example accounts set out in this chapter are entirely fictional.

The example accounts do not represent a comprehensive checklist of the statutory disclosure requirements nor do they purport to be definitive or exhaustive. The intention is to illustrate the more common situations. Other presentations may be equally acceptable, provided that they adhere to the rules set out in CA 2006 as applied to LLPs, supporting statutory regulations, relevant financial reporting accounting standards and the LLP SORP.

10.1 Accounts of an LLP

The illustrative example accounts of Richmond & Taylor LLP illustrate the audited accounts of a medium-sized LLP (as defined in **Chapter 4**) producing accounts under the provisions of the *Companies Act* 2006 as applied to LLPs. The example year end is 30 June 2016.

The example accounts comprise the 'Non-IAS individual accounts' of the LLP prepared in accordance with CA 2006 as applied to LLPs. A Members' Report has been produced (although not required) and includes the information required by the LLP SORP (**Chapter 5**) in the Members' Report rather than in the notes to the accounts, some additional information is also given in the Members' Report above the limited amount required by the LLP SORP as many LLPs choose to expand their Members' Report to include additional information.

The form of both the profit and loss account and the balance sheet are presented in Format 1.

**Registration Number
OC3422400
(England and Wales)**

RICHMOND & TAYLOR LLP

**MEMBERS' REPORT AND AUDITED
FINANCIAL STATEMENTS**

30 JUNE 2016

RICHMOND & TAYLOR LLP

Designated Members	*G Heggarty* *N J Purdon* *C F Ofdensen*
Registered office	32 Green Station Lane Swindon SN12 2BQ
Registration number	OC1234567 (England and Wales)
Bankers	The Royal Bank of Scotland Plc 45 London Road Swindon SN11 9SC
Independent auditor	Andrews LLP 10 Great Street Swindon SN31 9RC

RICHMOND & TAYLOR LLP   **Page [1]**
MEMBERS' REPORT

The members present their report with the financial statements for the year ended 30 June 2016.

Principal activity
The principal activity during the year was the provision of legal services.

Review of business and future developments
The results for the year and the financial position at the year end were considered satisfactory.

Designated members
The designated members during the year were as follows:

G Heggarty
N J Purdon
C F Ofdensen

Members' drawings and subscription and repayment of members' capital
The members are entitled to draw monthly, on account of profit, such sums as may from time to time be mutually agreed.

The capital requisite for carrying on this business of the LLP shall be agreed and contributed by the members from time to time. The total amount of and the respective contributions of the members to the fixed capital of the LLP shall be in the shares in which they are entitled to the net profits of the LLP. Partners moving up in relative profit sharing will contribute the relevant proportion of additional capital before being entitled to more shares.

Statement of members' responsibilities
The members are responsible for preparing the financial statements in accordance with applicable law and regulations.

Company law as applied to limited liability partnerships by the *Limited Liability Partnerships (Accounts and Audit) (Application of Companies Act 2006) Regulations* 2008 requires the members to prepare financial statements for each financial year. Under that law the members have elected to prepare the financial statements in accordance with United Kingdom Generally Accepted Accounting Practice (United Kingdom Accounting Standards and applicable law).

Under company law as applied to limited liability partnerships the members must not approve the financial statements unless they are satisfied that they give a true and fair view of the state of affairs of the LLP and of the profit or loss of the LLP for that period.

In preparing those financial statements, the members are required to:

- select suitable accounting policies and apply them consistently;
- make judgments and estimates that are reasonable and prudent; and
- prepare the financial statements on a going concern basis unless it is inappropriate to presume that the LLP will continue in business.

The members are responsible for keeping adequate accounting records that are sufficient to show and explain the LLP's transactions and disclose with reasonable accuracy at any time the financial position of the LLP and enable them to ensure that the financial statements comply with the *Companies Act* 2006 as modified by the *Limited Liability Partnerships (Accounts and Audit) (Application of Companies Act 2006) Regulations* 2008. They are also responsible for safeguarding the assets of the LLP and hence for taking reasonable steps for the prevention and detection of fraud and other irregularities.

[*Where the financial statements are published on the internet*] [The members are responsible for the maintenance and integrity of the corporate and financial information included on the LLP's website.

Legislation in the United Kingdom governing the preparation and dissemination of financial statements may differ from legislation in other jurisdictions.]

The responsibilities are exercised by the designated members on behalf of the members.

Signed on behalf of the members by:

C F Ofdensen

....

C F Ofdensen

Designated Member

Approved on: 10 November 2016

[Note: Inclusion of a Members' Report is not compulsory. Where such a report is not included the information above which is required by the LLP SORP should be shown in the notes to the financial statements and the statement of members responsibilities should be shown as a separate statement]

Independent auditor's report to the members of Richmond & Taylor LLP   **Page [3]**

We have audited the financial statements of Richmond & Taylor LLP for the year ended 30 June 2016, which comprise the profit and loss account, the balance sheet, the reconciliation of members' interest, the cash flow statement, principal accounting policies and the related notes. The financial reporting framework that has been applied in their preparation is applicable law and United Kingdom Accounting Standards (United Kingdom Generally Accepted Accounting Practice), including FRS 102 *The Financial Reporting Standard applicable in the UK and Republic of Ireland*.

This report is made solely to the LLP's members, as a body, in accordance with Chapter 3 of Part 16 of the *Companies Act* 2006 as applied to limited liability partnerships by the *Limited Liability Partnerships (Accounts and Audit) (Application of Companies Act 2006) Regulations* 2008. Our audit work has been undertaken so that we might state to the LLP's members those matters we are required to state to them in an auditor's report and for no other purpose. To the fullest extent permitted by law, we do not accept or assume responsibility to anyone other than the LLP and the LLP's members as a body, for our audit work, for this report, or for the opinions we have formed.

Respective responsibilities of members and auditor

As explained more fully in the Members' Responsibilities Statement set out in the Members' Report, the members are responsible for the preparation of the financial statements and for being satisfied that they give a true and fair view. Our responsibility is to audit and express an opinion on the financial statements in accordance with applicable law and International Standards on Auditing (UK and Ireland). Those standards require us to comply with the Auditing Practices Board's Ethical Standards for Auditors.

Scope of the audit of the financial statements

A description of the scope of an audit of financial statements is provided on the FRC's website at www.frc.org.uk/auditscopeukprivate.

Opinion on financial statements

In our opinion the financial statements:

- give a true and fair view of the state of the limited liability partnership's affairs as at 30 June 2016 and of its profit for the year then ended;
- have been properly prepared in accordance with United Kingdom Generally Accepted Accounting Practice; and
- have been prepared in accordance with the requirements of the *Companies Act* 2006 as applied to limited liability partnerships by the *Limited Liability Partnerships (Accounts and Audit) (Application of Companies Act 2006) Regulations* 2008.

Matters on which we are required to report by exception

We have nothing to report in respect of the following matters where the *Companies Act* 2006 as applied to limited liability partnerships requires us to report to you if, in our opinion:

- adequate accounting records have not been kept, or returns adequate for our audit have not been received from branches not visited by us; or
- the financial statements are not in agreement with the accounting records and returns; or
- we have not received all the information and explanations we require for our audit.

Samuel S Andrews
Senior Statutory Auditor for and on behalf of Andrews LLP, Statutory Auditor
10 Great Street
Swindon SN31 9RC
11 November 2016

RICHMOND & TAYLOR LLP   **Page [4]**
STATEMENT OF COMPREHENSIVE INCOME
FOR THE YEAR ENDED 30 JUNE 2016

	Notes	Year ended 30 June 2016	Year ended 30 June 2015 (as restated)
		£	£
Turnover	1	35,433,395	31,569,121
Cost of sales		(17,771,566)	(15,683,634)
Gross profit		17,661,829	15,885,487
Administrative expenses		(8,825,842)	(8,899,096)
Operating profit	2	8,835,987	6,986,391
Interest receivable and similar income	3	356	154
Interest payable and similar charges	4	(64,686)	(60,585)
Profit for the financial period before members' remuneration and profit shares		8,771,657	6,925,960
Members' remuneration charged as an expense	5	(8,771,657)	(6,930,960)
Profit for the financial period available for discretionary division among members		–	(5,000)
Other comprehensive income			
Revaluation of leasehold property		170,000	–
Total comprehensive income		170,000	(5,000)

[Note: This statement may, alternatively be presented as a separate, 'Income Statement' or 'Profit and Loss Account and Statement of Comprehensive Income' (showing only the items of other comprehensive income)]

RICHMOND & TAYLOR LLP   **Page [5]**
BALANCE SHEET 30 JUNE 2016

	Notes	30 June 2016	30 June 2016	30 June 2015 (as restated)	30 June 2015 (as restated)
		£	£	£	£
Fixed assets					
Tangible fixed assets	7		473,040		426,299
Current assets					
Debtors	8	10,035,200		10,150,293	
Cash at bank and in hand		1,835,000		455,164	
		11,870,200		10,605,457	
Creditors: amounts falling due within one year	9	(3,467,984)		(3,259,163)	
Net current assets			8,402,216		7,346,294
Total assets less current liabilities			8,875,256		7,772,593
Provisions for liabilities	10		(337,500)		(337,500)
Net assets attributable to members			8,537,756		7,435,093
Represented by: **Loans and other debts due to members within one year**					
Members' capital classified as debt			3,875,000		3,500,000
Other amounts			4,492,756		3,970,093
			8,367,756		7,470,093
Members' other interests					
Other reserves			170,000		(35,000)
			8,537,756		7,435,093
Total members interests					
Loans and other debts due to members			8,367,756		7,470,093
Members' other interests			170,000		(35,000)
			8,537,756		7,435,093

The financial statements were approved and authorised by the members on 10 November 2016 and were signed on their behalf by:

....

C F Ofdensen
Designated Member
Richmond & Taylor LLP
Registration number: OC1234567

The notes on pages 10 to 13 form part of these financial statements.

[Note: This statement is referred to as a 'Statement of Financial Position' in FRS 102, however the standard allows continued use of 'Balance Sheet' if desired]

RICHMOND & TAYLOR LLP
RECONCILIATION OF
MEMBERS' INTERESTS
FOR THE YEAR END 30 JUNE 2016

	EQUITY			DEBT			TOTAL
	Members' other interests						MEMBERS' INTERESTS
				Loans and other debts due to members less any amounts due from members in debtors			
	Revaluation reserve	Other reserves	Total equity	Members capital (classified as debt)	Other amounts	Total debts	
	£	£	£	£	£	£	£
Balance at 1 July 2014 (as restated)	–	(30,000)	(30,000)	2,812,500	3,418,878	6,231,378	6,201,378
Members' remuneration charged as an expense			–		6,930,960	6,930,960	6,930,960
Profit for the year available for discretionary division among members		(5,000)	(5,000)			–	(5,000)
Members' interests after profit for the period	–	(35,000)	(35,000)	2,812,500	10,349,838	13,162,338	13,127,338
Introduced by members			–	687,500		687,500	687,500
Drawings			–		(6,379,745)	(6,379,745)	(6,379,745)
Balance at 30 June 2015 (as restated)	–	(35,000)	(35,000)	3,500,000	3,970,093	7,470,093	7,435,093
Members' remuneration charged as an expense			–		8,771,657	8,771,657	8,771,657
Members' interests after profit for the period	–	(35,000)	(35,000)	3,500,000	12,741,750	16,241,750	16,206,750
Other division of profits		35,000	35,000		(35,000)	(35,000)	–
Surplus on revaluation of fixed assets	170,000		170,000			–	170,000
Introduced by members			–	735,000		735,000	735,000
Repayment of debt (including members capital classified as a liability)			–	(360,000)		(360,000)	(360,000)
Drawings			–		(8,213,994)	(8,213,994)	(8,213,994)
Balance at 30 June 2016	170,000	–	170,000	3,875,000	4,492,756	8,367,756	8,537,756

RICHMOND & TAYLOR LLP   **Page [7]**
STATEMENT OF CASH FLOWS
FOR THE YEAR END 30 JUNE 2016

	Notes	2016	2015
		£	£
Cash flow from operating activities	A	9,660,590	5,340,425
Interest paid		(64,686)	(60,585)
Members remuneration paid under an employment contract		(764,000)	(585,000)
Net cash flow from operating activities		8,831,904	4,694,840
Cash flow from investing activities			
Payments to acquire tangible fixed assets		(85,257)	(234,643)
Interest received		356	154
Net cash flow from investing activities		(84,901)	(234,489)
Cash flow from financing activities			
Capital introduced by members		735,000	687,500
Repayment of capital or debt to members		(7,809,994)	(5,794,745)
Net cash flow from financing activities		(7,074,994)	(5,107,245)
Net increase/(decrease) in cash and cash equivalents		1,672,009	(646,894)
Cash and cash equivalents at 1 July 2015		162,991	809,885
Cash and cash equivalents at 30 June 2016		1,835,000	162,991
Cash and cash equivalents consist of:		1,835,000	455,164
Cash in hand and at bank		–	(292,173)
Overdrafts			
		1,835,000	162,991

	2016	2015
A Reconciliation of profit to cash flow from operating activities		
	£	£
Profit for the period	8,771,657	6,925,960
Interest receivable and similar income	(356)	(154)
Interest payable and similar charges	64,686	60,585
Operating profit	8,835,987	6,986,391
Depreciation	208,516	219,829
Decease/(increase) in debtors	115,093	(1,998,876)
Increase in creditors	500,994	133,081
Cash flow from operating activities	9,660,590	5,340,425

General information and basis of preparation

Richmond and Taylor LLP is a Limited Liability Partnership incorporated in England and Wales. The address of the registered office is 32 Green Station Lane, Swindon, SN12 2BQ.

The annual report and financial statements have been prepared in accordance with applicable United Kingdom accounting standards including Financial Reporting Standard 102 The Financial Reporting Standard applicable in the UK and Republic of Ireland (FRS 102), the Statement of Recommended Practice 'Accounting by Limited Liability Partnerships' issued in July 2014 (SORP) and the *Companies Act* 2006 (as applied to LLPs). The financial statements have been prepared on a going concern basis under the historical cost convention, modified to include certain items at fair value.

The Financial Statements are prepared in sterling which is the functional currency of the LLP.

Turnover

Turnover represents the amounts recoverable for the services provided to clients, excluding value added tax, under contractual obligations which are performed gradually over time.

If, at the balance sheet date, completion of contractual obligations is dependent on external factors (and thus outside the control of the LLP), then revenue is recognised only if it is probable that the event will occur.

Depreciation of tangible fixed assets

Depreciation of tangible fixed assets is charged so as to write off their full costs less estimated residual value over their expected useful lives at the following rates:

- Office equipment – over three years straight line;
- Computer equipment – over three years straight line;
- Leasehold improvements – over lease term.

Leasing and hire purchase commitments

Assets obtained under hire purchase contracts and finance leases are capitalised as tangible assets and depreciated over the shorter of the lease term and their useful lives. Obligations under such agreements are included in creditors net of the finance charge allocated to future periods. The finance element of the rental payment is charged to the profit and loss account so as to produce a constant periodic rate of charge on the net obligation outstanding in each period.

Rentals payable under operating leases are charged against income on a straight line basis over the lease term.

Amounts recoverable under contracts

Amounts recoverable under contracts represent work done at the year end where a continuing right to receive income exists and is valued at the estimated amount recoverable in excess of fees already rendered on account.

RICHMOND & TAYLOR LLP   **Page [9]**
PRINCIPAL ACCOUNTING POLICIES *(continued)*

Pensions

The LLP pays contributions to qualifying individual pension schemes which are administered independently from the LLP. These are charged to the profit and loss as they become payable.

Foreign currency translation

Monetary assets and liabilities denominated in foreign currencies are translated into sterling at the rates of exchange ruling at the balance sheet date. Transactions in foreign currencies are translated into sterling at the rates of exchange ruling on the date of the transaction. Exchange differences are dealt with in the profit and loss account.

Provisions for retirement benefits and amounts due to former members

The LLP acts as agent for certain members who have an obligation to pay annuities to retired partners. These payments are treated as drawings of the relevant members.

Taxation

Taxation on all the LLP's profits is solely the personal liability of individual members and is not dealt with in these financial statements.

Provisions

Provisions relate to obligations of the LLP where there is uncertainty about the timing or amount of the future expenditure required in settlement of this obligation.

Judgments and key sources of estimation uncertainty

The following judgments (apart from those involving estimates) have been made:

Valuation of Property

The LLP's leasehold property is carried at market value, which is updated periodically by professional valuers.

Depreciation of tangible fixed assets

The depreciation charge on tangible fixed assets is affected by the LLP's estimate of the useful economic life and residual value of the assets, which are reviewed on a regular basis.

1 Turnover

All turnover arises from the principal activity of the LLP, undertaken in the following regions.

	2016 £	2015 £
Geographical analysis	10,620,293	10,156,621
– UK	16,007,340	14,342,500
– USA	8,805,762	7,070,000
– EU	35,433,395	31,569,121

2 Operating profit

Operating profit is stated after charging/(crediting):

	2016 £	2015 £
Depreciation of tangible assets	208,516	219,829
Profit on foreign exchange transactions	(1,176,521)	(1,202,705)
Operating lease rentals	1,022,499	1,063,973
Auditor's remuneration:		
– Audit services	31,250	27,500
– Taxation services	27,606	26,062
– Other services	32,250	42,919

3 Other interest receivable and similar income

	2016 £	2015 £
Bank interest	350	154

4 Interest payable and similar charges

	2016 £	2015 £
On bank loans and overdrafts	64,686	60,585

5 Members' remuneration charged as an expense

	2016 £	2015 £
Share of highest remunerated member	900,472	704,012
Average number of participating members	16	16

RICHMOND & TAYLOR LLP
Page [11]
NOTES TO THE FINANCIAL STATEMENTS 30 JUNE 2016 *(continued)*

6 Wages and salaries

	2016 £	2015 (as restated) £
Wages and salaries	5,461,412	4,363,793
Social security costs	637,193	650,286
Other pensions costs	254,782	268,059
	6,353,387	5,282,138

Employees

Average number of employees	2016	2015
Professional staff	46	48
Support staff	86	87
	132	135

7 Tangible fixed assets

	Leasehold property £	Office equipment £	Computer equipment £	Total £
Cost or valuation				
1 July 2015	337,500	1,062,990	1,144,917	2,545,407
Additions	–	37,751	47,506	85,257
Disposals	–	(41,326)	(588,217)	(629,543)
Revaluation	12,500	–	–	12,500
At 30 June 2016	350,000	1,059,415	604,206	2,013,621
Depreciation				
1 July 2015	143,182	932,682	1,043,244	2,119,108
Charge for the period	14,318	119,519	74,679	208,516
Disposals	–	(41,326)	(588,217)	(629,543)
Revaluation	(157,500)	–	–	(157,500)
At 30 June 2016	–	1,010,875	529,706	1,540,581
Net book value				
At 30 June 2016	350,000	48,540	74,500	473,040
At 30 June 2015	194,318	130,308	101,673	426,299

Leasehold land and buildings were subject to independent professional valuation on an open market basis at 30 June 2016 by Bartlett & Meeks, Chartered Surveyors. On an historical cost basis these assets would be included at £180,000.

8 Debtors

	2016 £	2015 £
Trade debtors	8,472,625	9,044,332
Amounts recoverable under contracts	365,700	6,001
Other debtors	598,948	464,286
Prepayments and accrued income	597,927	635,674
	10,035,200	10,150,293

RICHMOND & TAYLOR LLP   **Page [12]**
NOTES TO THE FINANCIAL STATEMENTS 30 JUNE 2016 *(continued)*

9   Creditors: amounts falling due within one year

	2016 £	2015 £ (as restated)
Bank overdraft	–	292,173
Trade creditors	2,382,021	2,001,637
Social security and other taxes	562,986	540,863
Other creditors	290,704	169,289
Accruals and deferred income	232,273	255,201
	3,467,984	3,259,163

10   Provision of liabilities

	2016 £	2015 £
Balance at 1 July 2015	337,500	337,500
Increase in provision	–	–
Balance at 30 June 2016	337,500	337,500

The provision relates to contractual obligations of the LLP which may give rise to a liability.

In the event of a winding up, any amounts owed to the LLP's bankers are secured by fixed and floating charges on the assets of the LLP.

Capital loans and other debts due to members rank behind creditors, in accordance with the members' agreement.

11   Financial Instruments

	2016 £	2015 £
Financial assets		
Debt instruments measured at amortised cost	9,437,273	9,514,619
Financial liabilities		
Measured at amortised cost	2,672,725	2,463,099

12   Leasing commitments

At 30 June 2016 the LLP had commitments under non-cancellable operating leases as follows:

	Land and buildings		Other	
Operating leases which expire:	2016	2015	2016	2015
Within one year	1,003,006	979,135	30,946	21,190
Between two and five years	3,009,018	3,961,540	61,892	53,490
	4,102,024	4,940,675	92,838	74,680

[Note: Under FRS 102 the amounts shown are the total commitments under the lease not the annual amounts payable]

RICHMOND & TAYLOR LLP **Page [13]**
NOTES TO THE FINANCIAL STATEMENTS 30 JUNE 2016 *(continued)*

13 Related parties

During the period, £36,500 of administrative expenses were paid by the LLP on behalf of a company under common control and £12,400 of administrative expenses were paid by them on behalf of the LLP. At the period end £24,100 is owed by them to the LLP.

Total Key Management Personnel compensation for the year was £4,008,647 (2015: £3,165,164).

14 Control

In the opinion of the members there is no ultimate controlling party.

15 Transition to FRS 102

The effects of changes to the LLP's accounting policies arising from the transition to FRS 102 were as follows:

	Note	At 1 July 2014			At 30 June 2015		
		As previously stated	Effect of transition	FRS 102 (as estated)	As previously stated	Effect of transition	FRS 102 (as restated)
Fixed assets		535,323		535,323	426,299		426,299
Current assets		9,499,743		9,499,743	10,605,457		10,605,457
Creditors: amounts falling due within one year	(a)	(4,141,188)	(30,000)	(4,171,188)	(3,224,163)	(35,000)	(3,259,163)
Net current assets		5,358,555	(30,000)	5,328,555	7,381,294	(35,000)	7,346,294
Total assets less current liabilities		5,893,878	(30,000)	5,863,878	7,807,593	(35,000)	7,772,593
Provisions for liabilities		337,500		337,500	(337,500)		(337,500)
Net assets attributable to members		6,231,378	(30,000)	6,201,378	7,470,093	(35,000)	7,435,093
Loans and other debts due to members		6,231,378		6,231,378	7,470,093		7,470,093
Members' other interests		–	(30,000)	(30,000)	–	(35,000)	(35,000)
		6,231,378	(30,000)	6,201,378	7,470,093	(35,000)	7,435,093

RICHMOND & TAYLOR LLP   **Page [14]**
NOTES TO THE FINANCIAL STATEMENTS 30 JUNE 2016 *(continued)*

15   Transition to FRS 102 *(continued)*

	Note	As previously stated	Effect of transition	Year ended 30 June 2015 FRS 102 (as restated)
Turnover		31,569,121		31,569,121
Cost of sales		(15,683,634)		(15,683,634)
Gross profit		15,885,487		15,885,487
Administrative expenses	(a)	(8,894,096)	(5,000)	(8,899,096)
Operating profit		6,991,391	(5,000)	6,986,391
Interest receivable and similar income		154		154
Interest payable and similar charges		(60,585)		(60,585)
Profit for the financial year before members remuneration and profit shares		6,930,960	(5,000)	6,925,960
Members remuneration charged as an expense		(6,930,960)		(6,930,960)
Profit for the year available for discretionary division among members		–	(5,000)	(5,000)

(a) Prior to applying FRS 102, the LLP did not make provision for holiday pay (i.e. holiday earned but not taken prior to the year-end). FRS 102 requires the cost of short-term compensated absences to be recognised when employees render the service that increases their entitlement. Consequently an additional accrual of £30,000 at 1 July 2014 has been made to reflect this. The additional provision at 30 June 2015 is £35,000 and the effect on profit for the year ended 30 June 2015 is an additional expense of £5,000.

10.2 Abbreviated accounts of a small LLP

The example abbreviated accounts comprise the 'Non-IAS abbreviated accounts' of the LLP prepared for filing with the Registrar of Companies in accordance with CA 2006, s. 444 as applied to LLPs, including a balance sheet complying with SI 2008/1912.

**Registered number:
OC7654321
England and Wales**

LITTLE LLP

ABBREVIATED [UNAUDITED] ACCOUNTS

YEAR ENDED 30 SEPTEMBER 2016

LITTLE LLP   **Page [1]**
BALANCE SHEET – 30 SEPTEMBER 2016

	Notes	2016 £	2016 £	2015 £	2015 £
Fixed assets					
Tangible fixed assets	1		210,471		304,047
Current assets					
Debtors	2	**2,242,183**		2,301,219	
Cash at bank and in hand		**1,347,574**		814,092	
		3,589,757		3,115,311	
Creditors: amounts falling due within one year		**(1,227,245)**		(822,519)	
Net current assets			**2,362,512**		2,292,792
Total assets less liabilities			**2,572,983**		2,596,839
Creditors: amounts falling due after more than one year			**—**		(15,976)
Net assets attributable to members			**2,572,983**		2,580,863
Represented by:					
Loans and other debts due to members within one year					
Members' capital classified as a liability			**651,344**		761,150
Other amounts			**1,921,639**		1,819,713
Total members' interests			**2,572,983**		2,580,863
Loans and other debts due to members					
			2,572,983		2,580,863

For the financial year ended 30 September 2016, the LLP was entitled to exemption from audit under the *Companies Act* 2006, s. 477 (as applied by the *Limited Liability Partnerships (Accounts and Audit) (Application of the Companies Act 2006) Regulations* 2008) applicable to LLPs subject to the small LLPs regime).

The members acknowledge their responsibilities for complying with the requirements of the Act with respect to accounting records and the preparation of accounts *[or (alternative): The members acknowledge their responsibilities for ensuring that the LLP keeps accounting records which comply with section 386 of the Act as applied to Limited Liability Partnerships and for preparing accounts which give a true and fair view of the state of affairs of the LLP as at the end of the financial year and of its profit or loss for the financial year in accordance with the requirements of s. 394–395 of the Act as applied to Limited Liability Partnerships and which otherwise comply with the requirements of the Companies Act 2006 as applied to Limited Liability Partnerships with respect to accounting records and the preparation of the accounts, so far as applicable to the LLP.]*

The accounts have been prepared in accordance with the provisions applicable to LLPs subject to the small LLPs regime.

The financial statements were approved by the members and signed on their behalf by:

S Bilboa
Designated Member
Date: 6 December 2016
Limited Liability Partnership registration number: OC7654321

LITTLE LLP
BALANCE SHEET – 30 SEPTEMBER 2014

NOTES TO THE FINANCIAL STATEMENTS – 30 SEPTEMBER 2016

1 Accounting policies

Basis of preparation

The financial statements are prepared under the historical cost convention, the Financial Reporting Standard for Smaller Entities (effective January 2015) (FRSSE) and the Statement of Recommended Practice 'Accounting by Limited Liability Partnerships' issued in January 2014 (SORP).

These financial statements reflect the results of the LLP for the year ended 30 September 2016.

Turnover

Turnover represents amounts due in respect of legal services provided during the year, net of Value Added Tax.

Services provided to clients during the year which, at the balance sheet date, have not been invoiced to clients have been recognised as turnover in accordance with the FRSSE. Turnover recognised in this manner is based on an assessment of the fair value of services provided by the balance sheet date as a proportion of the total value of the engagement. Provision is made against unbilled amounts on those engagements where the right to receive payment is contingent on factors outside the control of the LLP.

Tangible fixed assets

Tangible fixed assets are stated at cost or valuation less depreciation. Depreciation is provided at rates calculated to write off the cost or valuation less estimated residual value of each asset over its expected useful life, as follows:

- Leasehold improvements – over the term of the lease
- Fixtures and fittings – 20% on cost
- Computer equipment – 20% on cost

Tax provisions

Taxation on the profits of the LLP is solely the liability of individual members. Therefore, neither income tax nor deferred tax arising in respect of the LLP's profit is included in these financial statements.

Leased assets

Rentals applicable to operating leases where substantially all of the benefits and risks of ownership remain with the lessor are charged to the profit and loss account on a straight line basis over the lease term.

Assets held under finance leases and hire purchase contracts are capitalised and depreciated over their useful economic lives. The corresponding finance lease or hire purchase obligation is treated as a liability. The interest element of rental obligations is charged to the profit and loss account over the period of the lease at a constant proportion of the outstanding balance of capital repayments.

Pension costs

Contributions in respect of the LLP's defined contribution pension scheme are charged to the profit and loss account for the year in which they are payable to the scheme. Differences between contributions payable and contributions actually paid in the year are shown as either accruals or prepayments at the year end.

2 Tangible fixed assets

	Total *£*
Cost	**701,383**
At 1 October 2015	**24,458**
Additions	**725,841**
At 20 September 2016	
Depreciation	**397,336**
At 1 October 2015	**118,034**
Charge for the year	**515,370**
At 30 September 2016	
Net book values	
At 30 September 2016	**210,471**
At 30 September 2015	
	304,047

3 Debtors

Debtors include an amount of £2,000 (2015 – nil) falling due after more than one year.

4 Creditors

Creditors include a bank overdraft of £3,467 (2015 – £8,952). The bank overdraft is secured.

10.3 Unaudited accounts of Dormant LLP

The example Dormant LLP accounts illustrate the unaudited accounts of a dormant LLP suitable for filing with the Registrar of Companies.

**Registered number:
OC023461285
England and Wales**

DORMANT LLP

UNAUDITED ACCOUNTS

YEAR ENDED 30 JUNE 2016

DORMANT LLP   **Page [1]**
PROFIT AND LOSS ACCOUNT – 30 JUNE 2016

The LLP has not traded during the year or the preceding financial year. During these years, the LLP received no income and incurred no expenditure and therefore made neither profit nor loss.

BALANCE SHEET – 30 JUNE 2016

	2016 £	2015 £
CURRENT ASSETS		
Amounts due from members	100	100
NET ASSETS ATTRIBUTABLE TO MEMBERS	100	100
Represented by:		
Loans and other debts due to members within one year		
Members' capital classified as a liability	100	100
	100	100
TOTAL MEMBERS' INTERESTS		
Amounts due from members	(100)	(100)
Loans and other debts due to members within one year	100	100
	—	—

For the financial year ended 30 June 2016, the LLP was entitled to exemption from audit under the *Companies Act* 2006, s. 480 (as applied by the *Limited Liability Partnerships (Accounts and Audit) (Application of the Companies Act 2006) Regulations* 2008) as a dormant LLP.

The members acknowledge their responsibilities for complying with the requirements of the Act with respect to accounting records and the preparation of accounts *[or (alternative): The members acknowledge their responsibilities for ensuring that the LLP keeps accounting records which comply with section 386 of the Act as applied to Limited Liability Partnerships and for preparing accounts which give a true and fair view of the state of affairs of the LLP as at the end of the financial year and of its profit or loss for the financial year in accordance with the requirements of s. 394–395 of the Act as applied to Limited Liability Partnerships and which otherwise comply with the requirements of the Companies Act 2006 as applied to Limited Liability Partnerships with respect to accounting records and the preparation of the accounts, so far as applicable to the LLP].*

Signed on behalf of the members by:

N Pearce

....

N Pearce

Designated Member   Approved by the board: 1 November 2016

DORMANT LLP
NOTES TO THE ACCOUNTS – 30 JUNE 2016

Note to the accounts – Agency arrangements

Audit – exempt dormant LLP

The LLP was dormant and has not traded during the year. It has, however, acted in certain transactions as agent, for which it received no income.

Chapter 11 LLP audit and assurance reports

11.1 Available report types

Medium and large LLPs (as defined) are required to have an audit of their annual accounts. Some small LLPs are also required by law to have an audit, for example if they are part of a medium-sized group and have not taken advantage of the subsidiary audit exemption (see **Chapter 9**). Furthermore, some small LLPs may choose not to take advantage of the available audit exemption and undergo a statutory audit in order to provide assurance to third parties such as lenders.

If an LLP takes advantage of audit exemption in preparing its annual accounts, the members of the LLP may nevertheless wish to have the comfort of some form of report from independent accountants. Any report attached to the accounts of the LLP where no statutory report is required should be addressed to the members, since the accountants are engaged and instructed by the members.

An audit provides the highest level of assurance available. If a lower level of assurance is required, the other options can provide varying levels of comfort over the accounts.

The available options are as follows, in decreasing order of assurance level provided:

- Audit report (see **11.2**).
- Assurance review report – an accountants' report covering both the proper compilation of the accounts and the members' 'true and fair view' assertion. These reports are discussed in **11.6**.
- Agreed-upon procedures report – an accountants' report covering only some areas of the accounts. These reports are discussed in **11.7**.
- Accounts preparation/compilation report – an accountants' report on the compilation of the accounts. Reports on accounts prepared for unaudited LLPs are discussed in **11.8**.

11.2 Auditor's reports

This chapter comments on, and provides examples of, audit reports where an LLP is subject to audit. Audit reports must be prepared having regard to International Standards on Auditing – ISAs (UK and Ireland).

11.2.1 Audit – Part 16 of Companies Act 2006

Audit is covered in CA 2006, Pt. 16, which contains provisions (s. 475–539), concerning, *inter alia*, the requirement for audited accounts and the auditor's report. The summary of the statutory sections within Pt. 16 which apply to LLPs is shown in **Appendix B**.

11.2.2 Elements of an auditor's report

An auditor's report must include an introduction identifying the annual accounts and the financial reporting framework under which they are prepared, together with a description of the scope of the audit identifying the auditing standards adopted.

In essence, under CA 2006, s. 495, the auditor is required to report his opinion on these elements:

(1) *True and fair view* – whether the annual accounts show a 'true and fair view' (having regard to the members' statutory duty under CA 2006, s. 393(1))
(2) *Relevant reporting framework* – whether the accounts have been prepared in accordance with the relevant financial reporting framework.
(3) *Appropriate legislation* – whether the accounts have been prepared in accordance with CA 2006 (Pt. 15) as applied to LLPs.

The auditor's report must be either 'unqualified' or 'qualified' and contains reference to any emphasis of matters which the auditor may wish to include without modifying the report.

11.2.3 Auditor's report – s. 495

The form of report by auditors to be adopted with respect to non-IAS accounts is determined by the Regulations and by the International Standards on Auditing as applicable within the UK. Following the adoption of International Standards on Auditing (ISAs), an auditor's report on accounts is required to follow, ISA (UK and Ireland) 700 *The Auditor's Report on Financial Statements*. Example reports were issued by the Auditing Practices Board (APB*), and have been updated by the FRC – see **Example 11.1**.

Section 495 (Auditor's report on LLP's annual accounts) is reproduced in full in **Table 11.1**.

* Note that the APB was disbanded in July 2012. The function of the APB is now performed by the FRC's Audit and Assurance Council.

Table 11.1   Auditor's report on LLP's annual accounts

495 Auditor's report on LLP's annual accounts

(1) An LLP's auditor must make a report to the LLP's members on all annual accounts of the LLP of which copies are, during his tenure of office to be sent out to members under section 423;

(2) The auditor's report must include–
   (a) an introduction identifying the annual accounts that are the subject of the audit and the financial reporting framework that has been applied in their preparation, and
   (b) a description of the scope of the audit identifying the auditing standards in accordance with which the audit was conducted.

(3) The report must state clearly whether, in the auditor's opinion, the annual accounts–
   (a) give a true and fair view–
     (i) in the case of an individual balance sheet, of the state of affairs of the LLP as at the end of the financial year;
     (ii) in the case of an individual profit and loss account, of the profit or loss of the LLP for the financial year;
     (iii) in the case of group accounts, of the state of affairs as at the end of the financial year and of the profit or loss for the financial year of the undertakings included in the consolidation as a whole, so far as concerns members of the LLP;
   (b) have been properly prepared in accordance with the relevant financial reporting framework; and
   (c) have been prepared in accordance with the requirements of this Act.

Expressions used in this subsection that are defined for the purposes of Part 15 (see section 474) have the same meaning as in that Part.

(4) The auditor's report–
   (a) must be either unqualified or qualified; and
   (b) must include a reference to any matters to which the auditor wishes to draw attention by way of emphasis without qualifying the report.

Crown copyright is reproduced with the permission of the Controller of Her Majesty's Stationery Office.

11.2.4 Signature of auditor's report

The auditor's report must state the name of the auditor and be signed and dated. However, where the auditor is a firm, the report delivered to the members of the LLP must be signed by the 'senior statutory auditor' in his or her own name, for and on behalf of the auditor (CA 2006, s. 504).

Although the set of the accounts filed with the Registrar of Companies must contain the original signatures of the members who have signed the accounts on behalf of the members as a whole, a physical signature is not required on the auditor's report. In practice many auditors still prefer that the set submitted to the Registrar contains a signature. Where the auditor is a firm, the set filed with the Registrar can be signed in the name of the firm rather than in the name of the senior statutory auditor.

The Registrar has requested that all signatures in the auditor's report and accounts should be in black ink, although in practice the Registrar has accepted ink that is suitably dark to allow the pages to be scanned legibly.

11.3 ISA (UK and Ireland) 700 The Auditor's Report on Financial Statements

11.3.1 ISAs (UK and Ireland) and the auditor's report

The report of an auditor is required to follow ISA (UK and Ireland) 700 (Revised) *The Auditor's Report on Financial Statements*.

ISA (UK and Ireland) 700, although generally prescriptive as to the form and content of the auditor's report, does not preclude some flexibility when using the format and wording of the example reports prescribed by the ISA. The use of the term 'accounts', for example, in preference to 'financial statements' accords with CA 2006 and is essentially a question of personal choice, permissible provided the term is adequately defined.

From time to time, the APB* issued a Bulletin, providing illustrative examples of auditor's reports. The APB Bulletin 2010/2 (Revised), *Compendium of Illustrative Auditor's Reports on United Kingdom Private Sector Financial Statements for Periods ended on or after 15 December 2010 (Revised)* is the most recent bulletin and was revised by the APB in March 2012 and subsequently revised by FRC Bulletin 4 (April 2014, revised June 2015).

ISA (UK and Ireland) 700, *The Auditor's Report on Financial Statements*, facilitates, but does not mandate, a more concise auditor's report. This may be achieved by permitting the description of the scope of an audit and the auditor's reporting responsibilities to be made either within the body of the auditor's report (as was previously the norm) or by cross reference to the FRC's website (where a relevant statement of scope is maintained) or by cross reference to a 'Statement of the Scope of an Audit' that is included elsewhere within the Annual Report.

If it is decided to include the description of the scope of an audit with the auditor's report, the description should be presented as follows:

'An audit involves obtaining evidence about the amounts and disclosures in the accounts sufficient to give reasonable assurance that the accounts are free from material misstatement, whether caused by fraud or error. This includes an assessment of: whether the accounting policies are appropriate to the limited liability partnership's circumstances and have been consistently applied and adequately disclosed; the reasonableness of significant accounting estimates made by the members; and the overall presentation of the accounts. In addition, we read all the financial and non-financial information in the [describe the annual report] to identify material inconsistencies with the audited accounts and to identify any information that is apparently materially incorrect based on, or materially inconsistent with, the knowledge acquired by us in the course of performing the audit. If we become aware of any apparent material misstatements or inconsistencies we consider the implications for our report.'

If cross reference is made to the FRC's website, the following should be included:

'A description of the scope of an audit of financial statements is provided on the FRC's website at www.frc.org.uk/auditscopeukprivate'

11.4 Example Auditor's Report of an LLP

Example 11.1 is based on APB Bulletin 2010/2 (Revised) (at Bulletin Appendix 6) and illustrates an unmodified (that is, 'unqualified' and with no 'emphasis of matter' paragraph) auditor's report of an LLP performed in accordance with International Standards on Auditing (UK and Ireland). The example assumes:

- the LLP does not prepare group accounts; and
- the LLP adopts UK GAAP (and not IAS).

Amendments in the example made (by the author), for completeness and illustrative purposes, are presented in **[bold text]**.

Example 11.1

INDEPENDENT AUDITOR'S REPORT TO THE MEMBERS *[Author's note (1)]* OF XYZ LLP

We have audited the accounts of [name of Limited Liability Partnership] for the year ended [date], which comprise [the statement of financial position, the statement of comprehensive income, the reconciliation of members' interests, the statement of cash flows] and the related notes. The financial reporting framework that has been applied in their preparation is applicable law and United Kingdom Accounting Standards (United Kingdom Generally Accepted Accounting Practice), including FRS 102 The Financial Reporting Standard applicable in the UK and Republic of Ireland..

This report is made solely to the LLP's members, as a body, in accordance with the *Companies Act* 2006 as applied to limited liability partnerships by Part 12 of the *Limited Liability Partnerships (Accounts and Audit) (Application of Companies Act 2006) Regulations* 2008. Our audit work has been undertaken so that we might state to the LLP's members those matters we are required to state to them in an auditor's report and for no other purpose. To the fullest extent permitted by law, we do not accept or assume responsibility to anyone other than the LLP and the LLP's members as a body, for our audit work, for this report, or for the opinions we have formed. (Author's note 2)

Respective responsibilities of members and auditor

As explained more fully in the Statement of Members' Responsibilities, the members are responsible for the preparation of the accounts and for being satisfied that they give a true and fair view. Our responsibility is to audit and express an opinion on the accounts in accordance with applicable law and International Standards on Auditing (UK and Ireland). Those standards require us to comply with the Auditing Practices Board's Ethical Standards for Auditors [including 'APB Ethical Standard – Provisions Available for Small Entities (Revised)' in the circumstances set out in note x to the accounts]. (Author's note 3)

Scope of the audit of the accounts

A description of the scope of an audit of accounts is [provided on the FRC's website at www.frc.org/auditscopeukprivate]/[set out [on page x] **of the Members' Report**]. (Author's note 4)

[Or:]

An audit involves obtaining evidence about the amounts and disclosures in the accounts sufficient to give reasonable assurance that the accounts are free from material misstatement, whether caused by fraud or error. This includes an assessment of: whether the accounting policies are appropriate to the limited liability partnership's circumstances and have been consistently applied and adequately disclosed; the reasonableness of significant accounting estimates made by the designated members; and the overall presentation of the accounts. In addition, we read all the financial and non-financial information in the **Members' Report** to identify material inconsistencies with the audited accounts and to identify any information that is apparently materially incorrect based on, or materially inconsistent with, the knowledge acquired by us in the course of performing the audit. If we become aware of any apparent material misstatements or inconsistencies we consider the implications for our report.

Opinion on accounts

In our opinion the accounts:

- give a true and fair view of the state of the limited liability partnership's affairs as at [date] and of its [profit/loss] for the year then ended;
- have been properly prepared in accordance with United Kingdom Generally Accepted Accounting Practice [applicable to Smaller Entities] (Author's note 5); and
- have been prepared in accordance with the requirements of the *Companies Act* 2006 as applied to limited liability partnerships by the *Limited Liability Partnerships (Accounts and Audit) (Application of Companies Act 2006) Regulations* 2008.

Matters on which we are required to report by exception

We have nothing to report in respect of the following matters where the *Companies Act* 2006 as applied to limited liability partnerships requires us to report to you if, in our opinion:

- adequate accounting records have not been kept, or returns adequate for our audit have not been received from branches not visited by us; or
- the accounts are not in agreement with the accounting records and returns; or
- we have not received all the information and explanations we require for our audit [; or
- the members were not entitled to prepared accounts in accordance with the small limited liability partnerships regime] (Author's note 6).

Signature [Author's note (7)]

....

[Name] (Senior Statutory Auditor)
for and on behalf of [Firm name], Statutory Auditor
[Address]
[Date of signing]

Author's notes and commentary to **Example 11.1**

(1) **Report to the members** – The statutory auditor's report is made to the members of the LLP (CA2006, s. 495).

(2) **Duty of care to third parties** – the ICAEW recommends that auditors include additional wording in audit reports in order to clarify auditors' responsibilities to third parties – that is, other than to the members as a body. (Audit 1/03 – *The Audit Report and The Auditors' Duty of Care to Third Parties* (most recent update January 2010).)

[www.icaew.com/en/technical/audit-and-assurance/working-in-the-regulated-area-of-audit/audit-reports]

(3) **APB Ethical Standard – *Provisions Available for Small Entities (Revised)*** (ES PASE) – Paragraph 24 of ES PASE requires disclosure in the auditor's report where the audit firm has taken advantage of an exemption provided by ES PASE. The Appendix to ES PASE provides illustrative disclosures of relevant circumstances where the audit firm has taken advantage of an exemption (for example, where auditors have assisted in the preparation of accounts or provided tax advice). The words in square brackets in the above example should be deleted if the relief and exemptions provided by ES PASE are not utilised.

Copies of ES PASE and other ethical standards can be obtained from https://frc.org.uk/Our-Work/Codes-Standards/Audit-and-assurance/Standards-and-guidance/Standards-and-guidance-for-auditors/Ethical-standards-for-auditors.aspx

An example note for inclusion in the accounts illustrated within the APB ES PASE Appendix provides that 'In common with many other businesses of our size and nature we use our auditors to prepare and submit returns to the tax authorities and assist with the preparation of the financial statements'.

(4) **Description of the scope of an audit of accounts** – ISA (UK and Ireland) 700 (Revised) requires that an auditor's report should either: cross refer to Statement of the scope of an audit maintained on the APB's (now FRC's) website; or cross refer to such a scope statement that is included elsewhere within the Annual Report; or include a prescribed description of the scope of an audit.

The prescribed description of the scope of an audit (as illustrated in **Example 11.1**) is set out in ISA (UK and Ireland) 700 (Revised).

(5) Text in square brackets only required where the LLP has prepared the accounts in accordance with the FRSSE.

(6) Text in square brackets only required where the LLP has prepared the accounts in accordance with the small LLPs regime.

(7) **Signature and dating of auditor's report** – required by CA 2006, s. 503 and ISA (UK and Ireland) 700 *The Auditor's Report on Financial Statements* paras 23–26.

11.5   Special Auditor's Report – abbreviated accounts

Two examples below illustrate statutory reports on abbreviated accounts relating to a small LLP that has not taken advantage of audit exemption or a medium-sized LLP. The reports below are not appropriate (or required) if the LLP is exempt from audit (CA 2006, s. 477, 480).

The examples of special auditor's reports on abbreviated accounts comprise:

- **(Example 11.2)** – LLP abbreviated accounts (if small, advantage not taken (or available) of audit exemption);
- **(Example 11.3)** – LLP abbreviated accounts (qualified full audit opinion – if small, advantage not taken (or available) of audit exemption).

The example reports illustrated within the abbreviated accounts assume that the accounts are not published on a website.

APB Bulletin 2008/4 (April 2008) '*The special auditor's report on abbreviated accounts in the United Kingdom*' provides guidance for auditors regarding the filing obligations of small (and medium-sized) entities under the *Companies Act* 2006, and in particular, provides guidance concerning the 'Special Auditor's Report on Abbreviated Accounts' (CA 2006, s. 449). **Examples 11.2** and **11.3** reflect the guidance in APB Bulletin 2008/4.

Example 11.2

INDEPENDENT AUDITOR'S REPORT TO XYZ LLP UNDER SECTION 449 OF THE COMPANIES ACT 2006 AS APPLIED TO LLPs

We have examined the abbreviated accounts set out on pages [x] to [x], together with the accounts of [name of the LLP] for the year ended [30 June 2014] prepared under section 396 of the *Companies Act* 2006 as applied to limited liability partnerships by the Limited Liability Partnerships (Accounts and Audit) (Application of Companies Act 2006) Regulations 2008.

> This report is made solely to the LLP, in accordance with section 449 of the *Companies Act* 2006 as applied to limited liability partnerships by the Limited Liability Partnerships (Accounts and Audit) (Application of Companies Act 2006) Regulations 2008. Our work has been undertaken so that we might state to the LLP those matters we are required to state to it in a special auditors' report and for no other purpose. To the fullest extent permitted by law, we do not accept or assume responsibility to anyone other than the LLP, for our work, for this report, or for the opinions we have formed.

Respective responsibilities of members and auditor

The members are responsible for preparing the abbreviated accounts in accordance with section [444] or [445] of the *Companies Act* 2006 as applied to limited liability partnerships by the Limited Liability Partnerships (Accounts and Audit) (Application of Companies Act 2006) Regulations 2008. It is our responsibility to form an independent opinion as to whether the LLP is entitled to deliver abbreviated accounts to the Registrar of Companies and whether the abbreviated accounts have been properly prepared in accordance with the regulations made under that section and to report our opinion to you.

We conducted our work in accordance with Bulletin 2008/4 issued by the Auditing Practices Board. In accordance with that Bulletin we have carried out the procedures we consider necessary to confirm, by reference to the accounts, that the LLP is entitled to deliver abbreviated accounts and that the abbreviated accounts to be delivered are properly prepared. *The scope of our work for the purpose of this report did not include examining or dealing with events after the date of our report on the full statutory accounts.*

Opinion

In our opinion, the LLP is entitled to deliver abbreviated accounts prepared in accordance with section [444(3)] or [445(3)] of the *Companies Act* 2006 as applied to limited liability partnerships by the Limited Liability Partnerships (Accounts and Audit) (Application of Companies Act 2006) Regulations 2008 and the abbreviated accounts [on pages [x] to [x] have been properly prepared in accordance with [regulation 5 of the Small Limited Liability Partnerships (Accounts) Regulations 2008 (SI 2008/1912)] or [regulation 4 of the Large and Medium-sized Limited Liability Partnerships (accounts) Regulations 2008 (SI 2008/1913).]

Signature

....

[Name] (Senior Statutory Auditor)
for and on behalf of [Firm name], Statutory Auditors
[Address]
[Date]

s. 503 CA 2006

Author's notes and commentary to **Example 11.1**

Duty of care to third parties – boxed text contains additional wording as recommended by ICAEW (Audit 1/03 – *The Audit Report and The Auditors' Duty of Care to Third Parties*) (January 2003 as updated 2010). (See **12.5**.)

Events after the date of the report – Text in *italics* in the penultimate paragraph above is only appropriate where the special report is dated **after** the signing of the auditor's report on the full annual accounts.

Section numbers – section 444 relates to small LLPs and section 445 relates to medium-sized entities.

Example 11.3

INDEPENDENT AUDITOR'S REPORT TO XYZ LLP UNDER SECTION 449 OF THE COMPANIES ACT 2006 AS APPLIED TO LLPs [QUALIFIED FULL AUDIT OPINION]

We have examined the abbreviated accounts set out on pages [x] to [x], together with the [full statutory] accounts of the LLP for the year ended [30 June 2014] prepared under section 396 of the *Companies Act* 2006 as applied to limited liability partnerships by the Limited Liability Partnerships (Accounts and Audit) (Application of Companies Act 2006) Regulations 2008.

> This report is made solely to the LLP, in accordance with section 449 of the Companies Act 2006 as applied to limited liability partnerships by the Limited Liability Partnerships (Accounts and Audit) (Application of Companies Act 2006) Regulations 2008. Our work has been undertaken so that we might state to the LLP those matters we are required to state to it in a special auditor's report and for no other purpose. To the fullest extent permitted by law, we do not accept or assume responsibility to anyone other than the LLP, for our work, for this report, or for the opinions we have formed.

Respective responsibilities of members and auditor

The members are responsible for preparing the abbreviated accounts in accordance with section [444] or [445] of the *Companies Act* 2006 as applied to limited liability partnerships by the Limited Liability Partnerships (Accounts and Audit) (Application of Companies Act 2006) Regulations 2008. It is our responsibility to form an independent opinion as to whether the LLP is entitled to deliver abbreviated accounts to the Registrar of Companies and whether the abbreviated accounts have been properly prepared in accordance with the regulations made under that section and to report our opinion to you.

We conducted our work in accordance with Bulletin 2008/4 issued by the Auditing Practices Board. In accordance with that Bulletin we have carried out the procedures we consider necessary to confirm, by reference to the accounts, that the LLP is entitled to deliver abbreviated accounts and that the abbreviated accounts to be delivered are properly prepared. *The scope of our work for the purpose of this report did not include examining or dealing with events after the date of our report on the full statutory accounts.*

Opinion

In our opinion the LLP is entitled to deliver abbreviated accounts prepared in accordance with section [444(3)] or [445(3)] of the *Companies Act* 2006 as applied to limited liability partnerships by the Limited Liability Partnerships (Accounts and Audit) (Application of Companies Act 2006) Regulations 2008, and the abbreviated accounts [on pages x to x] have been properly prepared in accordance with [regulation 5 of the Small Limited Liability Partnerships (Accounts) Regulations 2008 (SI 2008/1912)] or [regulation 4 of the Large and Medium-sized Limited Liability Partnerships (Accounts) Regulations 2008 (SI 2008/1913).]

Other information

On 21 October 2014 we reported as auditor to the members of the LLP on the accounts prepared under section 396 of the *Companies Act* 2006 as applied to limited liability partnerships by the Limited Liability Partnerships (Accounts and Audit) (Application of Companies Act 2006) Regulations 2008 and our report was as follows [/included the following statement/paragraph]:

[Qualified audit report under section 495 *Companies Act* 2006 or Statements under section 498(2) [Inadequate accounting records] or section 498(3) [Failure to obtain necessary information] or Explanatory comment contained in Unqualified Audit Report under section 495 *Companies Act* 2006 concerning fundamental uncertainty to be set out in full]:

Signature
....

[Name] (Senior Statutory Auditor)
for and on behalf of [Firm] Statutory Auditors
[Address]
[Date]

s. 503 CA 2006

Example of other information: explanatory paragraph
Going concern. In forming our opinion, we have considered the adequacy of disclosures made in note 1 of the accounts concerning the uncertainty as to the continuation and renewal of the LLP's bank overdraft facility. In view of the significance of this uncertainty we consider that it should be drawn to your attention, but our opinion is not modified in this respect.

Qualified full audit opinion – The special auditor's report (where necessary) in connection with abbreviated accounts is not required to reproduce the full text of the auditor's report on the annual accounts, except (as illustrated above) in the circumstances of a qualification. This is explained further in **6.8**.

11.6 Assurance review reports

Guidance on the conduct of assurance reviews on accounts was published by the ICAEW in Technical Release (Audit and Assurance Faculty) TECH09/13 AAF *Assurance Review Engagements on Historical Financial Statements.* The objectives of a review report for a small LLP would be to provide comfort to the members and to enhance the credibility of the accounts of an LLP that is exempt from audit with third parties, including members and the Registrar of Companies.

The technical release states:

'Review engagements, like audit engagements, may help the accountant to report weaknesses and other issues that come to their attention to the directors. In other words, such engagements can generate much more value for the directors than just the assurance report itself. This represents a substantial degree of understanding of the client's circumstances. Further substantive testing is not required unless the chartered accountant has reason to be concerned about some aspect of the business. An assurance review engagement is therefore a flexible and proportionate service which can be adapted to suit different clients.' TECH09/13 AAF

The guidance is designed to assist with compliance with the International Standard for Review Engagements (ISRE) 2400 (Revised) issued by the IAASB which was revised in 2012 and came into effect for reviews of accounts for periods ending on or after 31 December 2013. It also provides example letters, statements and reports to support review engagements.

Further guidance can be found in the ICAEW's Assurance Sourcebook, published in July 2012.

Example 11.4 below reproduces the example Assurance Review Report from TECH09/13 AAF.

***Example 11.4   Example Assurance Review Report ICAEW Technical Release
(Audit and Assurance Faculty) – TECH09/13 AAF (September 2013)
Appendix 4: Illustrative Assurance Review Report***

INDEPENDENT CHARTERED ACCOUNTANTS' REVIEW REPORT TO THE MEMBERS OF [NAME OF ENTITY] ('THE LLP')

We have reviewed the financial statements of [name of entity] for the year ended [date], which comprise the [Profit and Loss Account, the Balance Sheet, the Cash Flow Statement, the Statement of Total Recognised Gains and Losses,] and the related notes 1 to [X]. The financial reporting framework that has been applied in their preparation is applicable law and the Financial Reporting Standard for Smaller Entities (effective April 2008) (United Kingdom Generally Accepted Accounting Practice applicable to Smaller Entities)

This report is made solely to the LLP's members, as a body, in accordance with the terms of our engagement letter dated [date]. Our review has been undertaken so that we may state to the members those matters that we have agreed to state to them in our engagement letter and for no other purpose. To the fullest extent permitted by law, we do not accept or assume responsibility to anyone other than the LLP and the LLP's members, as a body, for our work, for this report or for the conclusions we have formed.

Members' responsibility for the financial statements

As explained more fully in the members' responsibilities statement on page [] the members are responsible for the preparation of the financial statements and for being satisfied that they give a true and fair view.

Accountants' responsibility

Our responsibility is to express a conclusion based on our review of the financial statements. We conducted our review in accordance with International Standard on Review Engagements (ISRE) 2400 (Revised) *Engagements to review historical financial statements* and ICAEW Technical Release TECH 09/13AAF *Assurance review engagements on historical financial statements*. ISRE 2400 also requires us to comply with the ICAEW Code of Ethics.

Scope

A review of financial statements in accordance with ISRE 2400 (Revised) is a limited assurance engagement. We have performed additional procedures to those required under a compilation engagement. These primarily consist of making enquiries of management and others within the entity, as appropriate, applying analytical procedures and evaluating the evidence obtained. The procedures performed in a review are substantially less than those performed in an audit conducted in accordance with International Standards on Auditing (UK and Ireland). Accordingly, we do not express an audit opinion on these financial statements.

Conclusion

Based on our review, nothing has come to our attention that causes us to believe that the financial statements have not been prepared:

- so as to give a true and fair view of the state of the LLP's affairs as at [date], and of its profit [loss] for the year then ended;
- in accordance with United Kingdom Generally Accepted Accounting Practice [applicable to Smaller Entities]; and
- in accordance with the *Companies Act* 2006 as applied to limited liability partnerships by the Limited Liability Partnerships (Accounts and Audit) (Application of Companies Act 2006) Regulations 2008].

....

Name of firm
Chartered Accountants [**NOT** *'Statutory Auditors'*]
[Location]
[Date]

11.7 Agreed-upon procedures

The scope of an agreed-upon procedures engagement is formulated by discussion between the members of the LLP and the chartered accountant performing the work.

The accountant prepares a report based on the results of the procedures performed on a factual basis and does not express any opinion or conclusion.

Examples might include:

- Verification of existence and ownership of fixed assets;
- Stock valuation review; or
- Verification of controls being applied on purchase payments.

11.8 Compilation: reports on accounts prepared for unaudited LLPs – ICAEW Technical Release Audit 02/10

A Technical Release, issued by the Audit and Assurance Faculty of the Institute of Chartered Accountants in England and Wales in November 2010 (Audit 02/10 *Chartered Accountants' Reports on Compilation of Financial Statements of Incorporated Entities*) gives general guidance on the form and content of reports where accountants 'compile' (being the generally acknowledged term for 'prepare') accounts on behalf of client entities.

The example accountants' report (a non-statutory (or contractual) report) contained in the Technical Release Audit 02/10 adjusted by the author to make it appropriate to an LLP, is reproduced in **Example 11.5**.

The example is essentially appropriate in circumstances where the members wish the accountants to assist them in meeting the members' statutory obligation to prepare annual accounts showing a true and fair view. Where the accounts compiled by an accountant constitute abbreviated accounts, the form of report in **Example 11.5** may also be used to support the abbreviated accounts. Optional paragraphs (or text to be completed as appropriate) are indicated by [square brackets].

The use of the report remains voluntary – there is no requirement for LLPs to use professional accountants to help compile accounts or to obtain an accounts compilation report.

The special auditor's report under s. 449 is reflected within **Examples 11.2** and **11.3**, but is only required in the event of audited accounts.

Where accounts are compiled by a professional accountant and an accountants' report is prepared on the lines of **Example 11.5**, the Technical Release Audit 02/10 stresses the importance of agreeing terms of engagement between the members and the reporting accountants. The Technical Release provides example terms.

Example 11.5 Chartered Accountants' Reports on the Compilation of Financial Statements of Incorporated Entities (AAF 02/10)

Chartered Accountant's/Accountants' report to the members on the preparation of the unaudited statutory accounts of XYZ LLP for the year [/period] ended ...

In order to assist you to fulfil your duties under the *Companies Act* 2006 as applied to limited liability partnerships by the Limited Liability Partnerships (Accounts and Audit) (Application of Companies Act 2006) Regulations 2008, we have prepared for your approval the accounts of XYZ LLP for the year [/period] ended [date] [as set out on pages x-x/which comprise [insert statements]] from the LLP's accounting records and from information and explanations you have given us.

As a practising member [/member firm] of the Institute of Chartered Accountants in England and Wales (ICAEW), we are subject to its ethical and other professional requirements which are detailed at icaew. com/membershandbook.

[This report is made solely to the members of XYZ LLP, as a body, in accordance with the terms of our engagement letter dated [date].] Our work has been undertaken [solely to prepare for your approval the accounts of XYZ LLP and state those matters that we have agreed to state to you/the members of XYZ LLP, as a body, in this report] in accordance with AAF 2/10 as detailed at icaew.com/compilation. [To the fullest extent permitted by law, we do not accept or assume responsibility to anyone other than the XYZ LLP and its members as a body for our work or for this report.]

[It is your duty to ensure that XYZ LLP has kept adequate accounting records and to prepare statutory accounts that give a true and fair view of the assets, liabilities, financial position and profit[/loss] of XYZ LLP. You consider that XYZ LLP is exempt from the statutory audit requirement for the year [/period].]

[We have not been instructed to carry out an audit or a review of the accounts of XYZ LLP. For this reason, we have not verified the accuracy or completeness of the accounting records or information and explanations you have given to us and we do not, therefore, express any opinion on the statutory accounts.]

[Explanatory paragraph: e.g. records destroyed by fire] *Explanatory paragraph may be positioned in other places in the report depending on the nature of the matter described.*

Signature........................... *(The report is signed in the name of the professional accountant or, where appropriate, in the name of the accounting firm)*

Typed name of professional accountant

Chartered Accountants

Address

Date ....

Chapter 12 Filing accounts for LLPs

12.1 Introduction

This book does not aim to cover the finer details of the filing requirements for the accounts of LLPs but this chapter gives guidance on filing with the Registrar of Companies and explains some of the current filing methods which are introducing changes to the process which has existed for many years of paper filing of accounts with the Registrar.

Although it is available for some companies, online filing of accounts is not yet available for LLPs.

12.2 Filing deadlines

In general, LLPs are required to file accounts with the Registrar of Companies within nine months from the end of the accounting period (accounting reference date or ARD).

When filing the LLP's first accounts, the deadline for delivery is 21 months after the date of incorporation. The deadline remains the same even if the LLP extends its first accounting period to the maximum of 18 months. It is calculated to the exact corresponding date in the 21st month following the incorporation. For example, an LLP incorporated on 29 January 2014 has until midnight on 29 October 2015 to submit its first accounts.

When the accounting period is extended, other than for the first accounts, the filing deadline remains as nine months after the end of the period. However, when an LLP shortens the accounting period, the filing deadline for that period is the longer of the following:

- nine months after the new ARD; or
- three months after the date of the notice of the ARD change being delivered to the Registrar.

LLPs submitting their accounts after the filing deadline has passed will incur a late filing penalty of at least £150. The penalty increases in line with the period of late submission. The maximum penalty for an LLP which submits accounts six months after the normal filing deadline is £1,500. However, if the LLP files its accounts late two years in a row, the penalty in the second year is doubled.

12.3 Filing accounts with the Registrar of Companies

The Registrar of Companies is given authority under the CA 2006 to make rules governing the filing of documents at Companies House. These 'Registrar's Rules' are secondary legislation, made under section 1117 of the Act, and include the form, delivery and method of authentication for documents (including accounts) to be delivered to the Registrar.

The rules specify different filing requirements for hard copy and electronic filings. For example, although the Companies Act requirement for an original signature to be included on the accounts that are filed was repealed as from 1 October 2009, signatures are still required by the Registrar's Rules to be included on balance sheets filed in paper form.

Furthermore, Companies House has recently reviewed its policy on filing documents with original signatures and has concluded that the Registrar of Companies will 'accept in good faith that documents presented for filing which have automatically generated signatures have been properly approved by the signatory', and that 'documents will no longer be rejected simply because the signature does not appear to be original'.

A detailed list of the Registrar's rules, including when amendments came into force, is available at:

www.gov.uk/guidance/registrars-rules

Of particular relevance to the filing of accounts on paper at Companies House are the following rules relating to registered number, signatures and the form and content of documents.

Table 12.1   Filing accounts at Companies House

The Registrar's (requirements for paper documents) Rules 2009

Name and registered number

Paragraph 22(3) of Volume 2 of the amended Registrar's Rules 2009 lists the documents (delivered on paper) which must contain the name and registered number of the entity to which the document relates (but only one of the documents filed must show this information).

Only one of the following documents filed must contain the name and registered number of the LLP:

- copy of balance sheet or abbreviated accounts;
- (where applicable): copy of profit and loss account; or
- copy of auditor's report.

The LLP's name or registered number required as above must be in black typescript or handwritten in black ink in a 'prominent position' in the document filed; this does not, however, include, for example, the cover of an annual accounts package.

Paragraph 23(1) requires the following documents (filed in paper form) to be signed by a designated member:

- copy of balance sheet;
- abbreviated accounts; and
- annual accounts.

The signature must be applied to the document in a prominent position, at the end of the balance sheet.

Form and content of documents

Generally, paper documents sent to Companies House must state in a prominent position the registered name and number of the LLP. Paper documents must be:

- on A4 size, plain white paper with a matt finish (note – Companies House does usually accept accounts on US letter sized paper and off-white paper as long as the document can be scanned legibly to A4);
- black, clear and legible text, of uniform density; and
- clear and legible bold letters and numbers.

Documents should not be in poor lettering or photocopies, carbon copies, or produced from a dot matrix printer (as this may cause problems scanning the documents).

12.4 Common reasons for accounts rejections at Companies House

Common reasons why paper accounts are rejected by Companies House include:

- Company/LLP name or number is absent or incorrect;
- filing accounts with the same date as previously filed accounts (see **12.5** below);
- signatory name missing from the balance sheet;
- balance sheet signature missing;
- statement such as audit exemption missing or incorrect; and
- accounting reference date (ARD) absent or incorrect.

In 2010, the ICAEW issued a document entitled 'Rejected Accounts' which gives guidance on preventing accounts being rejected by the Registrar:

www.icaew.com/en/technical/financial-reporting/other-reporting-issues/other-uk-regulation/
briefing-on-companies-house-rejected-accounts-173847

If such accounts are submitted close to the filing deadline and the corrected accounts cannot be returned before the filing deadline expires, an automatic late filing penalty will be issued.

12.5 Filing amended accounts

If it is found that a set of accounts submitted to Companies House is defective (i.e. containing errors or not compliant with a requirement of the Companies Act as applied to LLPs), then the members may submit amending accounts to the Registrar of Companies. This may be because the LLP has realised that the accounts are defective or because the Registrar has written to the members to request that they either give a satisfactory explanation for the accounts or prepare revised accounts.

Revised accounts sent to Companies House must be marked as 'amending'. It is recommended that the 'amending' is very clearly marked (to prevent rejection by Companies House for being made up to the same date as a set of accounts that has previously been filed). The highlighting should not obscure any part of the accounts, however, as they could then be rejected if they do not scan legibly.

The amending accounts must contain the following statements (in a prominent position):

- the revised accounts replace the original accounts for the financial year (specifying it);
- the revised accounts are now the statutory accounts for that year; and
- the revised accounts have been prepared as at the date of the original accounts, and not as at the date of the revision and accordingly do not deal with events between those dates.

The accounts must also contain details (in a prominent position) of:

- the way in which the original accounts did not comply with the requirements of the CA 2006 as applied to LLPs; and
- any significant amendments made as a result of correcting the defects.

If the original accounts were audited, the amending accounts must contain an audit report on the revised accounts. This report differs from the original report and includes statements of whether:

- in the auditor's opinion, the revised accounts have been properly prepared in accordance with the CA 2006 as applied to LLPs;

- the revised accounts give a true and fair view of the individual balance sheet and profit and loss (consolidated in the case of group accounts), seen as at the date the original accounts were approved; and
- the original accounts failed to comply with the requirements of the CA 2006 as applied to LLPs in the respects identified by the members.

If the previous set of accounts was not audited, but the revised set is found not to be exempt from audit, the LLP must also deliver an auditor's report to Companies House within 28 days after the date of revision of the accounts.

The original (defective) accounts will remain on the public record. Removing incorrect documents from the public record requires a court order (unless Companies House, in error, accepted an item which should have been rejected).

12.6   Electronic filing of accounts

12.6.1   Online filing with the Registrar of Companies

Although Companies House's webfiling system can be used to submit many administrative forms, such as the Annual Return, Appointment or Termination of members or Change of accounting reference date, LLPs cannot file their annual accounts using the webfiling services.

LLPs also cannot file their accounts electronically by other means, unlike companies where audit exempt full accounts, small abbreviated accounts, dormant accounts and audited individual full accounts may be filed electronically in iXBRL format.

12.6.2   Electronic tagging of financial statements (iXBRL) for tax purposes

Inline Extensible Business Reporting Language (iXBRL) tagging of the UK statutory accounts of companies is required for corporation tax purposes. iXBRL is a tagging system which enables the accounts of a company to be read electronically. Although this has been mandatory for companies since accounting periods ending after 31 March 2010 which are filing their tax return after 31 March 2011, these requirements **do not apply** to LLPs as LLPs do not file corporation tax returns.

It is only if the combined annualised turnover of an LLP is more than £15m, that LLPs are required to send their accounts with the partnership tax return to HMRC. Further guidance is given in the Partnership Tax Return Guide which applies to LLPs and partnerships. In cases where the accounts are required to be sent to HMRC, HMRC do not require these to be electronically tagged.

Chapter 13 Future of UK financial reporting for LLPs

13.1 Changes to financial reporting for LLPs

When LLPs were introduced, the financial reporting regime that was applied to them was the same as the existing regime for private limited companies, with certain adaptations which were required in order to allow for the differences between the two types of entity.

However, in recent years various changes have been made to the financial reporting regime for private limited companies which have not been applied to LLPs. In November 2015, the Department for Business Innovation and Skills (BIS) issued a consultation *De-regulatory changes for Limited Liability Partnerships (LLPs) and Qualifying Partnerships* which, amongst other things, proposed to extend those changes to LLPs. The consultation closed on 21 December 2015 and on 19 February 2016, the department confirmed that the changes would be extended to LLPs.

The main changes to the financial reporting regime for private limited companies, which apply for periods commencing on or after 1 January 2016, are:

- changes to the size limits for small and medium-sized companies;
- changes to the content of small company accounts;
- introduction of the option to prepare abridged accounts instead of full statutory accounts;
- removal of the option to file abbreviated accounts for small and medium-sized companies;
- the withdrawal of the FRSSE and its replacement by section 1A of FRS 102.

In addition, the smallest private limited companies have for some time been able to prepare micro entity accounts, with greatly simplified accounting and disclosure requirements. This regime will also be made available to LLPs.

The effect of these changes, referring to companies which will also be applied to LLPs, is summarised below.

13.1.1 Size limits

The revised size limits for small and medium-sized companies and the unchanged size limits for micro companies are:

	Micro	Small	Medium
Turnover	£632k	£10.2m	£36m
Gross assets	£316k	£5.1m	£18m
Employees	10	50	250

The method of applying the above limits in order to determine the size of a company has not changed (see **Chapter 4**).

The size limits for small and medium-sized groups (see **Chapter 7**) have also been revised, as follows:

	Small		Medium	
	Net	Gross	Net	Gross
Turnover	£10.2m	£12.2m	£36m	£43.2m
Gross assets	£5.1m	£6.1m	£18m	£21.6m
Employees	50	50	250	250

These limits apply for periods commencing on or after 1 January 2016, but companies can early adopt the limits for any period commencing on or after 1 January 2015 provided that all of the other changes to financial reporting are adopted at the same time. If the same provisions are applied to LLPs, this could be particularly attractive to those medium-sized LLPs which would qualify as small under the revised limits (however, see **13.2** below regarding timing of early adoption as this is not possible for LLPs until issuance of the statutory instrument and **13.3** for the effect on audit exemption).

13.1.2   Small company accounts

From 1 January 2016, or for companies early adopting the new size limits, the FRSSE has been withdrawn and small companies must account in accordance with FRS 102 (unless they opt to apply FRS 101 or even full IFRS as set out in the scope of this book). This will mean that the accounting will be the same as for medium-sized and large companies, however there are extensive disclosure exemptions which are contained in section 1A of FRS 102 which they could opt to take.

The disclosure exemptions mean that accounts prepared under section 1A of FRS 102 are likely to have less disclosure than the accounts currently prepared under the FRSSE. However, unlike micro entities, for small companies compliance with the minimum disclosure requirements in company law and section 1A of FRS 102 is not deemed to give a true and fair view. As a result directors are required to consider whether additional disclosures are required.

In addition, if all of the members agree, a small company can prepare abridged accounts as its statutory accounts instead of preparing accounts with all of the disclosures required by section 1A. This will mean that most notes to the balance sheet are not required and the profit and loss account can start with gross profit.

13.1.3   Filing requirements

The option to file abbreviated accounts is removed and, in principle, small companies are required to file the full statutory accounts that they have prepared. Where their full accounts are abridged accounts these will be the accounts that are filed, along with a statement that all members of the company have consented to the abridgement.

However, small companies are allowed to omit the directors' report and profit and loss account (or either of them) from their filed accounts. Where this is the case the filed accounts must note that the profit and loss account is not included and must state in a prominent position that they have been delivered in accordance with the provisions applicable to companies subject to the small companies regime.

Where small company accounts have been audited, the accounts delivered to Companies House must contain the audit report if they are the full accounts (i.e. they contain the profit and loss account as well as the balance sheet). If the profit and loss account is omitted then the audit report is not filed, however the notes to the accounts are required to state whether the audit report was qualified or unqualified, give details of any qualification or emphasis of matter and give the name of the audit firm and the senior statutory auditor.

13.1.4   Micro entity accounts

Companies which meet the micro entity size limits (see **13.1.1** above) are permitted to prepare simplified accounts as their statutory accounts. Such companies are allowed to prepare statutory accounts which only consist of:

Balance sheet:	Profit and loss account:
Called up share capital not paid	Turnover
Fixed assets	Other income
Current assets	Cost of raw materials and consumables
Prepayments and accrued income	Staff costs
Creditors: amounts falling due within one year	Depreciation and other amounts written off assets
Net current assets (liabilities)	
Total assets less current liabilities	Other charges
Creditors: amounts falling due after more than one year	Tax
	Profit or loss
Provisions for liabilities	
Accruals and deferred income	NB. Micro entities are not permitted to use a format 1
Capital and reserves	Profit and loss (showing cost of sales and gross profit)

Notes are not required so, for example, the split of fixed assets into tangible and intangible is not given. However, micro entities are required to give details of advances, credits and guarantees granted to directors and financial commitments, guarantees and contingencies at the foot of the balance sheet.

These accounts are deemed by law to give a true and fair view, so there is no need to consider whether additional disclosures are needed in order to actually give a true and fair view.

As well as simplified disclosures, micro entities are also subject to simplified accounting requirements. For periods commencing on or after 1 January 2016 (with early adoption permitted) these micro entity reporting is governed by FRS 105 *The Financial Reporting Standard applicable to the Micro-entities Regime*. Simplifications include all fixed assets (including investment properties) being carried at cost rather than being allowed or required to carry them at fair value and also not accounting for deferred tax.

13.2   Timing of the application of the financial reporting changes to LLPs

Micro entity accounts are already available to companies. The other financial reporting changes, as noted above, are applicable to companies for periods commencing on or after 1 January 2016, with early adoption allowed for periods commencing on or after 1 January 2015 provided that all of the changes are adopted.

BIS has announced that the changes will be available to LLPs from the same date and that early adoption will be allowed on the same basis. However, LLPs will not be able to early adopt until the changes have been approved by a statutory instrument, which is not expected to happen until mid 2016. Given the nine month deadline for filing accounts this will mean that LLPs with 31 December 2015 year ends that wish to early adopt the new provisions (for example because they are medium-sized, but will be small under the new size limits and wish to take advantage of the disclosure exemptions in section 1A of FRS 102) will have a short window in which to file their accounts.

13.3 Proposed changes to audit exemption

BIS also consulted on whether to increase the thresholds for audit exemption in order that they remain aligned with the small company thresholds. This consultation *Auditor Regulation: Discussion document on the implications of the EU and wider reforms* closed on 19 March 2015 and on 26 January 2016 BIS announced that the thresholds for audit exemption would be increased to the new small company thresholds. BIS indicated in its consultation on LLP changes (see above) that it intends to apply whatever changes are made to the audit thresholds for companies to LLPs as well.

It is also proposed that LLPs which are part of a group which includes a public limited company will no longer lose their audit exemption as part of an 'ineligible group'.

The effective date for any changes to the audit thresholds will be for periods commencing 1 January 2016. It should be noted that early adoption of the new accounting thresholds for periods commencing before this date but after 1 January 2015 will not affect the audit exemption thresholds, so LLPs that qualify as small under the new limits but not under the previous ones will continue to require an audit.

Chapter 14 Transition to FRS 102

14.1   Disclosure on transition

As set out in Chapter 1, most LLPs will use FRS 102 as their underlying accounting standard for periods commencing on or after 1 January 2015.

As there are various differences between the accounting required by FRS 102 and previous UK GAAP, LLPs will need to change their accounting policies. Subject to certain exemptions set out in section 35 of FRS 102 *Transition to this FRS*, LLPs are required to deal with these changes in accounting policy by restating their opening balances and comparative figures.

As part of the transition process LLPs will need to establish their transition date, which is the first day of the comparative accounting period in their first set of FRS 102 accounts. So, for an LLP with a year end of 31 March, the first set of FRS 102 accounts will be for the year ended 31 March 2016 and the transition date will be 1 April 2014.

The LLP will then restate its members' interests at the transition date to what they would have been if FRS 102 had always applied (subject to the exemptions contained in section 35) and restate the profit and loss account for the comparative year and the balance sheet at that year end under FRS 102.

Section 35 requires LLPs to present a reconciliation of their equity at the transition date and at the end of the comparative year between the amounts shown in their previous accounts, determined under previous UK GAAP, and the restated amounts under FRS 102 (para 35.13). It also requires a similar reconciliation of the profit for the comparative year between the amounts shown in their previous accounts, determined under previous UK GAAP, and the restated amounts under FRS 102.

The FRS has given examples of the format of such disclosures for companies in Staff Education Note 13, which is available from its website (www.frc.org.uk). An example of this, adapted for LLPs is shown below.

	Note	At 1 Jan 2014			At 31 Dec 2014		
		As previously stated	Effect of transition	FRS 102 (as restated)	As previously stated	Effect of transition	FRS 102 (as restated)
		£000	£000	£000	£000	£000	£000
Fixed assets		5,868	-	5,868	5,416	-	5,416
Current assets	1,2	2,475	15	2,490	2,520	17	2,537
Creditors: amounts falling due within one year	1,3	(2,355)	(16)	(2,371)	(1,824)	(20)	(1,844)
Net current assets		120	(1)	119	696	(3)	693
Total assets less current liabilities		5,988	(1)	5,987	6,112	(3)	6,109

	Note	At 1 Jan 2014			At 31 Dec 2014		
		As previously stated	Effect of transition	FRS 102 (as restated)	As previously stated	Effect of transition	FRS 102 (as restated)
		£000	£000	£000	£000	£000	£000
Creditors: amounts falling due after more than one year	1	(2,900)	(6)	(2,906)	(2,840)	(3)	(2,843)
Provisions for liabilities		(410)	-	(410)	(465)	-	(465)
Net assets attributable to members		2,678	(7)	2,671	2,807	(6)	2,801
Loans and other debts due to members		2,151	-	2,151	2,402	-	2,402
Members' other interests		527	(7)	520	405	(6)	399
		2,678	(7)	2,671	2,807	(6)	2,801

	Note	Year ended 31 Dec 2014		
		As previously stated	Effect of transition	FRS 102 (as restated)
		£000	£000	£000
Turnover		832	-	832
Cost of sales	1,2	(520)	1	(519)
Gross profit		312	1	313
Administrative expenses	1,2,3	(65)	-	(65)
Other operating income		42	-	42
Operating profit		289	1	290
Interest receivable and similar income		5	-	5
Interest payable and similar charges		(130)	-	(130)
Profit for the financial year before members remuneration and profit shares		164	1	165
Members remuneration charged as an expense		(35)	-	(35)
Profit for the year available for discretionary division among members		129	1	130

Notes to the above tables are also required to explain the transitional adjustments.

As an alternative to the above presentation, LLPs could present a reconciliation of their equity at the transition date and the comparative year end and their comparative profit for the year in total.

14.2 Effect on previously allocated profits

Where transitional adjustments are made it is likely that cumulative profits up to the transition date and profits for the comparative year calculated under FRS 102 accounting policies will be different from those previously calculated.

In many cases, LLPs will have allocated their profits in previous years based on the profits calculated under previous UK GAAP, either by automatic allocation of the profits as they arise or by a specific allocation of the profits once they have been determined.

How profits are allocated is a matter for the LLP members' agreement. Where the agreement makes an allocation to members based on profit this will, subject to any clarification of this in the members' agreement, be the profit determined in accordance with the UK GAAP which applied at that time. Therefore if an LLP automatically divides profits as they arise, the allocated profits for the comparative year (and earlier) will be those calculated under previous GAAP and the allocation will not be changed by the restatement of the comparative profit.

Similarly, LLPs that make specific allocations of profit, even if these are based on the accounting profit for the previous year, will not restate these.

This is consistent with the requirement in paragraph 35.8 of FRS 102 to recognise the transitional adjustments in retained earnings or another component of equity.

How this adjustment to equity is then allocated in the first year under FRS 102 will be a matter for the LLP members' agreement. Where there are specific provisions dealing with prior year adjustments in general or with the transition to FRS 102 specifically these must be followed, otherwise the general provisions of the agreement will apply.

For an LLP that allocates profits as they arise this may result in equity being shown in the balance sheet at the previous year end (and at the transition date), whereas such an LLP would normally have no equity.

If there will be changes in the membership of the LLP during the transitional period, the members should consider specifically agreeing how any transitional profit adjustments will be allocated.

14.3   General effects of FRS 102

FRS 102 makes various changes to the required accounting under UK GAAP, some of which have led to changes specific to LLPs in the LLP SORP.

The effects of changes specific to LLPs are considered in **Chapter 8** and it is beyond the scope of this book to consider all of the changes to general accounting under FRS 102. However, a summary of the areas which are the most common effects is shown below.

Further guidance on transition to FRS 102 can be found in *Applying New UK GAAP 2015–16* (formerly *CCH New UK GAAP In-depth*) published by Wolters Kluwer UK, on CCH Online and in the FRC's Staff Education Notes (SENs), which can be found at www.frc.org.uk/Our-Work/Codes-Standards/Accounting-and-Reporting-Policy/New-UK-GAAP/Staff-Education-Notes.aspx.

14.3.1   *Revalued property, plant and equipment*

On transition to FRS 102, entities may elect to treat the revalued amount of certain assets, arrived at using UK GAAP before the transition date, as the deemed cost at the date of revaluation.

This applies to tangible fixed assets, investment properties or intangible assets (other than goodwill).

Alternatively, assets can be revalued at fair value on the date of transition, even if this was not included in the previous UK GAAP accounts.

Rules on the prescribed frequency of revaluations have also been relaxed.

14.3.2 Investment properties

There have been some changes to the definition of investment properties, for example a property which had previously been accounted for as a tangible fixed asset because it was used by another group company may now be an investment property.

Both FRS 102 and the previous UK standards require the revaluation of investment properties every year. However, under FRS 102 this revaluation will be included in the profit and loss account for the year, rather than the STRGL. In addition, entities which are themselves subject to tax will need to account for deferred tax based on the amount of tax that they would have to pay if they disposed of the property at the revalued amount.

However, under FRS 102 where the fair value of the investment properties cannot be determined without undue cost or effort, such properties can be accounted for at cost less depreciation, but this is expected to be rare.

14.3.3 Financial instruments

FRS 102 divides financial instruments into basic and other. Basic financial instruments (other than investments in shares), such as trade creditors, trade debtors and basic bank loans, are stated at amortised cost. However, for short term items discounting is not applied and they will be stated at the amount of cash expected to be paid.

Other financial instruments, such as interest rate swaps and foreign exchange forward contracts, are recognised in the accounts at fair value, with any changes during the year being taken to the profit and loss account. However, there are some exceptions to this when the financial instrument meets the conditions for the LLP to be allowed to opt to apply the hedging provisions.

For LLPs that have hedging arrangements, then it will be important to ensure that they have the relevant paperwork in place.

Many of the financial instruments in the 'other' category are not currently recognised under current UK standards, their effect being shown when they mature.

14.3.4 Business combinations, goodwill and other intangible assets

The requirement for consolidated accounts is not changed by FRS 102, however the use of merger accounting for transactions other than group reconstructions is not allowed.

It is likely that the goodwill calculated on acquisitions under FRS 102 will be lower as more intangible fixed assets are allowed to be separately identified as part of the purchase. There is no need to recalculate the goodwill on acquisitions before the transition to FRS 102, as there is a specific exemption from the need to do this. However, entities can choose to adopt a point of time prior to the transition date and apply the new provisions to all acquisitions subsequent to that date.

In addition, goodwill and other intangible assets must be amortised over a finite period; they cannot be considered to have an indefinite useful life.

14.3.5 Defined benefit pension schemes

The method of valuing the defined benefit pension scheme liability or asset remains the same under FRS 102. However, the split between those movements which are taken to the profit and loss account and those included in 'other comprehensive income' are different, so the reported profit will be affected.

For multi-employer schemes where the individual employers are unable to identify their share of the assets and liabilities under previous UK GAAP, the individual entities could account for the schemes as if they were defined contribution schemes in their individual accounts. Typically in these cases, the defined benefit liability or asset is only shown in the group accounts.

FRS 102 splits these into multi-employer schemes (where several unrelated employers participate in a pension scheme, e.g. an industry wide scheme) and group schemes (where the employers are part of the same group). For multi-employer schemes and most of the LLPs in a group scheme, the previous accounting will continue for most of the entities involved, although they will now be required to recognise a liability for any committed deficit funding. However, the entity which is legally responsible for a group scheme will recognise the defined benefit liability on its individual balance sheet.

14.3.6   Interest free loans

Where entities have given interest free loans or loans with interest below a commercial rate (typically to other group entities) where previously the non-commercial nature of the arrangement could be ignored for accounting purposes, under FRS 102 adjustments will be made to recognise this.

The lender is required to account for the loan at the present value of the cash flows that it expects to receive (discounted using a market rate of interest). It will then show an 'interest' income over the period of the loan; so that when it comes to be repaid the debtor is equal to the amount received. The treatment by the borrower will mirror this.

Where a loan is repayable on demand discounting will not be required, however such loans must be shown as due within one year.

14.3.7   Lease incentives

Under current standards, lease incentives are spread over the period up to the point when the rentals revert to the market rate (generally taken to be the first rent review). However, under FRS 102 they are spread over the non-cancellable period for which the lessee has contracted to lease the asset together with any further terms for which the lessee has an option to continue to lease the asset when, at the inception of the lease, it is reasonably certain that the lessee will exercise that option.

14.3.8   Holiday pay accruals

Where an entity's holiday year is not the same as its financial year an accrual will need to be made for any holiday accrued in the period which has not been taken by the period end (and a prepayment in respect of any taken which will only accrue in respect of service after the period end).

14.3.9   Related parties

FRS 102 does not require the publication of the names of the related parties with whom the entity has transactions.

14.3.10   Disclosure exemptions for Qualifying Entities

FRS 102 contains a number of disclosure exemptions for Qualifying Entities (i.e. members of groups where the parent of that group prepares publicly available consolidated financial statements). These are similar to the disclosure exemptions from full IFRS for those adopting FRS 101. However, as described in the scope section of this book, this will only arise for LLPs that are themselves parent entities preparing group accounts (who can take the exemptions only in their individual accounts) or those LLPs with a corporate member, because of the need to have a parent that prepares consolidated financial statements. Therefore only a small subset of LLPs might consider applying these disclosure exemptions. In addition, the exemptions for subsidiaries are conditional on the 'shareholders' being informed that the entity intends to use the exemptions and objections not having been received from the holders of 5% of the entity's allotted shares or 50% of those not held by the parent. For an LLP the reference to shareholders should be read as referring to the members.

These are set out in paragraph 1.12 of FRS 102 and include exemption from the following requirements:

- preparation of a Statement of Cash Flows;
- disclosure of Key Management Compensation (however, the statutory requirements on Directors' Remuneration as required by CA 2006 remain);
- most of the disclosures on share based payments, provided that these are included in the parent's consolidated accounts;
- most of the disclosures on financial instruments, provided that these are included in the parent's consolidated accounts.

14.3.11 *Transitional exemptions*

The general principle is that the balances at the opening date of the preceding period are restated based on the new accounting framework, however there are some exemptions from this.

The exemptions are set out in paragraph 35.10 of FRS 102 and include:

- Goodwill on business combinations before the transition date (see above).
- Share based payments where the LLP previously adopted the FRSSE.
- Previously revalued assets (see above).
- Some arrangements containing a lease.
- Decommissioning liabilities included in the cost of property, plant and equipment may be measured at the transition date rather than the date of acquisition.
- Dormant LLPs may retain their UK GAAP accounting policies until there is any change to their assets or liabilities or they undertake new transactions.
- LLPs may elect to treat deferred development costs calculated under UK GAAP as the deemed cost at the transition date.
- LLPs may commence capitalisation of borrowing costs from the date of transition without restating to capitalise borrowing costs prior to this.
- Lease incentives entered into before the transition date may continue to be accounted for over the period that would have applied under UK GAAP (see above).
- Financial instruments may be designated as at fair value through the profit and loss at the transition date even if they were not designated as such on initial recognition.
- Hedging transactions which are documented before the date that the first FRS 102 accounts are approved may be treated as meeting the documentation requirements for hedge accounting.

Appendix A Guidelines and definitions

This appendix gives brief guidelines on statutory definitions, interpretation and analysis. Comment is not necessarily comprehensive but aims to cover those headings or terms that tend to present difficulty in practice. The text contains references to statute and accounting standards from where further guidance may be available

Definitions are provided by accounting standards and the LLP SORP as well as legislation.

Where there are no definitions or rules laid down in the Regulations or provided by accounting standards (including IAS), it is necessary to:

- determine a reasonable interpretation of the requirement;
- ensure the proposed interpretation is sensible and appropriate to the business; and
- adopt the interpretation consistently from year to year.

1   Accounts

Definitions of statutory terms concerning an LLP's accounts, prepared to show a 'true and fair view', are set out below.

1.1   Annual accounts s. 471

Individual accounts – the accounts of an LLP prepared by the members, for each financial year: *s. 394*

- comprising a balance sheet (as at the last day of the year), a profit and loss account, and notes to the accounts;   *s. 396*
- showing a 'true and fair view'; and   *s. 393*
- complying with the provisions of reg. 3 of SI 2008/1912 (small LLPs) or reg. 3 and 4 of SI 2008/1913 (large and medium-sized LLPs).   *s. 396*

Individual accounts must be prepared in accordance with the appropriate framework and accordingly may be prepared: *s. 395*

- in accordance with s. 396 ('non-IAS individual accounts'); or
- in accordance with international accounting standards ('IAS individual accounts').

Group accounts – the accounts prepared, in addition to 'individual accounts', by the members of a parent LLP: *s. 398–399*

- comprising consolidated accounts (consolidated balance sheet and consolidated profit and loss account of the parent and its 'subsidiary undertakings' and related notes); and
- showing a 'true and fair view' of the consolidated undertakings as a whole (so far as concerns members of the parent entity).   *s. 404 (1)*

Group accounts must (with exceptions) be prepared either:

- in accordance with SI 2008/1912, Sch. 4 (Small LLP) or SI 2008/1913, Sch. 3 (Large and medium-sized LLPs) (non-IAS group accounts'); or
- in accordance with international accounting standards or if required by Article 4 of the IAS Regulation ('IAS group accounts').   *s. 403*

Group accounts exemptions – the following exemptions from preparing group accounts are available:

- eligible small groups (s. 383) – see **Chapter 7**;
- parent LLPs included in accounts of larger EEA group (s. 400);
- parent LLPs included in accounts of larger non-EEA group (s. 401); and
- if all subsidiary undertakings excluded from consolidation (s. 402).

Entitlement to exemptions in all cases is determined upon conditions – see **Chapter 7**.

IAS accounts – accounts ('IAS individual accounts' or 'IAS group accounts') prepared in accordance with international accounting standards adopted by the EU (EC Regulation No. 1606/2002).

An LLP's 'annual accounts', in relation to a financial year, means the LLP's individual accounts for that year (CA 2006, s. 394) and any group accounts prepared by the LLP for that year (s. 398–399). Section 408 provides an option to omit the individual profit and loss account from annual accounts where information is given in group accounts.

s. 408 Individual profit and loss account where group accounts prepared – the profit and loss account of a parent entity:

- prepared in addition to, but omitted from, 'group accounts'; and
- omitting the supplemental information required by s. 411 (information about employee numbers and costs).

The fact of omission and the amount of the parent entity's profit or loss for the year must be disclosed, and the individual profit and loss account of the parent entity must be approved by the members (in accordance with s. 414(1)).

Notes to the accounts – notes forming part of the annual accounts (or annexed thereto) giving information required by any provision of CA 2006 as applied to LLPs or International Accounting *s. 472* Standards.

1.2 Statutory accounts

The accounts that must be prepared for members and/or filed with the Registrar of Companies. These will be either:

- annual accounts and (if required) an auditor's report; or
- abbreviated accounts, prepared in accordance with s. 444(3) or 445(3), together with (if appropriate) a special auditor's report, and members' statement.

(As explained in **Chapter 6**, some LLPs can file abbreviated accounts with the Registrar. This set will be in addition to the full accounts prepared for members).

1.3 Abbreviated accounts

The accounts prepared in accordance with special provisions for small (or medium-sized) LLPs, as the case may be (see **Chapter 6**).

2 Profit and loss account (income statement)

Two formats for the profit and loss account (which may alternatively be titled the Income Statement) may be adopted. Format 1 headings include 'Turnover', 'Cost of sales', 'Distribution costs' and 'Administrative expenses', whereas the Format 2 headings include 'Turnover', 'Change in stocks and work in progress', 'Purchases of raw materials and consumables', 'Staff costs' and 'Depreciation'.

Format 1 is generally used by businesses which produce goods, as it includes a total for gross profit, whereas service businesses generally use Format 2 as this total is not relevant for them.

2.1 Turnover

'The amounts derived from the provision of goods and services falling within the LLP's ordinary activities, after deduction of trade discounts, value added tax and any other taxes based on the amounts so derived.'

s. 474(1)

Sales of fixed assets are not normally revenue transactions giving rise to 'turnover'.

Section 23 of FRS 102 provides guidance on the principles of revenue recognition and the treatment of turnover (see **8.6**).

2.2 Staff costs

The information required by s. 411 ('Information about employee numbers and costs') applies only to LLPs other than those subject to the small LLPs regime.

s. 411

'Staff costs' are wages and salaries, social security costs and other pension costs paid or payable to, or incurred by, the LLP on behalf of persons employed under contracts of service, i.e. employees of the LLP (including directors who are employees). This heading will not include subcontractors' costs or consultants, etc.

Social security costs: LLP (employers') contributions to any compulsory state, social security, National Insurance, or pension scheme, fund or arrangement.

Other pension costs: all other costs incurred by an LLP towards employee pensions (for example, employer pension scheme).

The disclosure of the average number of employees within categories is to be determined by the members 'having regard to the manner in which the LLP's activities are organised'. The average number is determined by dividing the total relevant annual number of employees by the number of months in the year. The relevant annual number is determined by ascertaining for each month in the year the number of persons employed by the LLP.

The following definitions (**2.3–2.9**) are based on the definitions contained in FRS 102.

2.3 Ordinary activities

Any activities which are undertaken by a reporting entity as part of its business and such related activities in which the reporting entity engages in furtherance of, incidental to, or arising from, these activities.

FRS 102 para 5.10

Ordinary activities include the effects on the reporting entity of any event in the various environments in which it operates, including the political, regulatory, economic and geographical environments, irrespective of the frequency or unusual nature of the events.

2.4   Continuing operations

Operations other than 'discontinued operations'.

2.5   Discontinued operations

A component of the reporting entity (i.e. operations that can be clearly distinguished, operationally and for financial reporting purposes from the rest of the entity) that has been disposed of and:

- represented a separate major line of business or geographical area of operations;
- was part of a single coordinated plan to dispose of a separate major line of business or geographical area of operations; or
- was a subsidiary acquired exclusively with a view to resale.

2.6   Material items

FRS 102 para 5.9A

FRS 102 requires material items included in profit or loss for the year or other comprehensive income to be separately disclosed on the face of the profit and loss account or statement of comprehensive income or in the notes.

Items are material if their omission could, individually or collectively, influence the economic decisions of users taken on the basis of the financial statements. Materiality depends on the size and nature of the omission or misstatement judged in the surrounding circumstances. The size or nature of the item, or a combination of both, could be the determining factor.

It will therefore be necessary to consider for each material item whether inclusion on the face of the profit and loss account or statement of comprehensive income is necessary to ensure that users are sufficiently informed or whether a note will be sufficient.

Where such items are shown on the face of the profit and loss account, they should be included alongside their natural line item and further explanation should be given in a note.

The requirements in FRS 3 to show profits and losses on the sale or termination of an operation, the costs of the fundamental reorganisation and profits or losses on disposal of fixed assets as 'exceptional items' separately on the face of the profit and loss account, have not been carried forward to FRS 102. They will therefore only be shown separately if they are considered to be material.

In addition, the specific 'exceptional items' referred to above were presented after 'operating profit' under FRS 3. However, under FRS 102 they, if material, would be presented alongside the natural line item to which they belong rather than being presented separately at the end of the profit and loss account.

2.7   Extraordinary items

FRS 102 para 5.10A

Material items possessing a high degree of abnormality which arise from events or transactions that fall outside the ordinary activities of the reporting entity and which are not expected to recur. They do not include prior period items merely because they relate to a prior period, nor would the material items, required to be separately disclosed, be included as these are almost certain to fall within the definition of ordinary activities.

Extraordinary items are extremely rare. Although it remains a statutory format heading (see **Table 5.3**), the extraordinary item has effectively been abolished by accounting standards.

2.8 Prior period adjustments

Material adjustments applicable to prior periods arising from changes in accounting policies or from the correction of material errors. They do not include normal recurring adjustments or corrections of accounting estimates made in prior periods. Prior period adjustments should be accounted for by restating comparative figures and adjusting the opening balance of reserves.

2.9 Total comprehensive income

The changes in equity during a period resulting from transactions and other events, other than those changes resulting from transactions with equity participants (equal to the sum of profit or loss and other comprehensive income). This is the total of all gains and losses of the reporting entity that are recognised in a period and are attributable to members or shareholders.

3 Balance sheet (Statement of financial position)

Commentary on selected balance sheet headings is set out below. FRS 102 uses different names for some headings (which are given in brackets below), however it also allows LLPs to use the statutory headings and, in practice, most LLPs are likely to do so.

3.1 Fixed assets

Assets of an entity which are intended for use on a continuing basis in the entity's activities. 'Fixed assets' include assets and property which cannot easily be converted into cash, i.e. not current assets; this includes tangible fixed assets (property, plant and equipment under FRS 102), investments and intangible assets such as goodwill.

Assets awaiting disposal: a fixed asset intended for disposal at the balance sheet date and not intended for use on a continuing basis in the entity's activities may be reclassified as a 'current asset' (this does not apply to assets which it is intended to replace in the normal course of business).

'Development costs' may be capitalised in special circumstances as defined in Section 18 of FRS 102. Otherwise, 'costs of research' must not be treated as an asset.

'Preliminary expenses', 'expenses of, and commission on, any issue of debentures' and 'costs of research' may not be treated as assets.

SI 2008/1912 and SI 2008/1913, Sch 1.3(2)

3.2 Goodwill

'Amounts representing goodwill shall only be included to the extent that goodwill was acquired for valuable consideration' (SI 2008/1912, Sch. 1 – balance sheet format Note 1 and SI 2008/1913, Sch. 1 – balance sheet format Note 2). Any goodwill valued and created by an LLP itself, therefore, cannot be capitalised and included in an LLP's balance sheet.

Acquired goodwill should be systematically depreciated over the useful economic life of the goodwill. The period of write-off and the reasons for choosing that period must be disclosed.

SI 2008/1912 and SI 2008/1913, Sch 1.22

3.3 Tangible assets: headings

The SI 2008/1912, Sch. 1 balance sheet format heading A II 2 for small LLPs is 'plant and machinery etc.'

Otherwise in practice, there is some latitude in the formats generally, with headings: for example, 'equipment' would not generally be included in 'plant and machinery'but may be aggregated with 'motor vehicles'. Strict interpretation would not allow, for example, 'plant and machinery' to be changed to 'plant and equipment'. However, in a situation where 'equipment' is immaterial, this might acceptably be aggregated with plant and machinery under a heading 'plant, machinery and equipment'. Additional headings may be given but doing so increases the amount of disclosure required.

'Payments on account' and 'Assets in course of construction' have to be shown separately from other items but individually may be aggregated.

In the balance sheet format shown in SI 2008/1913, the headings for fixed assets also include 'Fixtures, fittings, tools and equipment' and 'Payments on account and assets in the course of construction'. As for small LLPs, in practice the heading names are amended to be appropriate for the entity.

3.4   Cash at bank and in hand; bank loans and overdrafts

The heading 'Cash at bank and in hand' comprises the amounts as recorded in the LLP's accounting records, not those as shown necessarily in the bank statements.

Bank balances and bank overdrafts, etc. should not be offset to show a net balance *unless* there is a legal right of set-off.

Cash is defined in FRS 102 as 'cash on hand and demand deposits'. Deposits are repayable on demand if they can be withdrawn at any time without notice and without penalty. In practice a maturity or period of notice of not more than 24 hours or one working day should be classified as cash. Cash includes cash in hand and deposits denominated in foreign currencies.

3.5   Current assets

Assets which are not intended for use on a continuing basis in the LLP's activities (assets which are not fixed assets). Current assets include cash, debtors, stock, short-term investments, prepaid expenses and other liquid assets.

3.6   Contingent asset

A possible asset that arises from past events and whose existence will be confirmed only by the occurrence of one or more uncertain future events not wholly within the entity's control.

Contingent assets are not included as assets in the balance sheet. Disclosure of a contingent asset is required by FRS 102 para 21.16 where an inflow of economic benefits is probable.

3.7   Stock (Inventory under FRS 102)

Assets:

  (a)   held for sale in the ordinary course of business;
  (b)   in the process of production for such sale; or
  (c)   in the form of materials or supplies to be consumed in the production process or in the rendering of services.

These are an LLP's merchandise, raw materials, and finished and unfinished products which have not yet been sold. These are considered current assets since individual stock items are not intended to be held on continuing basis.

Stock and work in progress is generally valued at the lower of cost and net realisable value. The basis of arriving at the cost of 'stock' must be a reasonable approximation to actual cost (appropriate, in the opinion of the members, to the circumstances of the members), e.g. FIFO (first in, first out), weighted average or other similar method.

Sch 1.28

When considering work in progress for service providers, it is necessary to consider whether the amounts should be recognised as accrued income rather than deferring the costs within work in progress (see **8.6**).

3.8 Provisions for liabilities

A 'provision' is a liability of uncertain timing or amount, to be settled by the transfer of economic benefits. These are only recognised where the obligation at the year end arises as a result of a past event, it is probable (more likely than not) that the entity will be required to settle the obligation and it can be estimated reliably.

3.9 Contingent liability

A disclosable contingent liability is either:

- A possible obligation that arises from past events and whose existence will be confirmed only by the occurrence or non-occurrence of one or more uncertain future events not wholly within the entity's control; or
- A present obligation that arises from past events but is not recognised because:
    (a) it is not probable that a transfer of economic benefits will be required to settle the obligation; or
    (b) the amount of the obligation cannot be measured with sufficient reliability.

Contingent liabilities are not recognised on the balance sheet as liabilities but will be disclosed in the notes to the accounts.

4 Definitions

Below are the definitions which are included in the LLP SORP.

4.1 Allocated profit

Profits (after deducting members' remuneration charged as an expense) that have been allocated during the year as a result of the members deciding on a division of profits.

SORP para 9

The decision to divide profits, which gives rise to a liability in respect of allocated profits, must be distinguished from the arrangements for profit sharing. A provision in an agreement between the members which sets out the profit shares of the members does not of itself constitute an agreement for the division of profits. It merely sets out the respective profit shares of the members that will apply to those profits that the members decide to divide among themselves. Accordingly, the default rule that is applied by virtue of the *Limited Liability Partnerships Regulations* 2001 (SI 2001/1090), reg. 7(1) (which provides for the members of an LLP to share equally in the capital and profits of an LLP in the absence of agreement to the contrary) does not constitute a default rule as to the automatic division of profits between the members. (Where the agreement between the members provides for the automatic division of profits, those divided profits will form part of members' remuneration charged as an expense and will be credited directly to the current accounts of the members without being first shown under the balance sheet heading 'Other reserves'.) Allocated profits are debts due to members which, unless otherwise agreed by the members, rank pari passu with ordinary creditors in the event of a winding up. The total amount of profit allocated following a decision to divide may be less (or more) than the amount of profit earned by the LLP in the relevant year.

4.2 Automatic division of profits

An automatic division of profits is one where the LLP has an unconditional obligation to divide those profits based on the LLP agreement in force at the time. Such a pre-agreed automatic division of profits could be in respect either of the entire profits for the year or a portion or fixed amount thereof. The fact that the actual amount to be divided is contingent on the existence of profits in the first place does not negate the LLP's unconditional obligation in respect of those profits nor the member's unconditional entitlement to those profits should they come into existence. A division of profits that requires a decision of the LLP does not constitute an automatic division because the *SORP para 10* LLP has an unconditional right to refuse payment of profits for a particular year.

4.3 Designated members

Designated members are those members specified as such in the incorporation document or otherwise in accordance with an agreement with the other members, as required under s. 8 of the 2000 Act. Designated members perform certain duties in relation to the legal administration of an LLP that would, for a company, be performed by the secretary or directors. If there would otherwise *SORP para 11* be no designated members, or only one, all members are deemed to be designated members.

4.4 Drawings

The payment in cash (or kind) of amounts to members. Drawings may consist of regular monthly payments or ad hoc payments; for example, in respect of current year's and/or prior years' *SORP para 12* remuneration (as defined).

4.5 Limited liability partnership (LLP)

An LLP incorporated in the United Kingdom under the 2000 Act, or incorporated prior to *SORP para 13* 1 October 2009 under the *Limited Liability Partnerships Act (Northern Ireland) 2002*.

4.6 Loans and other debts due to members

Members' interests that are debts of the LLP and are included in balance sheet item J in the *SORP para 14* accounts formats set out in the LLP Regulations.

4.7 Members

On incorporation, the members of an LLP are the persons who subscribe their names to the incorporation document. Persons may become or cease to be members in accordance with an *SORP para 15* agreement between existing members.

144

4.8 Members' agreement

Any express or implied agreement between an LLP and its members that determines the mutual rights and duties of the members in their capacity as such and their rights and duties in relation to the LLP. An agreement between the members, to which the LLP is not party – for example, an agreement to guarantee a minimum or specified remuneration for a particular member – does not constitute a members' agreement for the purposes of the SORP.

SORP para 16

4.9 Members' capital

Amounts subscribed or otherwise contributed by members that are classified as capital by the constitutional arrangements of the LLP. Such amounts will require analysis as to whether they are considered equity or debt in accordance with Section 22 of FRS 102. Members' capital is a component of 'Members' other interests' or 'Loans and other debts due to members' depending on its classification under this section of FRS 102.

SORP para 17

4.10 Members' other interests

Members' interests other than debt due to them by the LLP, which constitute equity in the LLP and are included in balance sheet item K in the accounts formats set out in the Regulations. Members' other interests include 'Members' capital' that is classified as equity in accordance with Section 22 of FRS 102, 'Revaluation reserve' and 'Other reserves'.

SORP para 18

4.11 Members' participation rights

All the rights of a member against the LLP that arise under the members' agreement (for example, in respect of amounts subscribed or otherwise contributed, remuneration and profits).

SORP para 19

4.12 Members' remuneration

Any outflow of benefits to a member. It may include or comprise, but is not limited to, one or more of the following elements: salary, interest, bonus, risk premium and allocated share of profits. The form that remuneration takes will be a matter of agreement between the members.

SORP para 20

4.13 Members' remuneration charged as an expense

Remuneration that is payable to a member, which falls to be treated as a charge against profits and not an allocation of profits. The treatment of members' remuneration is determined by reference to the nature of the participation rights that give rise to the remuneration. If those rights were to give the members an unconditional right to the division of profits or to other forms of remuneration, for example those items set out in paragraph 20 of the LLP SORP, then they give rise to a liability for that remuneration in accordance with Section 22 of FRS 102, and the remuneration is charged as an expense. Members' remuneration charged as an expense is not restricted to amounts that are payable by the LLP regardless of the existence or extent of profits; it also includes, for example, any profits that are automatically divided between members by virtue of a members' agreement. Members' remuneration charged as an expense may in some exceptional circumstances be a negative amount. A member can also legally be an employee of an LLP – in this case, there will be a contract of employment between the two parties – and such remuneration covered by the employment contract is classified as members' remuneration charged as an expense, including amounts relating to pension obligations and share-based payments (if any).

SORP para 21

4.14 Post-retirement payments to members

Any post-retirement payments, whether in cash, in kind or any other benefits, including annuities and payments for goodwill, payable by the LLP as principal to former members of the LLP, other than where the payments are properly made in return for post-retirement services performed by the recipient for the LLP's benefit. Members who retire by or at the balance sheet date are regarded as former members. Such post-retirement payments include, but are not limited to, amounts payable to, for example, spouses, children and the estates of former members. In this context, former members may include former partners in a predecessor partnership of the LLP, where the LLP assumes responsibility for the post-retirement payments to the former partners.

SORP para 22

4.15 Puttable instrument

The definition of 'puttable instrument' is contained in Section 22 of FRS 102. A puttable instrument is a financial instrument that gives the holder the right to sell that instrument back to the issuer for cash or another financial asset or is automatically redeemed or repurchased by the issuer on the occurrence of an uncertain future event or the death or retirement of the instrument holder (paragraph 22.4(a) of FRS 102). In practice for LLPs, puttable instruments may include certain types of capital or member's loan that carry rights for the member (or other holder) to obtain repayment from the LLP.

SORP para 23

(See **5** (below) for the definition of puttable instruments from FRS 102 and the general description of financial instruments.)

4.16 Unallocated profit

Profits of the LLP (after deducting members' remuneration charged as an expense) that have been ascertained but which are not yet divided among the members. After the profits have been ascertained, in the absence of any agreement between members to the contrary, the balance will be unallocated profit and will need to be shown under 'Other reserves' on the balance sheet, pending a decision to divide the profits among the members. It is open to the members of an LLP to agree that all, or a proportion of, the profits of the LLP shall be automatically divided between the members after they have been ascertained; in that event, the LLP will not have an unconditional right to avoid delivering cash or other assets to a member in respect of those amounts. This is a matter of construction of the members' agreement. Where this is the case, any amounts automatically divided will form part of members' remuneration charged as an expense, i.e. they will be deducted in arriving at retained profit or loss for the financial year available for discretionary division among members. Accordingly, where all the profits are automatically divided, a nil amount will be reported as retained profit or loss for the financial year available for discretionary division among members, and there will be no unallocated profits.

SORP para 24

5 Financial instruments

Section 11 *Basic Financial Instruments*, Section 12 *Other Financial Instruments Issues* and Section 22 *Liabilities and Equity* of FRS 102 deal with the classification, presentation and disclosure of capital instruments.

Basically, every financial instrument or constituent is recognised as a 'financial asset', a 'financial liability' or an 'equity instrument'. The definitions set out here (in **5.1–5.9**) are based on those contained in FRS 102.

5.1 Financial instrument

A financial instrument is any contract that gives rise to a financial asset of one entity and a financial liability or equity instrument of another entity.

FRS 102
para 11.3

5.2 Financial asset

A financial asset is any asset that is:

- cash;
- an equity instrument of another entity;
- a contractual right to receive cash or another financial asset from another entity or to exchange financial assets or financial liabilities with another entity under conditions that are potentially favourable to the entity; or
- a contract that will or may be settled in the entity's own equity instruments and (i) under which the entity is or may be obliged to receive a variable number of the entity's own equity instruments; or (ii) that will or may be settled other than by the exchange of a fixed amount of cash or another financial asset for a fixed number of the entity's own equity instruments. For this purpose, the entity's own equity instruments do not include instruments that are themselves contracts for the future receipt or delivery of the entity's own equity instruments.

5.3 Financial liability

A financial liability is any liability that is:

- a contractual obligation to deliver cash or another financial asset to another entity or to exchange financial assets or financial liabilities with another entity under conditions that are potentially unfavourable to the entity; or
- a contract that will or may be settled in the entity's own equity instruments and:
  - (i) under which the entity is or may be obliged to deliver a variable number of the entity's own equity instruments; or
  - (ii) will or may be settled other than by the exchange of a fixed amount of cash or another financial asset for a fixed number of the entity's own equity instruments. For this purpose the entity's own equity instruments do not include instruments that are themselves contracts for the future receipt or delivery of the entity's own equity instruments.

FRS 102
para 22.3

5.4 Equity

Equity is the residual interest in the assets of an entity after deducting all of its liabilities

FRS 102
para 22.3

5.5 Fair value

Fair value is the amount for which an asset could be exchanged, a liability settled or an equity instrument granted could be exchanged, between knowledgeable and willing parties in an arm's length transaction.

Where a fair value is needed in the absence of any specific guidance provided in the relevant section of FRS 102, the use of a quoted price for an identical asset in an active market is required, if this is available. Otherwise the price of a recent transaction for an identical asset can be used, as long as there has not been a significant change in economic circumstances or a significant lapse of time since the transaction took place. Otherwise a valuation technique will need to be used. Further guidance is in paragraphs 11.27 to 11.32 of FRS 102.

FRS 102
para 11.27

5.6   Derivative

A derivative is a financial instrument or other contract with all three of the following characteristics:

(a)   its value changes in response to the change in a specified interest rate, financial instrument price, commodity price, foreign exchange rate, index of prices or rates, credit rating or credit index, or other variable (sometimes called the 'underlying'), provided, in the case of a non-financial variable, that the variable is not specific to a party to the contract;

(b)   it requires no initial net investment or an initial net investment that is smaller than would be required for other types of contracts that would be expected to have a similar response to changes in market factors; and

(c)   it is settled at a future date.

Examples of derivative financial instruments are futures, options, forward contracts, interest rate and currency swaps, interest rate caps, collars and floors, forward interest rate agreements, commitments to purchase shares or bonds, note issuance facilities and letters of credit.

5.7   Basic financial instruments

The definition of basic financial instruments in paragraph 11.8 of FRS 102 is:

(a)   cash;

(b)   a debt instrument (such as an account, note, or loan receivable or payable) that meets the conditions in paragraph 11.9 and is not a financial instrument described in paragraph 11.6(b);

(c)   commitments to receive or make a loan to another entity that:

(i)   cannot be settled net in cash; and

(ii)   when the commitment is executed, are expected to meet the conditions in paragraph 11.9; and

(d)   an investment in non-convertible preference shares and non-puttable ordinary shares or preference shares.

Paragraph 11.9 of FRS 102 then goes on to set out detailed conditions for debt instruments to be regarded as basic financial instruments. These are intended to ensure that normal loan arrangements are classified as basic and therefore includes within the definition interest free loans, fixed rate loans, positive variable rate loans, loans with and initial fixed rate which revert to a variable rate and loans linked to general inflation (e.g. CPI or RPI, but not house price inflation). Leveraged loans (e.g. twice the base rate) are not considered to be basic.

Some examples of financial instruments that would and would not qualify as basic are given in paragraphs 11.9 to 11.11 of FRS 102.

When an LLP enters into a basic financial instrument it is initially recorded at the transaction price unless it is, in effect, a financing transaction (e.g. an interest free loan). If it is a financing transaction then it is initially recorded at the present value of the future payments discounted at a market rate of interest for a similar debt instrument, however, discounting is not required if the term of the instrument is less than one year (so an interest free loan repayable on demand would be included at the undiscounted amount).

At each year end financial instruments, other than non-convertible preference shares and non-puttable ordinary shares and preference shares (which are measured at fair value except for subsidiaries, associates, and joint ventures) are then measured at amortised cost, using the effective interest method.

Details of the effective interest method are given in paragraphs 11.15 to 11.20 of FRS 102, however in general it will mean that normal interest bearing financial instruments will be recorded in the same way as before, but those where there is an arrangement fee will need to include this in the finance charge and calculate an effective interest rate to take account of this.

5.8   Other financial instruments

Other financial instruments are those which are not classified as basic. They are initially included at fair value, which is normally the transaction price, and are also included at fair value at each year end, if this can be measured reliably (otherwise they are included at cost).

5.9   The FRS 102 definition of a puttable instrument

The following definition is taken from FRS 102 (para 22.4):

A puttable instrument is a financial instrument that gives the holder the right to sell that instrument back to the issuer for cash or another financial asset or is automatically redeemed or repurchased by the issuer on the occurrence of an uncertain future event or the death or retirement of the instrument holder. A puttable instrument that has all of the following features is classified as an equity instrument:

(i)   It entitles the holder to a pro rata share of the entity's net assets in the event of the entity's liquidation. The entity's net assets are those assets that remain after deducting all other claims on its assets.

(ii)   The instrument is in the class of instruments that is subordinate to all other classes of instruments.

(iii)   All financial instruments in the class of instruments that is subordinate to all other classes of instruments have identical features.

(iv)   Apart from the contractual obligation for the issuer to repurchase or redeem the instrument for cash or another financial asset, the instrument does not include any contractual obligation to deliver cash or another financial asset to another entity, or to exchange financial assets or financial liabilities with another entity under conditions that are potentially unfavourable to the entity, and it is not a contract that will or may be settled in the entity's own equity instruments as set out in paragraph 22.3(b) of the definition of a financial liability.

(v)   The total expected cash flows attributable to the instrument over the life of the instrument are based substantially on the profit or loss, the change in the recognised net assets or the change in the fair value of the recognised and unrecognised net assets of the entity over the life of the instrument (excluding any effects of the instrument).

5.10   Financial instruments and the FRSSE

The detailed requirements for financial instruments in FRS 102 are not included in the FRSSE and they are therefore included at historical cost, which in some cases will be nil (e.g. forward contracts).

6   Alternative accounting rules

FRS 102 requires certain items, such as investment properties and some types of financial instrument, to be carried at fair value, with any changes in the fair value of these being shown in the profit and loss account. This is permitted by SI 2008/1912, Sch. 1, para. 39–40 and forms part of the normal basis of accounting.

Accounting standards also permit, but do not require the revaluation of tangible fixed assets, using the alternative accounting rules basis of accounting (SI 2008/1912, Sch. 1, para. 32). An LLP may choose whether to revalue fixed assets and may decide to revalue only some categories. It is common practice, for example, to revalue properties but to show other fixed assets at cost.

Where revaluations are carried out under the alternative accounting rules the change in fair value is not shown in the profit and loss account. It is shown within other comprehensive income and taken to a revaluation reserve.

Under the FRSSE, revaluations of fixed asset investments and investment properties are not shown in the profit and loss account. Instead such revaluations (which are compulsory for investment properties) are made under the alternative accounting rules.

Where an LLP has chosen to revalue fixed assets it is required to keep the valuation up to date.

6.1 Purchase price

SI 2008/1912 &
SI 2008/1913,
Sch 1.27

The purchase price of an asset is to be determined by adding to the actual price paid any expenses incidental to its acquisition.

6.2 Production cost

SI 2008/1912 &
SI 2008/1913,
Sch 1.27

The price of raw materials and consumables together with costs directly attributable to the production of the asset; a reasonable proportion of indirect costs (relating to the period of production); and interest on capital borrowed to finance the production of the asset (to the extent that it is accrued during the period of production).

6.3 Revaluation reserve

SI 2008/1912 &
SI 2008/1913,
sch 1.35

This is the amount arising from a revaluation of fixed assets other than investment properties. The difference between the amount of any item determined according to one of the alternative accounting rules and the amount at which it would be determined on the historical cost accounting rules should be debited or credited, as applicable, to a 'revaluation reserve'.

Appendix B Companies Act 2006 accounts and audit sections applicable to LLPs

Companies Act 2006

Those familiar with the Companies Act will recognise that many of the requirements of the *Companies Act* 2006 in relation to the accounts and audit of companies are also applicable to Limited Liability Partnerships.

SI 2008/1911 (*Limited Liability Partnerships (Accounts and Audit) (Application of Companies Act 2006) Regulations* 2008) states which sections of the *Companies Act* 2006 are applicable to LLPs. Within some of the sections, apart from changing 'company' to 'LLP', there are other amendments which have been made to ensure that they are appropriately worded for LLPs. The 2008 Regulations give the amended text for each of the *Companies Act* 2006 sections which are applicable to LLPs.

As a quick reference guide, set out below is a table showing which sections of Part 15 'Accounts and Reports' and Part 16 'Audit' of the *Companies Act* 2006 are applicable to LLPs.

Companies Act 2006 Part 15 – Accounts and Reports

		Applicable to LLP (as modified by SI 2008/1911)
INTRODUCTION		
General		
380	Scheme of this Part	✓
Companies subject to the small companies regime		
381	Companies subject to the small companies regime	✓
382	Companies qualifying as small: general	✓
383	Companies qualifying as small: parent companies	✓
384	Companies excluded from the small companies regime	✓
384A	Companies qualifying as micro-entities	✗
384B	Companies excluded from being treated as micro-entities	✗
Quoted and unquoted companies		
385	Quoted and unquoted companies	✗
ACCOUNTING RECORDS		
386	Duty to keep accounting records	✓
387	Duty to keep accounting records: offence	✓
388	Where and for how long records to be kept	✓
389	Where and for how long records to be kept: offences	✓

A COMPANY'S FINANCIAL YEAR

390	A company's financial year	✓
391	Accounting reference periods and accounting reference date	✓
392	Alteration of accounting reference date	✓

ANNUAL ACCOUNTS

General

393	Accounts to give true and fair view	✓

Individual accounts

394	Duty to prepare individual accounts	✓
394A	Individual accounts: exemption for dormant subsidiaries	✓
394B	Companies excluded from the dormant subsidiaries exemption	✓
394C	Dormant subsidiaries exemption: parent undertaking declaration of guarantee	✓
395	Individual accounts: applicable accounting framework	✓
396	Companies Act individual accounts	✓
397	IAS individual accounts	✓

Group accounts: small companies

398	Option to prepare group accounts	✓

Group accounts: other companies

399	Duty to prepare group accounts	✓
400	Exemption for company included in EEA group accounts of larger group	✓
401	Exemption for company included in non-EEA group accounts of larger group	✓
402	Exemption if no subsidiary undertakings need be included in the consolidation	✓

Group accounts: general

403	Group accounts: applicable accounting framework	✓
404	Companies Act group accounts	✓
405	Companies Act group accounts: subsidiary undertakings included in the consolidation	✓
406	IAS group accounts	✓
407	Consistency of financial reporting within group	✓
408	Individual profit and loss account where group accounts prepared	✓

Information to be given in notes to the accounts

409	Information about related undertakings	✓
410	Information about related undertakings: alternative compliance	✓
410A	Information about off-balance sheet arrangements	✓
411	Information about employee numbers and costs	✓
412	Information about directors' benefits: remuneration	✗
413	Information about directors' benefits: advances, credit and guarantees	✗

Approval and signing of accounts

414	Approval and signing of accounts	✓

STRATEGIC REPORT

Strategic report

DIRECTORS' REPORT

Directors' report

QUOTED COMPANIES: DIRECTORS' REMUNERATION REPORT

PUBLICATION OF ACCOUNTS AND REPORTS

Duty to circulate copies of accounts and reports

Option to provide strategic report with supplementary material

Quoted companies: requirements as to website publication

Right of member or debenture holder to demand copies of accounts and reports

Requirements in connection with publication of accounts and reports

PUBLIC COMPANIES: LAYING OF ACCOUNTS AND REPORTS BEFORE GENRAL MEETING

437	Public companies: laying of accounts and reports before general meeting	✗
438	Public companies: offence of failure to lay accounts and reports	✗

QUOTED COMPANIES: MEMBERS' APPROVAL OF DIRECTORS' REMUNERATION REPORT

439	Quoted companies: members' approval of directors' remuneration report	✗
439A	Quoted companies: members' approval of directors' remuneration policy	✗
440	Quoted companies: offences in connection with procedure for approval	✗

FILING OF ACCOUNTS AND REPORTS

Duty to file accounts and reports

441	Duty to file accounts and reports with the registrar	✓
442	Period allowed for filing accounts	✓
443	Calculation of period allowed	✓

Filing obligations of different descriptions of company

444	Filing obligations of companies subject to small companies regime	✓
444A	Filing obligations of companies entitled to small companies exemption in relation to directors' report	✗
445	Filing obligations of medium-sized companies	✓
446	Filing obligations of unquoted companies	✓
447	Filing obligations of quoted companies	✗
448	Unlimited companies exempt from obligation to file accounts	✗
448A	Dormant subsidiaries exempt from obligation to file accounts	✓
448B	Companies excluded from the dormant subsidiaries exemption	✓
448C	Dormant subsidiaries filing exemption: parent undertaking declaration of guarantee	✓

Requirements where abbreviated accounts delivered

449	Special auditor's report where abbreviated accounts delivered	✓
450	Approval and signing of abbreviated accounts	✓

Failure to file accounts and reports

451	Default in filing accounts and reports: offences	✓
452	Default in filing accounts and reports: court order	✓
453	Civil penalty for failure to file accounts and reports	✓

REVISION OF DEFECTIVE ACCOUNTS AND REPORTS

Voluntary revision

454	Voluntary revision of accounts etc.	✓

Secretary of State's notice

455	Secretary of State's notice in respect of accounts or reports	✓

Application to court

456	Application to court in respect of defective accounts or reports	✓
457	Other persons authorised to apply to the court	✗
458	Disclosure of information by tax authorities	✓

Companies Act 2006 Part 16 – Audit

Exemption from audit: dormant companies

480	Dormant companies: conditions for exemption from audit	✓
481	Companies excluded from dormant companies exemption	✓

Companies subject to public sector audit

482	Non-profit-making companies subject to public sector audit	✗
483	Scottish public sector companies: audit by Auditor General for Scotland	✗

General power of amendment by regulations

484	General power of amendment by regulations	✗

APPOINTMENT OF AUDITORS

Private companies

485	Appointment of auditors of private company: general	✓
486	Appointment of auditors of private company: default power of Secretary of State	✓
487	Term of office of auditors of private company	✓
488	Prevention by members of deemed re-appointment of auditor	✓

Public companies

489	Appointment of auditors of public company: general	✗
490	Appointment of auditors of public company: default power of Secretary of State	✗
491	Term of office of auditors of public company	✗

General provisions

492	Fixing of auditor's remuneration	✓
493	Disclosure of terms of audit appointment	✗
494	Disclosure of services provided by auditor or associates and related remuneration	✓

FUNCTIONS OF AUDITOR

Auditor's report

495	Auditor's report on company's annual accounts	✓
496	Auditor's report on directors' report	✗
497	Auditor's report on auditable part of directors' remuneration report	✗
497A	Auditor's report on separate corporate governance statement	✗

Duties and rights of auditors

498	Duties of auditor	✓
498A	Auditor's duties in relation to separate corporate governance statement	✗
499	Auditor's general right to information	✓
500	Auditor's right to information from overseas subsidiaries	✓
501	Auditor's rights to information: offences	✓
502	Auditor's rights in relation to resolutions and meetings	✓

Signature of auditor's report

503	Signature of auditor's report	✓
504	Senior statutory auditor	✓
505	Names to be stated in published copies of auditor's report	✓
506	Circumstances in which names may be omitted	✓

Liability limitation agreements

534	Liability limitation agreements	✕
535	Terms of liability limitation agreement	✕
536	Authorisation of agreement by members of the company	✕
537	Effect of liability limitation agreement	✕
538	Disclosure of agreement by company	✕
538A	Meaning of 'corporate governance statement' etc	✕
SUPPLEMENTARY PROVISIONS		
539	Minor definitions	✓

Note: Amendments were made to the *Companies Act* 2006 by SI 2015/980 *The Companies, Partnerships and Groups (Accounts and Reports) Regulations* 2015. However, regulation 3 disapplied these changes in respect of LLPs, therefore the above sections are those before the changes made by that regulation.

Note: SI 2008/1911 has been amended several times, therefore reference should be made to an up to date copy. The following statutory instruments have amended SI 2008/1911:

2009/1342 *The Financial Services and Markets Act 2000 (Regulated Activities) (Amendment) Order* 2009

2009/1804 *The Limited Liability Partnerships (Application of Companies Act 2006) Regulations* 2009

2011/99 *The Electronic Money Regulations* 2011

2011/245 *The Investment Bank Special Administration Regulations* 2011

2012/1741 *The Statutory Auditors (Amendment of Companies Act 2006 and Delegation of Functions etc) Order* 2012

2012/2301 *The Companies and Limited Liability Partnerships (Accounts and Audit Exemptions and Change of Accounting Framework) Regulations* 2012

2013/472 *The Financial Services Act 2012 (Consequential Amendments and Transitional Provisions) Order* 2013

2013/2005 *The Companies and Partnerships (Accounts and Audit) Regulations* 2013

2014/1815 *The Co-operative and Community Benefit Societies and Credit Unions Act 2010 (Consequential Amendments) Regulations* 2014

Appendix C   Small Limited Liability Partnerships (Accounts) Regulations 2008 (SI 2008/1912)

This appendix reproduces in full SI 2008/1912 *Small Limited Liability Partnerships (Accounts) Regulations* 2008. It is also available at: www.legislation.gov.uk/uksi/2008/1912/contents/made

In summary, as set out in the Contents below, the statutory instrument comprises:

Part 1 Introduction

Part 2 Form and content of individual accounts

Part 3 Form and content of group accounts

Part 4 Interpretation

Schedule 1 – Non-IAS individual accounts

Schedule 2 – Information about related undertakings where LLP not preparing group accounts (non-IAS or IAS individual accounts)

Schedule 3 – Non-IAS abbreviated accounts for delivery to registrar of companies

Schedule 4 – Group accounts

Schedule 5 – General interpretation

STATUTORY INSTRUMENTS

2008 No. 1912

LIMITED LIABILITY PARTNERSHIPS

The Small Limited Liability Partnerships (Accounts)
Regulations 2008

Made - - - -		*17th July 2008*
Coming into force - -		*1st October 2008*

CONTENTS

PART 1

INTRODUCTION

PART 2

FORM AND CONTENT OF INDIVIDUAL ACCOUNTS

PART 3

FORM AND CONTENT OF GROUP ACCOUNTS

PART 4

INTERPRETATION

The Secretary of State makes the following Regulations in exercise of the powers conferred by sections 15 and 17 of the Limited Liability Partnerships Act 2000**(a)**.

In accordance with section 17(4) and (5)(b) of the Limited Liability Partnerships Act 2000, a draft of this instrument was laid before Parliament and approved by a resolution of each House of Parliament.

PART 1

INTRODUCTION

Citation and interpretation

1.—(1) These Regulations may be cited as the Small Limited Liability Partnerships (Accounts) Regulations 2008.

(2) In these Regulations—

"the 2006 Act" means the Companies Act 2006**(b)**;

"LLP" means a limited liability partnership formed under the Limited Liability Partnerships Act 2000 or the Limited Liability Partnerships Act (N.I.) 2002**(c)**;

"the Small Companies Accounts Regulations" means the Small Companies and Groups (Accounts and Directors' Report) Regulations 2008**(d)**.

(3) Any reference in these Regulations to a numbered Part or section of the 2006 Act is a reference to that Part or section as applied to LLPs by the Limited Liability Partnerships (Accounts and Audit) (Application of Companies Act 2006) Regulations 2008**(e)**.

Commencement and application

2.—(1) These Regulations come into force on 1st October 2008.

(2) They apply in relation to financial years beginning on or after 1st October 2008.

(a) 2000 c.12.
(b) 2006 c.46.
(c) 2002 (N.I.) (c.12).
(d) S.I. 2008/409.
(e) S.I. 2008/1911.

(3) They apply to LLPs which are subject to the small LLPs regime under Part 15 of the 2006 Act (see section 381 of that Act**(a)**) provisions of the Small Companies Accounts Regulations, with modifications.

PART 2

FORM AND CONTENT OF INDIVIDUAL ACCOUNTS

Non-IAS individual accounts

3.—(1) Regulation 3 of the Small Companies Accounts Regulations applies to LLPs, modified so that it reads as follows—

> **"Non-IAS individual accounts**
>
> **3.**—(1) Non-IAS individual accounts under section 396 of the 2006 Act (non-IAS individual accounts) must comply with the provisions of Schedule 1 to the Small Limited Liability Partnerships (Accounts) Regulations 2008**(b)** as to the form and content of the balance sheet and profit and loss account, and additional information to be provided by way of notes to the accounts.
>
> (2) The profit and loss account of an LLP that falls within section 408 of the 2006 Act (individual profit and loss account where group accounts prepared)**(c)** need not contain the information specified in paragraphs 57 to 59 of Schedule 1 to the Small Limited Liability Partnerships (Accounts) Regulations 2008 (information supplementing the profit and loss account).
>
> (3) Accounts are treated as having complied with any provision of Schedule 1 to the Small Limited Liability Partnerships (Accounts) Regulations 2008 if they comply instead with the corresponding provision of Schedule 1 to the Large and Medium-sized Limited Liability Partnerships (Accounts) Regulations 2008**(d)**."

(2) The provisions of Schedule 1 to the Small Companies Accounts Regulations apply to LLPs, modified so that they are the provisions set out in Schedule 1 to these Regulations.

Information about related undertakings (non-IAS or IAS individual accounts)

4.—(1) Regulation 4 of the Small Companies Accounts Regulations applies to LLPs, modified so that it reads as follows—

> **"Information about related undertakings (non-IAS or IAS individual accounts)**
>
> **4.**—(1) Non-IAS or IAS individual accounts must comply with the provisions of Schedule 2 to the Small Limited Liability Partnerships (Accounts) Regulations 2008 as to information about related undertakings to be given in notes to the LLP's accounts.
>
> (2) Information otherwise required to be given by Schedule 2 to the Small Limited Liability Partnerships (Accounts) Regulations 2008 need not be disclosed with respect to an undertaking that—
>
>   (a) is established under the law of a country outside the United Kingdom, or
>
>   (b) carries on business outside the United Kingdom,
>
> if the conditions specified in section 409(4) of the 2006 Act are met (see section 409(5) of the 2006 Act for disclosure required where advantage taken of this exemption)."

(a)   Section 381 is amended by regulation 6(1) of S.I. 2008/393.
(b)   S.I. 2008/1912.
(c)   Section 408 is amended by regulation 10 of S.I. 2008/393.
(d)   S.I. 2008/1913.

(2) The provisions of Schedule 2 to the Small Companies Accounts Regulations apply to LLPs, modified so that they are the provisions set out in Schedule 2 to these Regulations.

Accounts for delivery to registrar of companies (non-IAS individual accounts)

5.—(1) Regulation 6 of the Small Companies Accounts Regulations applies to LLPs, modified so that it reads as follows—

"Accounts for delivery to registrar of companies (non-IAS individual accounts)

6. The designated members of an LLP for which non-IAS individual accounts are being prepared may deliver to the registrar of companies under section 444 of the 2006 Act (filing obligations of LLPs subject to small LLPs regime) a copy of a balance sheet which complies with Schedule 3 to the Small Limited Liability Partnerships (Accounts) Regulations 2008 rather than Schedule 1 to those Regulations."

(2) The provisions of Schedule 4 to the Small Companies Accounts Regulations apply to LLPs, modified so that they are the provisions set out in Schedule 3 to these Regulations.

PART 3

FORM AND CONTENT OF GROUP ACCOUNTS

Non-IAS group accounts

6.—(1) Regulation 8 of the Small Companies Accounts Regulations applies to LLPs, modified so that it reads as follows—

"Non-IAS group accounts

8.—(1) Where the members of a parent LLP which—

    (a) is subject to the small LLPs regime, and

    (b) has prepared non-IAS individual accounts in accordance with regulation 3,

prepare non-IAS group accounts under section 398 of the 2006 Act (option to prepare group accounts), those accounts must comply with the provisions of Part 1 of Schedule 4 to the Small Limited Liability Partnerships (Accounts) Regulations 2008 as to the form and content of the consolidated balance sheet and consolidated profit and loss account, and additional information to be provided by way of notes to the accounts.

    (2) Accounts are treated as having complied with any provision of Part 1 of Schedule 4 to the Small Limited Liability Partnerships (Accounts) Regulations 2008 if they comply instead with the corresponding provision of Schedule 3 to the Large and Medium-sized Limited Liability Partnerships (Accounts) Regulations 2008."

(2) The provisions of Part 1 of Schedule 6 to the Small Companies Accounts Regulations apply to LLPs, modified so that they are the provisions set out in Part 1 of Schedule 4 to these Regulations.

Information about related undertakings (Non-IAS or IAS group accounts)

7.—(1) Regulation 10 of the Small Companies Accounts Regulations applies to LLPs, modified so that it reads as follows—

"Information about related undertakings (Non-IAS or IAS group accounts)

10.—(1) Non-IAS or IAS group accounts must comply with the provisions of Part 2 of Schedule 4 to the Small Limited Liability Partnerships (Accounts) Regulations 2008 as to information about related undertakings to be given in notes to the LLP's accounts.

(2) Information otherwise required to be given by Part 2 of Schedule 4 to the Small Limited Liability Partnerships (Accounts) Regulations 2008 need not be disclosed with respect to an undertaking that—

    (a) is established under the law of a country outside the United Kingdom, or

    (b) carries on business outside the United Kingdom,

if the conditions specified in section 409(4) of the 2006 Act are met (see section 409(5) of the 2006 Act for disclosure required where advantage taken of this exemption)."

(2) The provisions of Part 2 of Schedule 6 to the Small Companies Accounts Regulations apply to LLPs, modified so that they are the provisions set out in Part 2 of Schedule 4 to these Regulations.

PART 4

INTERPRETATION

General interpretation

8.—(1) Regulation 13 of the Small Companies Accounts Regulations applies to LLPs, modified so that it reads as follows—

"General interpretation

13. Schedule 5 to the Small Limited Liability Partnerships (Accounts) Regulations 2008 contains general definitions for the purposes of these Regulations."

(2) The provisions of Schedule 8 to the Small Companies Accounts Regulations apply to LLPs, modified so that they are the provisions set out in Schedule 5 to these Regulations.

Gareth Thomas
Parliamentary Under Secretary of State for Trade and Consumer Affairs,
17th July 2008   Department for Business, Enterprise and Regulatory Reform

SCHEDULE 1

NON-IAS INDIVIDUAL ACCOUNTS

PART 1

GENERAL RULES AND FORMATS

SECTION A

GENERAL RULES

1.—(1) Subject to the following provisions of this Schedule—

(a) every balance sheet of an LLP must show the items listed in either of the balance sheet formats in Section B of this Part, and

(b) every profit and loss account must show the items listed in either of the profit and loss account formats in Section B.

(2) References in this Schedule to the items listed in any of the formats in Section B are to those items read together with any of the notes following the formats which apply to those items.

(3) The items must be shown in the order and under the headings and sub-headings given in the particular format used, but—

(a) the notes to the formats may permit alternative positions for any particular items, and

(b) the heading or sub-heading for any item does not have to be distinguished by any letter or number assigned to that item in the format used.

2.—(1) Where in accordance with paragraph 1 an LLP's balance sheet or profit and loss account for any financial year has been prepared by reference to one of the formats in Section B, the members of the LLP must use the same format in preparing non-IAS individual accounts for subsequent financial years, unless in their opinion there are special reasons for a change.

(2) Particulars of any such change must be given in a note to the accounts in which the new format is first used, and the reasons for the change must be explained.

3.—(1) Any item required to be shown in an LLP's balance sheet or profit and loss account may be shown in greater detail than required by the particular format used.

(2) The balance sheet or profit and loss account may include an item representing or covering the amount of any asset or liability, income or expenditure not otherwise covered by any of the items listed in the format used, save that none of the following may be treated as assets in any balance sheet—

(a) preliminary expenses,

(b) expenses of, and commission on, any issue of debentures,

(c) costs of research.

4.—(1) Where the special nature of the LLP's business requires it, the members of the LLP must adapt the arrangement, headings and sub-headings otherwise required in respect of items given an Arabic number in the balance sheet or profit and loss account format used.

(2) The members may combine items to which Arabic numbers are given in any of the formats set out in Section B if—

(a) their individual amounts are not material to assessing the state of affairs or profit or loss of the LLP for the financial year in question, or

(b) the combination facilitates that assessment.

(3) Where sub-paragraph (2)(b) applies, the individual amounts of any items which have been combined must be disclosed in a note to the accounts.

5.—(1) Subject to sub-paragraph (2), the members must not include a heading or sub-heading corresponding to an item in the balance sheet or profit and loss account format used if there is no amount to be shown for that item for the financial year to which the balance sheet or profit and loss account relates.

(2) Where an amount can be shown for the item in question for the immediately preceding financial year that amount must be shown under the heading or sub-heading required by the format for that item.

6. Every profit and loss account must show the amount of an LLP's profit or loss on ordinary activities before taxation.

7.—(1) For every item shown in the balance sheet or profit and loss account the corresponding amount for the immediately preceding financial year must also be shown.

(2) Where that corresponding amount is not comparable with the amount to be shown for the item in question in respect of the financial year to which the balance sheet or profit and loss account relates, the former amount may be adjusted, and particulars of the non-comparability and of any adjustment must be disclosed in a note to the accounts.

8. Amounts in respect of items representing assets or income may not be set off against amounts in respect of items representing liabilities or expenditure (as the case may be), or vice versa.

9. The members of the LLP must, in determining how amounts are presented within items in the profit and loss account and balance sheet, have regard to the substance of the reported transaction or arrangement, in accordance with generally accepted accounting principles or practice.

SECTION B

THE REQUIRED FORMATS FOR ACCOUNTS(a)

Balance sheet formats

Format 1

A.   Fixed assets
- I. Intangible assets
  1. Goodwill *(1)*
  2. Other intangible assets *(2)*
- II. Tangible assets
  1. Land and buildings
  2. Plant and machinery etc.
- III. Investments
  1. Shares in group undertakings and participating interests
  2. Loans to group undertakings and undertakings in which the LLP has a participating interest
  3. Other investments other than loans
  4. Other investments

B.   Current assets
- I. Stocks
  1. Stocks
  2. Payments on account

(a) A number in brackets following any item is a reference to the note of that number in the notes following the formats.

    II. Debtors *(3)*
- 1. Trade debtors
- 2. Amounts owed by group undertakings and undertakings in which the LLP has a participating interest
- 3. Other debtors

    III. Investments
- 1. Shares in group undertakings
- 2. Other investments

    IV. Cash at bank and in hand

C.   Prepayments and accrued income *(4)*

D.   Creditors: amounts falling due within one year
- 1. Bank loans and overdrafts
- 2. Trade creditors
- 3. Amounts owed to group undertakings and undertakings in which the LLP has a participating interest
- 4. Other creditors *(5)*

E.   Net current assets (liabilities) *(6)*

F.   Total assets less current liabilities

G.   Creditors: amounts falling due after more than one year
- 1. Bank loans and overdrafts
- 2. Trade creditors
- 3. Amounts owed to group undertakings and undertakings in which the LLP has a participating interest
- 4. Other creditors *(5)*

H.   Provisions for liabilities

I.   Accruals and deferred income *(5)*

J.   Loans and other debts due to members *(7)*

K.   Members' other interests
- I. Members' capital
- II. Revaluation reserve
- III. Other reserves

Balance sheet formats

Format 2

ASSETS

A.   Fixed assets
- I. Intangible assets
  - 1. Goodwill *(1)*
  - 2. Other intangible assets *(2)*
- II. Tangible assets
  - 1. Land and buildings
  - 2. Plant and machinery etc.
- III. Investments
  - 1. Shares in group undertakings and participating interests
  - 2. Loans to group undertakings and undertakings in which the LLP has a participating interest

  3. Other investments other than loans
  4. Other investments

B. Current assets
  I. Stocks
    1. Stocks
    2. Payments on account
  II. Debtors *(3)*
    1. Trade debtors
    2. Amounts owed by group undertakings and undertakings in which the LLP has a participating interest
    3. Other debtors
  III. Investments
    1. Shares in group undertakings
    2. Other investments
  IV. Cash at bank and in hand

C. Prepayments and accrued income *(4)*

LIABILITIES

A. Loans and other debts due to members *(7)*

B. Members' other interests
  I. Members' capital *(7)*
  II. Revaluation reserve
  III. Other reserves

C. Provisions for liabilities

D. Creditors *(8)*
    1. Bank loans and overdrafts
    2. Trade creditors
    3. Amounts owed to group undertakings and undertakings in which the LLP has a participating interest
    4. Other creditors *(5)*

E. Accruals and deferred income *(5)*

Notes on the balance sheet formats

(1) Goodwill

(Formats 1 and 2, item A.I.1.)

Amounts representing goodwill must only be included to the extent that the goodwill was acquired for valuable consideration.

(2) Other intangible assets

(Formats 1 and 2, item A.I.2.)

Amounts in respect of concessions, patents, licences, trade marks and similar rights and assets must only be included in an LLP's balance sheet under this item if either—
  (a) the assets were acquired for valuable consideration and are not required to be shown under goodwill, or
  (b) the assets in question were created by the LLP itself.

(3)   Debtors

(Formats 1 and 2, items B.II.1 to 3.)

The amount falling due after more than one year must be shown separately for each item included under debtors unless the aggregate amount of debtors falling due after more than one year is disclosed in the notes to the accounts.

(4)   Prepayments and accrued income

(Formats 1 and 2, item C.)

This item may alternatively be included under item B.II.3 in Format 1 or 2.

(5)   Other creditors

(Format 1, items D.4, G.4 and I and Format 2, items D.4 and E.)

There must be shown separately—
- (a)   the amount of any convertible loans, and
- (b)   the amount for creditors in respect of taxation and social security.

Payments received on account of orders must be included in so far as they are not shown as deductions from stocks.

In Format 1, accruals and deferred income may be shown under item I or included under item D.4 or G.4, or both (as the case may require). In Format 2, accruals and deferred income may be shown under item E or within item D.4 under Liabilities.

(6)   Net current assets (liabilities)

(Format 1, item E.)

In determining the amount to be shown under this item any prepayments and accrued income must be taken into account wherever shown.

(7)   Loans and other debts due to members

(Format 1, item J and Format 2, Liabilities item A)

The following amounts must be shown separately under this item—
- (a)   the aggregate amount of money advanced to the LLP by the members by way of loan,
- (b)   the aggregate amount of money owed to members by the LLP in respect of profits,
- (c)   any other amounts.

(8)   Creditors

(Format 2, Liabilities items D.1 to 4.)

Amounts falling due within one year and after one year must be shown separately for each of these items and for the aggregate of all of these items unless the aggregate amount of creditors falling due within one year and the aggregate amount of creditors falling due after more than one year is disclosed in the notes to the accounts.

Profit and loss account formats

Format 1
(see note (12) below)

1. Turnover
2. Cost of sales *(9)*
3. Gross profit or loss
4. Distribution costs *(9)*
5. Administrative expenses *(9)*
6. Other operating income
7. Income from shares in group undertakings
8. Income from participating interests
9. Income from other fixed asset investments *(10)*
10. Other interest receivable and similar income *(10)*
11. Amounts written off investments
12. Interest payable and similar charges *(11)*
13. Tax on profit or loss on ordinary activities
14. Profit or loss on ordinary activities after taxation
15. Extraordinary income
16. Extraordinary charges
17. Extraordinary profit or loss
18. Tax on extraordinary profit or loss
19. Other taxes not shown under the above items
20. Profit or loss for the financial year before members' remuneration and profit shares

Profit and loss account formats

Format 2

1. Turnover
2. Change in stocks of finished goods and in work in progress
3. Own work capitalised
4. Other operating income
5. (a) Raw materials and consumables
   (b) Other external charges
6. Staff costs
   (a) wages and salaries
   (b) social security costs
   (c) other pension costs
7. (a) Depreciation and other amounts written off tangible and intangible fixed assets
   (b) Exceptional amounts written off current assets

8.   Other operating charges

9.   Income from shares in group undertakings

10. Income from participating interests

11. Income from other fixed asset investments *(10)*

12. Other interest receivable and similar income *(10)*

13. Amounts written off investments

14. Interest payable and similar charges *(11)*

15. Tax on profit or loss on ordinary activities

16. Profit or loss on ordinary activities after taxation

17. Extraordinary income

18. Extraordinary charges

19. Extraordinary profit or loss

20. Tax on extraordinary profit or loss

21. Other taxes not shown under the above items

22. Profit or loss for the financial year before members' remuneration and profit shares

Notes on the profit and loss account formats

(9)   *Cost of sales: distribution costs: administrative expenses*

(Format 1, items 2, 4 and 5.)

These items must be stated after taking into account any necessary provisions for depreciation or diminution in value of assets.

(10)   *Income from other fixed asset investments: other interest receivable and similar income*

(Format 1, items 9 and 10; Format 2, items 11 and 12.)

Income and interest derived from group undertakings must be shown separately from income and interest derived from other sources. Interest receivable from members must not be included under this item.

(11)   *Interest payable and similar charges*

(Format 1, item 12; Format 2, item 14.)

The amount payable to group undertakings must be shown separately. Interest payable to members must not be included under this item.

(12)   *Format 1*

The amount of any provisions for depreciation and diminution in value of tangible and intangible fixed assets falling to be shown under item 7(a) in Format 2 must be disclosed in a note to the accounts in any case where the profit and loss account is prepared using Format 1.

PART 2

ACCOUNTING PRINCIPLES AND RULES

SECTION A
ACCOUNTING PRINCIPLES

Preliminary

10.—(1) The amounts to be included in respect of all items shown in an LLP's accounts must be determined in accordance with the principles set out in this Section.

(2) But if it appears to the members of the LLP that there are special reasons for departing from any of those principles in preparing the LLP's accounts in respect of any financial year they may do so, in which case particulars of the departure, the reasons for it and its effect must be given in a note to the accounts.

Accounting principles

11. The LLP is presumed to be carrying on business as a going concern.

12. Accounting policies must be applied consistently within the same accounts and from one financial year to the next.

13. The amount of any item must be determined on a prudent basis, and in particular—

(a) only profits realised at the balance sheet date must be included in the profit and loss account, and

(b) all liabilities which have arisen in respect of the financial year to which the accounts relate or a previous financial year must be taken into account, including those which only become apparent between the balance sheet date and the date on which it is signed on behalf of the members in accordance with section 414 of the 2006 Act (approval and signing of accounts).

14. All income and charges relating to the financial year to which the accounts relate must be taken into account, without regard to the date of receipt or payment.

15. In determining the aggregate amount of any item, the amount of each individual asset or liability that falls to be taken into account must be determined separately.

SECTION B
HISTORICAL COST ACCOUNTING RULES

Preliminary

16. Subject to Sections C and D of this Part of this Schedule, the amounts to be included in respect of all items shown in an LLP's accounts must be determined in accordance with the rules set out in this Section.

Fixed assets

General rules

17.—(1) The amount to be included in respect of any fixed asset must be its purchase price or production cost.

(2) This is subject to any provision for depreciation or diminution in value made in accordance with paragraphs 18 to 20.

Rules for depreciation and diminution in value

18. In the case of any fixed asset which has a limited useful economic life, the amount of—

(a) its purchase price or production cost, or

(b) where it is estimated that any such asset will have a residual value at the end of the period of its useful economic life, its purchase price or production cost less that estimated residual value,

must be reduced by provisions for depreciation calculated to write off that amount systematically over the period of the asset's useful economic life.

19.—(1) Where a fixed asset investment of a description falling to be included under item A.III of either of the balance sheet formats set out in Part 1 of this Schedule has diminished in value, provisions for diminution in value may be made in respect of it and the amount to be included in respect of it may be reduced accordingly.

(2) Provisions for diminution in value must be made in respect of any fixed asset which has diminished in value if the reduction in its value is expected to be permanent (whether its useful economic life is limited or not), and the amount to be included in respect of it must be reduced accordingly.

(3) Any provisions made under sub-paragraph (1) or (2) which are not shown in the profit and loss account must be disclosed (either separately or in aggregate) in a note to the accounts.

20.—(1) Where the reasons for which any provision was made in accordance with paragraph 19 have ceased to apply to any extent, that provision must be written back to the extent that it is no longer necessary.

(2) Any amounts written back in accordance with sub-paragraph (1) which are not shown in the profit and loss account must be disclosed (either separately or in aggregate) in a note to the accounts.

Development costs

21.—(1) Notwithstanding that an item in respect of "development costs" is included under "fixed assets" in the balance sheet formats set out in Part 1 of this Schedule, an amount may only be included in an LLP's balance sheet in respect of development costs in special circumstances.

(2) If any amount is included in an LLP's balance sheet in respect of development costs the following information must be given in a note to the accounts—

(a) the period over which the amount of those costs originally capitalised is being or is to be written off, and

(b) the reasons for capitalising the development costs in question.

Goodwill

22.—(1) The application of paragraphs 17 to 20 in relation to goodwill (in any case where goodwill is treated as an asset) is subject to the following.

(2) Subject to sub-paragraph (3), the amount of the consideration for any goodwill acquired by an LLP must be reduced by provisions for depreciation calculated to write off that amount systematically over a period chosen by the members of the LLP.

(3) The period chosen must not exceed the useful economic life of the goodwill in question.

(4) In any case where any goodwill acquired by an LLP is shown or included as an asset in the LLP's balance sheet there must be disclosed in a note to the accounts—

(a) the period chosen for writing off the consideration for that goodwill, and

(b) the reasons for choosing that period.

Current assets

23. Subject to paragraph 24, the amount to be included in respect of any current asset must be its purchase price or production cost.

24.—(1) If the net realisable value of any current asset is lower than its purchase price or production cost, the amount to be included in respect of that asset must be the net realisable value.

(2) Where the reasons for which any provision for diminution in value was made in accordance with sub-paragraph (1) have ceased to apply to any extent, that provision must be written back to the extent that it is no longer necessary.

Miscellaneous and supplementary provisions

Excess of money owed over value received as an asset item

25.—(1) Where the amount repayable on any debt owed by an LLP is greater than the value of the consideration received in the transaction giving rise to the debt, the amount of the difference may be treated as an asset.

(2) Where any such amount is so treated—

(a) it must be written off by reasonable amounts each year and must be completely written off before repayment of the debt, and

(b) if the current amount is not shown as a separate item in the LLP's balance sheet, it must be disclosed in a note to the accounts.

Assets included at a fixed amount

26.—(1) Subject to sub-paragraph (2), assets which fall to be included—

(a) amongst the fixed assets of an LLP under the item "tangible assets", or

(b) amongst the current assets of an LLP under the item "raw materials and consumables", may be included at a fixed quantity and value.

(2) Sub-paragraph (1) applies to assets of a kind which are constantly being replaced where—

(a) their overall value is not material to assessing the LLP's state of affairs, and

(b) their quantity, value and composition are not subject to material variation.

Determination of purchase price or production cost

27.— (1) The purchase price of an asset is to be determined by adding to the actual price paid any expenses incidental to its acquisition.

(2) The production cost of an asset is to be determined by adding to the purchase price of the raw materials and consumables used the amount of the costs incurred by the LLP which are directly attributable to the production of that asset.

(3) In addition, there may be included in the production cost of an asset—

(a) a reasonable proportion of the costs incurred by the LLP which are only indirectly attributable to the production of that asset, but only to the extent that they relate to the period of production, and

(b) interest on capital borrowed to finance the production of that asset, to the extent that it accrues in respect of the period of production, provided, however, in a case within paragraph (b), that the inclusion of the interest in determining the cost of that asset and the amount of the interest so included is disclosed in a note to the accounts.

(4) In the case of current assets distribution costs may not be included in production costs.

28.—(1) The purchase price or production cost of—

    (a) any assets which fall to be included under any item shown in an LLP's balance sheet under the general item "stocks", and

    (b) any assets which are fungible assets (including investments),

may be determined by the application of any of the methods mentioned in sub-paragraph (2) in relation to any such assets of the same class, provided that the method chosen is one which appears to the members to be appropriate in the circumstances of the LLP.

(2) Those methods are—

    (a) the method known as "first in, first out" (FIFO),

    (b) the method known as "last in, first out" (LIFO),

    (c) a weighted average price, and

    (d) any other method similar to any of the methods mentioned above.

(3) For the purposes of this paragraph, assets of any description must be regarded as fungible if assets of that description are substantially indistinguishable one from another.

Substitution of original stated amount where price or cost unknown

29.—(1) This paragraph applies where—

    (a) there is no record of the purchase price or production cost of any asset of an LLP or of any price, expenses or costs relevant for determining its purchase price or production cost in accordance with paragraph 27, or

    (b) any such record cannot be obtained without unreasonable expense or delay.

(2) In such a case, the purchase price or production cost of the asset must be taken, for the purposes of paragraphs 17 to 24, to be the value ascribed to it in the earliest available record of its value made on or after its acquisition or production by the LLP.

SECTION C
ALTERNATIVE ACCOUNTING RULES

Preliminary

30.—(1) The rules set out in Section B are referred to below in this Schedule as the historical cost accounting rules.

(2) Those rules, with the omission of paragraphs 16, 22 and 26 to 29, are referred to below in this Part of this Schedule as the depreciation rules; and references below in this Schedule to the historical cost accounting rules do not include the depreciation rules as they apply by virtue of paragraph 33.

31. Subject to paragraphs 33 to 35, the amounts to be included in respect of assets of any description mentioned in paragraph 32 may be determined on any basis so mentioned.

Alternative accounting rules

32.—(1) Intangible fixed assets, other than goodwill, may be included at their current cost.

(2) Tangible fixed assets may be included at a market value determined as at the date of their last valuation or at their current cost.

(3) Investments of any description falling to be included under item A III of either of the balance sheet formats set out Part 1 of this Schedule may be included either—

    (a) at a market value determined as at the date of their last valuation, or

    (b) at a value determined on any basis which appears to the members to be appropriate in the circumstances of the LLP.

But in the latter case particulars of the method of valuation adopted and of the reasons for adopting it must be disclosed in a note to the accounts.

(4) Investments of any description falling to be included under item B III of either of the balance sheet formats set out in Part 1 of this Schedule may be included at their current cost.

(5) Stocks may be included at their current cost.

Application of the depreciation rules

33.—(1) Where the value of any asset of an LLP is determined on any basis mentioned in paragraph 32, that value must be, or (as the case may require) be the starting point for determining, the amount to be included in respect of that asset in the LLP's accounts, instead of its purchase price or production cost or any value previously so determined for that asset.

The depreciation rules apply accordingly in relation to any such asset with the substitution for any reference to its purchase price or production cost of a reference to the value most recently determined for that asset on any basis mentioned in paragraph 32.

(2) The amount of any provision for depreciation required in the case of any fixed asset by paragraphs 18 to 20 as they apply by virtue of sub-paragraph (1) is referred to below in this paragraph as the adjusted amount, and the amount of any provision which would be required by any of those paragraphs in the case of that asset according to the historical cost accounting rules is referred to as the historical cost amount.

(3) Where sub-paragraph (1) applies in the case of any fixed asset the amount of any provision for depreciation in respect of that asset—

    (a) included in any item shown in the profit and loss account in respect of amounts written off assets of the description in question, or

    (b) taken into account in stating any item so shown which is required by note *(9)* of the notes on the profit and loss account formats set out in Part 1 of this Schedule to be stated after taking into account any necessary provision for depreciation or diminution in value of assets included under it,

may be the historical cost amount instead of the adjusted amount, provided that the amount of any difference between the two is shown separately in the profit and loss account or in a note to the accounts.

Additional information to be provided in case of departure from historical cost accounting rules

34.—(1) This paragraph applies where the amounts to be included in respect of assets covered by any items shown in an LLP's accounts have been determined on any basis mentioned in paragraph 32.

(2) The items affected and the basis of valuation adopted in determining the amounts of the assets in question in the case of each such item must be disclosed in a note to the accounts.

(3) In the case of each balance sheet item affected (except stocks) either—

    (a) the comparable amounts determined according to the historical cost accounting rules, or

(b) the differences between those amounts and the corresponding amounts actually shown in the balance sheet in respect of that item,

must be shown separately in the balance sheet or in a note to the accounts.

(4) In sub-paragraph (3), references in relation to any item to the comparable amounts determined as there mentioned are references to—

(a) the aggregate amount which would be required to be shown in respect of that item if the amounts to be included in respect of all the assets covered by that item were determined according to the historical cost accounting rules, and

(b) the aggregate amount of the cumulative provisions for depreciation or diminution in value which would be permitted or required in determining those amounts according to those rules.

Revaluation reserve

35.—(1) With respect to any determination of the value of an asset of an LLP on any basis mentioned in paragraph 32, the amount of any profit or loss arising from that determination (after allowing, where appropriate, for any provisions for depreciation or diminution in value made otherwise than by reference to the value so determined and any adjustments of any such provisions made in the light of that determination) must be credited or (as the case may be) debited to a separate reserve ("the revaluation reserve").

(2) The amount of the revaluation reserve must be shown in the LLP's balance sheet under a separate sub-heading in the position given for the item "revaluation reserve" in Format 1 or 2 of the balance sheet formats set out in Part 1 of this Schedule, but need not be shown under that name.

(3) The treatment for taxation purposes of amounts credited or debited to the revaluation reserve must be disclosed in a note to the accounts.

SECTION D

FAIR VALUE ACCOUNTING

Inclusion of financial instruments at fair value

36.—(1) Subject to sub-paragraphs (2) to (5), financial instruments (including derivatives) may be included at fair value.

(2) Sub-paragraph (1) does not apply to financial instruments that constitute liabilities unless—

(a) they are held as part of a trading portfolio,

(b) they are derivatives, or

(c) they are financial instruments falling within sub-paragraph (4).

(3) Unless they are financial instruments falling within sub-paragraph (4), sub-paragraph (1) does not apply to—

(a) financial instruments (other than derivatives) held to maturity,

(b) loans and receivables originated by the LLP and not held for trading purposes,

(c) interests in subsidiary undertakings, associated undertakings and joint ventures,

(d) equity instruments issued by the LLP,

(e) contracts for contingent consideration in a business combination, or

(f) other financial instruments with such special characteristics that the instruments, according to generally accepted accounting principles or practice, should be accounted for differently from other financial instruments.

(4) Financial instruments that, under international accounting standards adopted by the European Commission on or before 5th September 2006 in accordance with the IAS Regulation, may be

included in accounts at fair value, may be so included, provided that the disclosures required by such accounting standards are made.

(5) If the fair value of a financial instrument cannot be determined reliably in accordance with paragraph 37, sub-paragraph (1) does not apply to that financial instrument.

(6) In this paragraph—

"associated undertaking" has the meaning given by paragraph 19 of Schedule 4 to these Regulations;

"joint venture" has the meaning given by paragraph 18 of that Schedule.

Determination of fair value

37.—(1) The fair value of a financial instrument is its value determined in accordance with this paragraph.

(2) If a reliable market can readily be identified for the financial instrument, its fair value is to be determined by reference to its market value.

(3) If a reliable market cannot readily be identified for the financial instrument but can be identified for its components or for a similar instrument, its fair value is determined by reference to the market value of its components or of the similar instrument.

(4) If neither sub-paragraph (2) nor (3) applies, the fair value of the financial instrument is a value resulting from generally accepted valuation models and techniques.

(5) Any valuation models and techniques used for the purposes of sub-paragraph (4) must ensure a reasonable approximation of the market value.

Hedged items

38. An LLP may include any assets and liabilities, or identified portions of such assets or liabilities, that qualify as hedged items under a fair value hedge accounting system at the amount required under that system.

Other assets that may be included at fair value

39.—(1) This paragraph applies to—

      (a) investment property, and

      (b) living animals and plants,

that, under international accounting standards, may be included in accounts at fair value.

(2) Such investment property and such living animals and plants may be included at fair value, provided that all such investment property or, as the case may be, all such living animals and plants are so included where their fair value can reliably be determined.

(3) In this paragraph, "fair value" means fair value determined in accordance with relevant international accounting standards.

Accounting for changes in value

40.—(1) This paragraph applies where a financial instrument is valued in accordance with paragraph 36 or 38 or an asset is valued in accordance with paragraph 39.

(2) Notwithstanding paragraph 13 in this Part of this Schedule, and subject to sub-paragraphs (3) and (4), a change in the value of the financial instrument or of the investment property or living animal or plant must be included in the profit and loss account.

(3) Where—

(a) the financial instrument accounted for is a hedging instrument under a hedge accounting system that allows some or all of the change in value not to be shown in the profit and loss account, or

(b) the change in value relates to an exchange difference arising on a monetary item that forms part of an LLP's net investment in a foreign entity,

the amount of the change in value must be credited to or (as the case may be) debited from a separate reserve ("the fair value reserve").

(4) Where the instrument accounted for—

(a) is an available for sale financial asset, and

(b) is not a derivative,

the change in value may be credited to or (as the case may be) debited from the fair value reserve.

The fair value reserve

41.—(1) The fair value reserve must be adjusted to the extent that the amounts shown in it are no longer necessary for the purposes of paragraph 40(3) or (4).

(2) The treatment for taxation purposes of amounts credited or debited to the fair value reserve must be disclosed in a note to the accounts.

PART 3

NOTES TO THE ACCOUNTS

Preliminary

42. Any information required in the case of any LLP by the following provisions of this Part of this Schedule must (if not given in the LLP's accounts) be given by way of a note to those accounts.

Reserves

43. Any amount set aside or proposed to be set aside to, or withdrawn or proposed to be withdrawn from, reserves must be stated.

Disclosure of accounting policies

44. The accounting policies adopted by the LLP in determining the amounts to be included in respect of items shown in the balance sheet and in determining the profit or loss of the LLP must be stated (including such policies with respect to the depreciation and diminution in value of assets).

Information supplementing the balance sheet

45. Paragraphs 46 to 56 require information which either supplements the information given with respect to any particular items shown in the balance sheet or is otherwise relevant to assessing the LLP's state of affairs in the light of the information so given.

Loans and other debts due to members

46. The following information must be given—

(a) the aggregate amount of loans and other debts due to members as at the date of the beginning of the financial year,

   (b)   the aggregate amounts contributed by members during the financial year,

   (c)   the aggregate amounts transferred to or from the profit and loss account during that year,

   (d)   the aggregate amounts withdrawn by members or applied on behalf of members during that year,

   (e)   the aggregate amount of loans and other debts due to members as at the balance sheet date, and

   (f)   the aggregate amount of loans and other debts due to members that fall due after one year.

Fixed assets

47.—(1) In respect of each item which is or would but for paragraph 4(2)(b) be shown under the general item "fixed assets" in the LLP's balance sheet the following information must be given—

   (a)   the appropriate amounts in respect of that item as at the date of the beginning of the financial year and as at the balance sheet date respectively,

   (b)   the effect on any amount shown in the balance sheet in respect of that item of—

      (i)   any revision of the amount in respect of any assets included under that item made during that year on any basis mentioned in paragraph 32,

      (ii)   acquisitions during that year of any assets,

      (iii)   disposals during that year of any assets, and

      (iv)   any transfers of assets of the LLP to and from that item during that year.

(2) The reference in sub-paragraph (I)(a) to the appropriate amounts in respect of any item as at any date there mentioned is a reference to amounts representing the aggregate amounts determined, as at that date, in respect of assets falling to be included under that item on either of the following bases, that is to say—

   (a)   on the basis of purchase price or production cost (determined in accordance with paragraphs 27 and 28), or

   (b)   on any basis mentioned in paragraph 32,
(leaving out of account in either case any provisions for depreciation or diminution in value).

(3) In respect of each item within sub-paragraph (1) there must also be stated—

   (a)   the cumulative amount of provisions for depreciation or diminution in value of assets included under that item as at each date mentioned in sub-paragraph (I)(a),

   (b)   the amount of any such provisions made in respect of the financial year,

   (c)   the amount of any adjustments made in respect of any such provisions during that year in consequence of the disposal of any assets, and

   (d)   the amount of any other adjustments made in respect of any such provisions during that year.

48. Where any fixed assets of the LLP (other than listed investments) are included under any item shown in the LLP's balance sheet at an amount determined on any basis mentioned in paragraph 32, the following information must be given—

   (a)   the years (so far as they are known to the members) in which the assets were severally valued and the several values, and

   (b)   in the case of assets that have been valued during the financial year, the names of the persons who valued them or particulars of their qualifications for doing so and (whichever is stated) the bases of valuation used by them.

Investments

49.—(1) In respect of the amount of each item which is or would but for paragraph 4(2)(b) be shown in the LLP's balance sheet under the general item "investments" (whether as fixed assets or as current assets) there must be stated how much of that amount is ascribable to listed investments.

(2) Where the amount of any listed investments is stated for any item in accordance with subparagraph (1), the following amounts must also be stated—

    (a) the aggregate market value of those investments where it differs from the amount so stated, and

    (b) both the market value and the stock exchange value of any investments of which the former value is, for the purposes of the accounts, taken as being higher than the latter.

Information about fair value of assets and liabilities

50.—(1) This paragraph applies where financial instruments have been valued in accordance with paragraph 36 or 38.

(2) There must be stated—

    (a) the significant assumptions underlying the valuation models and techniques used where the fair value of the instruments has been determined in accordance with paragraph 37(4),

    (b) for each category of financial instrument, the fair value of the instruments in that category and the changes in value—

        (i) included in the profit and loss account, or

        (ii) credited to or (as the case may be) debited from the fair value reserve, in respect of those instruments, and

    (c) for each class of derivatives, the extent and nature of the instruments, including significant terms and conditions that may affect the amount, timing and certainty of future cash flows.

(3) Where any amount is transferred to or from the fair value reserve during the financial year, there must be stated in tabular form—

    (a) the amount of the reserve as at the date of the beginning of the financial year and as at the balance sheet date respectively,

    (b) the amount transferred to or from the reserve during that year, and

    (c) the source and application respectively of the amounts so transferred.

51.—(1) This paragraph applies if—

    (a) the LLP has financial fixed assets that could be included at fair value by virtue of paragraph 36,

    (b) the amount at which those items are included under any item in the LLP's accounts is in excess of their fair value, and

    (c) the LLP has not made provision for diminution in value of those assets in accordance with paragraph 19(1) of this Schedule.

(2) There must be stated—

    (a) the amount at which either the individual assets or appropriate groupings of those individual assets are included in the LLP's accounts,

    (b) the fair value of those assets or groupings, and

    (c) the reasons for not making a provision for diminution in value of those assets, including the nature of the evidence that provides the basis for the belief that the amount at which they are stated in the accounts will be recovered.

Information where investment property and living animals and plants included at fair value

52.—(1) This paragraph applies where the amounts to be included in an LLP's accounts in respect of investment property or living animals and plants have been determined in accordance with paragraph 39.

(2) The balance sheet items affected and the basis of valuation adopted in determining the amounts of the assets in question in the case of each such item must be disclosed in a note to the accounts.

(3) In the case of investment property, for each balance sheet item affected there must be shown, either separately in the balance sheet or in a note to the accounts—

(a) the comparable amounts determined according to the historical cost accounting rules, or

(b) the differences between those amounts and the corresponding amounts actually shown in the balance sheet in respect of that item.

(4) In sub-paragraph (3), references in relation to any item to the comparable amounts determined in accordance with that sub-paragraph are to—

(a) the aggregate amount which would be required to be shown in respect of that item if the amounts to be included in respect of all the assets covered by that item were determined according to the historical cost accounting rules, and

(b) the aggregate amount of the cumulative provisions for depreciation or diminution in value which would be permitted or required in determining those amounts according to those rules.

Reserves and provisions

53.—(1) This paragraph applies where any amount is transferred—

(a) to or from any reserves, or

(b) to any provision for liabilities, or

(c) from any provision for liabilities otherwise than for the purpose for which the provision was established,

and the reserves or provisions are or would but for paragraph 4(2)(b) be shown as separate items in the LLP's balance sheet.

(2) The following information must be given in respect of the aggregate of reserves or provisions included in the same item—

(a) the amount of the reserves or provisions as at the date of the beginning of the financial year and as at the balance sheet date respectively,

(b) any amounts transferred to or from the reserves or provisions during that year, and

(c) the source and application respectively of any amounts so transferred.

(3) Particulars must be given of each provision included in the item "other provisions" in the LLP's balance sheet in any case where the amount of that provision is material.

Details of indebtedness

54.—(1) For the aggregate of all items shown under "creditors" in the LLP's balance sheet there must be stated the aggregate of the following amounts—

(a) the amount of any debts included under "creditors" which are payable or repayable otherwise than by instalments and fall due for payment or repayment after the end of the period of five years beginning with the day next following the end of the financial year, and

(b) in the case of any debts so included which are payable or repayable by instalments, the amount of any instalments which fall due for payment after the end of that period.

(2) In respect of each item shown under "creditors" in the LLP's balance sheet there must be stated the aggregate amount of any debts included under that item in respect of which any security has been given by the LLP.

(3) References above in this paragraph to an item shown under "creditors" in the LLP's balance sheet include references, where amounts falling due to creditors within one year and after more than one year are distinguished in the balance sheet—

(a) in a case within sub-paragraph (1), to an item shown under the latter of those categories,

(b) in a case within sub-paragraph (2), to an item shown under either of those categories.

References to items shown under "creditors" include references to items which would but for paragraph 4(2)(b) be shown under that heading.

Guarantees and other financial commitments

55.—(1) Particulars must be given of any charge on the assets of the LLP to secure the liabilities of any other person, including, where practicable, the amount secured.

(2) The following information must be given with respect to any other contingent liability not provided for—

(a) the amount or estimated amount of that liability,

(b) its legal nature, and

(c) whether any valuable security has been provided by the LLP in connection with that liability and if so, what.

(3) There must be stated, where practicable, the aggregate amount or estimated amount of contracts for capital expenditure, so far as not provided for.

(4) Particulars must be given of—

(a) any pension commitments included under any provision shown in the LLP's balance sheet, and

(b) any such commitments for which no provision has been made,

and where any such commitment relates wholly or partly to pensions payable to past members of the LLP separate particulars must be given of that commitment so far as it relates to such pensions.

(5) Particulars must also be given of any other financial commitments that—

(a) have not been provided for, and

(b) are relevant to assessing the LLP's state of affairs.

(6) Commitments within any of sub-paragraphs (1) to (5) which are undertaken on behalf of or for the benefit of—

(a) any parent undertaking or fellow subsidiary undertaking, or

(b) any subsidiary undertaking of the LLP,

must be stated separately from the other commitments within that sub-paragraph, and commitments within paragraph (a) must also be stated separately from those within paragraph (b).

Miscellaneous matters

56. Particulars must be given of any case where the purchase price or production cost of any asset is for the first time determined under paragraph 29.

Information supplementing the profit and loss account

57. Paragraphs 58 and 59 require information which either supplements the information given with respect to any particular items shown in the profit and loss account or otherwise provides particulars of income or expenditure of the LLP or of circumstances affecting the items shown in the profit and loss account (see regulation 3 for exemption for LLP falling within section 408 of the 2006 Act).

Particulars of turnover

58.—(1) If the LLP has supplied geographical markets outside the United Kingdom during the financial year in question, there must be stated the percentage of its turnover that, in the opinion of the members, is attributable to those markets.

(2) In analysing for the purposes of this paragraph the source of turnover, the members of the LLP must have regard to the manner in which the LLP's activities are organised.

Miscellaneous matters

59.—(1) Where any amount relating to any preceding financial year is included in any item in the profit and loss account, the effect must be stated.

(2) Particulars must be given of any extraordinary income or charges arising in the financial year.

(3) The effect must be stated of any transactions that are exceptional by virtue of size or incidence though they fall within the ordinary activities of the LLP.

Sums denominated in foreign currencies

60. Where sums originally denominated in foreign currencies have been brought into account under any items shown in the balance sheet or profit and loss account, the basis on which those sums have been translated into sterling (or the currency in which the accounts are drawn up) must be stated.

Dormant LLPs acting as agents

61. Where the members of an LLP take advantage of the exemption conferred by section 480 of the 2006 Act (dormant LLPs: exemption from audit), and the LLP has during the financial year in question acted as an agent for any person, the fact that it has so acted must be stated.

SCHEDULE 2

Regulation 4

INFORMATION ABOUT RELATED UNDERTAKINGS WHERE LLP NOT PREPARING GROUP
ACCOUNTS (NON-IAS OR IAS INDIVIDUAL ACCOUNTS)

Subsidiary undertakings

1.—(1) The following information must be given where at the end of the financial year the LLP
has subsidiary undertakings.

(2) The name of each subsidiary undertaking must be stated.

(3) There must be stated with respect to each subsidiary undertaking—

    (a) if it is incorporated outside the United Kingdom, the country in which it is incorporated,

    (b) if it is unincorporated, the address of its principal place of business.

Holdings in subsidiary undertakings

2.—(1) There must be stated in relation to shares of each class held by the LLP in a subsidiary
undertaking—

    (a) the identity of the class, and

    (b) the proportion of the nominal value of the shares of that class represented by those
shares.

(2) The shares held by or on behalf of the LLP itself must be distinguished from those attributed
to the LLP which are held by or on behalf of a subsidiary undertaking.

Financial information about subsidiary undertakings

3.—(1) There must be disclosed with respect to each subsidiary undertaking—

    (a) the aggregate amount of its capital and reserves as at the end of its relevant financial
year, and

    (b) its profit or loss for that year.

(2) That information need not be given if the LLP would (if it were not subject to the small LLP
regime) be exempt by virtue of section 400 or 401 of the 2006 Act (parent LLP included in accounts
of larger group) from the requirement to prepare group accounts.

(3) That information need not be given if the LLP's investment in the subsidiary undertaking is
included in the LLP's accounts by way of the equity method of valuation.

(4) That information need not be given if—

    (a) the subsidiary undertaking is not required by any provision of the 2006 Act to deliver a
copy of its balance sheet for its relevant financial year and does not otherwise publish that
balance sheet in the United Kingdom or elsewhere, and

    (b) the LLP's holding is less than 50% of the nominal value of the shares in the undertaking.

(5) Information otherwise required by this paragraph need not be given if it is not material.

(6) For the purposes of this paragraph the "relevant financial year" of a subsidiary undertaking
is—

    (a) if its financial year ends with that of the LLP, that year, and

    (b) if not, its financial year ending last before the end of the LLP's financial year.

Significant holdings in undertakings other than subsidiary undertakings

4.—(1) The information required by paragraphs 5 and 6 must be given where at the end of the financial year the LLP has a significant holding in an undertaking which is not a subsidiary undertaking of the LLP.

(2) A holding is significant for this purpose if—

    (a) it amounts to 20% or more of the nominal value of any class of shares in the undertaking, or

    (b) the amount of the holding (as stated or included in the LLP's accounts) exceeds 20% of the amount (as so stated) of the LLP's assets.

5.—(1) The name of the undertaking must be stated.

(2) There must be stated—

    (a) if the undertaking is incorporated outside the United Kingdom, the country in which it is incorporated,

    (b) if it is unincorporated, the address of its principal place of business.

(3) There must also be stated—

    (a) the identity of each class of shares in the undertaking held by the LLP, and

    (b) the proportion of the nominal value of the shares of that class represented by those shares.

6.—(1) There must also be stated—

    (a) the aggregate amount of the capital and reserves of the undertaking as at the end of its relevant financial year, and

    (b) its profit or loss for that year.

(2) That information need not be given if—

    (a) the LLP would (if it were not subject to the small LLP regime) be exempt by virtue of section 400 or 401 of the 2006 Act (parent LLP included in accounts of larger group) from the requirement to prepare group accounts, and

    (b) the investment of the LLP in all undertakings in which it has such a holding as is mentioned in sub-paragraph (1) is shown, in aggregate, in the notes to the accounts by way of the equity method of valuation.

(3) That information need not be given in respect of an undertaking if—

    (a) the undertaking is not required by any provision of the 2006 Act to deliver to the registrar a copy of its balance sheet for its relevant financial year and does not otherwise publish that balance sheet in the United Kingdom or elsewhere, and

    (b) the LLP's holding is less than 50% of the nominal value of the shares in the undertaking.

(4) Information otherwise required by this paragraph need not be given if it is not material.

(5) For the purposes of this paragraph the "relevant financial year" of an undertaking is—

    (a) if its financial year ends with that of the LLP, that year, and

    (b) if not, its financial year ending last before the end of the LLP's financial year.

Parent undertaking drawing up accounts for larger group

7.—(1) Where the LLP is a subsidiary undertaking, the following information must be given with respect to the parent undertaking of—

    (a) the largest group of undertakings for which group accounts are drawn up and of which the LLP is a member, and

    (b) the smallest such group of undertakings.

  (2) The name of the parent undertaking must be stated.

  (3) There must be stated—

    (a) if the undertaking is incorporated outside the United Kingdom, the country in which it is incorporated,

    (b) if it is unincorporated, the address of its principal place of business.

  (4) If copies of the group accounts referred to in sub-paragraph (1) are available to the public, there must also be stated the addresses from which copies of the accounts can be obtained.

Identification of ultimate parent

8.—(1) Where the LLP is a subsidiary undertaking, the following information must be given with respect to the body corporate (if any) regarded by the members as being the LLP's ultimate parent.

  (2) The name of that body corporate must be stated.

  (3) If that body corporate is incorporated outside the United Kingdom, the country in which it is incorporated must be stated (if known to the members).

Construction of references to shares held by LLP

9.—(1) References in this Part of this Schedule to shares held by an LLP are to be construed as follows.

  (2) For the purposes of paragraphs 2 and 3 (information about subsidiary undertakings)—

    (a) there must be attributed to the LLP any shares held by a subsidiary undertaking, or by a person acting on behalf of the LLP or a subsidiary undertaking; but

    (b) there must be treated as not held by the LLP any shares held on behalf of a person other than the LLP or a subsidiary undertaking.

  (3) For the purposes of paragraphs 4 to 6 (information about undertakings other than subsidiary undertakings)—

    (a) there must be attributed to the LLP shares held on its behalf by any person; but

    (b) there must be treated as not held by an LLP shares held on behalf of a person other than the LLP.

  (4) For the purposes of any of those provisions, shares held by way of security must be treated as held by the person providing the security—

    (a) where apart from the right to exercise them for the purpose of preserving the value of the security, or of realising it, the rights attached to the shares are exercisable only in accordance with his instructions, and

    (b) where the shares are held in connection with the granting of loans as part of normal business activities and apart from the right to exercise them for the purpose of preserving the value of the security, or of realising it, the rights attached to the shares are exercisable only in his interests.

SCHEDULE 3

Regulation 5

NON-IAS ABBREVIATED ACCOUNTS FOR DELIVERY TO REGISTRAR OF COMPANIES

PART 1

THE REQUIRED BALANCE SHEET FORMATS

1.—(1) An LLP may deliver to the registrar a copy of the balance sheet showing the items listed in either of the balance sheet formats set out below, in the order and under the headings and subheadings given in the format adopted, but in other respects corresponding to the full balance sheet.

(2) The copy balance sheet must contain in a prominent position a statement that it has been prepared in accordance with the provisions applicable to LLP subject to the small LLP regime.

Balance sheet formats

Format 1

A.   Fixed assets
      I.   Intangible assets
      II. Tangible assets
      III. Investments

B.   Current assets
      I.   Stocks
      II. *Debtors (1)*
      III. Investments
      IV. Cash at bank and in hand

C.   Prepayments and accrued income

D.   Creditors: amounts falling due within one year

E.   Net current assets (liabilities)

F.   Total assets less current liabilities

G.   Creditors: amounts falling due after more than one year

H.   Provisions for liabilities

I.   Accruals and deferred income

J.   Loans and other debts due to members

K.   Members' other interests
      I.   Members' capital
      II. Revaluation reserve
      III. Other reserves

Balance sheet formats

Format 2

ASSETS

A.   Fixed assets
      I.   Intangible assets
      II.   Tangible assets
      III. Investments

B.   Current assets
      I.   Stocks
      II.   *Debtors (1)*
      III. Investments
      IV.   Cash at bank and in hand

C.   Prepayments and accrued income

LIABILITIES

A.   Loans and other debts due to members

B.   Members' other interests
      I.   Members' capital
      II.   Revaluation reserve
      III. Other reserves

C.   Provisions for liabilities

D.   Creditors *(2)*

E.   Accruals and deferred income

Notes on the balance sheet formats

(1)   *Debtors*

(Formats 1 and 2, items B.II.)

The aggregate amount of debtors falling due after more than one year must be shown separately, unless it is disclosed in the notes to the accounts.

(2)   *Creditors*

(Format 2, Liabilities item D.)

The aggregate amount of creditors falling due within one year and of creditors falling due after more than one year must be shown separately, unless it is disclosed in the notes to the accounts.

PART 2
NOTES TO THE ACCOUNTS

Preliminary

2. Any information required in the case of any LLP by the following provisions of this Part of this Schedule must (if not given in the LLP's accounts) be given by way of a note to those accounts.

Disclosure of accounting policies

3. The accounting policies adopted by the LLP in determining the amounts to be included in respect of items shown in the balance sheet and in determining the profit or loss of the LLP must be stated (including such policies with respect to the depreciation and diminution in value of assets).

Information supplementing the balance sheet

Fixed assets

4.—(1) In respect of each item to which a letter or Roman number is assigned under the general item "fixed assets" in the LLP's balance sheet the following information must be given—

(a) the appropriate amounts in respect of that item as at the date of the beginning of the financial year and as at the balance sheet date respectively,

(b) the effect on any amount shown in the balance sheet in respect of that item of—

(i) any revision of the amount in respect of any assets included under that item made during that year on any basis mentioned in paragraph 32 of Schedule 1 to these Regulations,

(ii) acquisitions during that year of any assets,

(iii) disposals during that year of any assets, and

(iv) any transfers of assets of the LLP to and from that item during that year.

(2) The reference in sub-paragraph (I)(a) to the appropriate amounts in respect of any item as at any date there mentioned is a reference to amounts representing the aggregate amounts determined, as at that date, in respect of assets falling to be included under that item on either of the following bases, that is to say—

(a) on the basis of purchase price or production cost (determined in accordance with paragraphs 27 and 28 of Schedule 1 to these Regulations), or

(b) on any basis mentioned in paragraph 32 of that Schedule,
(leaving out of account in either case any provisions for depreciation or diminution in value).

(3) In respect of each item within sub-paragraph (1) there must also be stated—

(a) the cumulative amount of provisions for depreciation or diminution in value of assets included under that item as at each date mentioned in sub-paragraph (I)(a),

(b) the amount of any such provisions made in respect of the financial year,

(c) the amount of any adjustments made in respect of any such provisions during that year in consequence of the disposal of any assets, and

(d) the amount of any other adjustments made in respect of any such provisions during that year.

Financial fixed assets

5.—(1) This paragraph applies if—

(a) the LLP has financial fixed assets that could be included at fair value by virtue of paragraph 36 of Schedule 1 to these Regulations,

(b) the amount at which those items are included under any item in the LLP's accounts is in excess of their fair value, and

(c) the LLP has not made provision for diminution in value of those assets in accordance with paragraph 19(1) of that Schedule.

(2) There must be stated—

(a) the amount at which either the individual assets or appropriate groupings of those individual assets are included in the LLP's accounts,

(b) the fair value of those assets or groupings, and

(c) the reasons for not making a provision for diminution in value of those assets, including the nature of the evidence that provides the basis for the belief that the amount at which they are stated in the accounts will be recovered.

Details of indebtedness

6.—(1) For the aggregate of all items shown under "creditors" in the LLP's balance sheet there must be stated the aggregate of the following amounts—

(a) the amount of any debts included under "creditors" which are payable or repayable otherwise than by instalments and fall due for payment or repayment after the end of the period of five years beginning with the day next following the end of the financial year, and

(b) in the case of any debts so included which are payable or repayable by instalments, the amount of any instalments which fall due for payment after the end of that period.

(2) In respect of each item shown under "creditors" in the LLP's balance sheet there must be stated the aggregate amount of any debts included under that item in respect of which any security has been given by the LLP.

Sums denominated in foreign currencies

7. Where sums originally denominated in foreign currencies have been brought into account under any items shown in the balance sheet or profit and loss account, the basis on which those sums have been translated into sterling (or the currency in which the accounts are drawn up) must be stated.

Dormant LLPs acting as agents

8. Where the members of an LLP take advantage of the exemption conferred by section 480 of the 2006 Act (dormant LLPs: exemption from audit), and the LLP has during the financial year in question acted as an agent for any person, the fact that it has so acted must be stated.

SCHEDULE 4

GROUP ACCOUNTS

Regulations 6 and 7

PART 1

FORM AND CONTENT OF NON-IAS GROUP ACCOUNTS

General rules

1.—(1) Subject to sub-paragraphs (1) and (2), group accounts must comply so far as practicable with the provisions of Schedule 1 to these Regulations (non-IAS individual accounts) as if the undertakings included in the consolidation ("the group") were a single LLP.

(2) For item A.III in each balance sheet format set out in that Schedule substitute—

"A. III. Investments
1. Shares in group undertakings
2. Interests in associated undertakings
3. Other participating interests
4. Loans to group undertakings and undertakings in which a participating interest is held
5. Other investments other than loans
6. Others".

(3) In the profit and loss account formats replace the items headed "Income from participating interests", that is—

(a) in Format 1, item 8, and

(b) in Format 2, item 10,

by two items: "Income from interests in associated undertakings" and "Income from other participating interests".

2.—(1) The consolidated balance sheet and profit and loss account must incorporate in full the information contained in the individual accounts of the undertakings included in the consolidation, subject to the adjustments authorised or required by the following provisions of this Schedule and to such other adjustments (if any) as may be appropriate in accordance with generally accepted accounting principles or practice.

(2) If the financial year of a subsidiary undertaking included in the consolidation does not end with that of the parent LLP, the group accounts must be made up—

(a) from the accounts of the subsidiary undertaking for its financial year last ending before the end of the parent LLP's financial year, provided that year ended no more than three months before that of the parent LLP, or

(b) from interim accounts prepared by the subsidiary undertaking as at the end of the parent LLP's financial year.

3.—(1) Where assets and liabilities to be included in the group accounts have been valued or otherwise determined by undertakings according to accounting rules differing from those used for the group accounts, the values or amounts must be adjusted so as to accord with the rules used for the group accounts.

(2) If it appears to the members of the parent LLP that there are special reasons for departing from sub-paragraph (1) they may do so, but particulars of any such departure, the reasons for it and its effect must be given in a note to the accounts.

(3) The adjustments referred to in this paragraph need not be made if they are not material for the purpose of giving a true and fair view.

4. Any differences of accounting rules as between a parent LLP's individual accounts for a financial year and its group accounts must be disclosed in a note to the latter accounts and the reasons for the difference given.

5. Amounts that in the particular context of any provision of this Schedule are not material may be disregarded for the purposes of that provision.

Elimination of group transactions

6.—(1) Debts and claims between undertakings included in the consolidation, and income and expenditure relating to transactions between such undertakings, must be eliminated in preparing the group accounts.

(2) Where profits and losses resulting from transactions between undertakings included in the consolidation are included in the book value of assets, they must be eliminated in preparing the group accounts.

(3) The elimination required by sub-paragraph (2) may be effected in proportion to the group's interest in the shares of the undertakings.

(4) Sub-paragraphs (1) and (2) need not be complied with if the amounts concerned are not material for the purpose of giving a true and fair view.

Acquisition and merger accounting

7.—(1) The following provisions apply where an undertaking becomes a subsidiary undertaking of the parent LLP.

(2) That event is referred to in those provisions as an "acquisition", and references to the "undertaking acquired" are to be construed accordingly.

8. An acquisition must be accounted for by the acquisition method of accounting unless the conditions for accounting for it as a merger are met and the merger method of accounting is adopted.

9.—(1) The acquisition method of accounting is as follows.

(2) The identifiable assets and liabilities of the undertaking acquired must be included in the consolidated balance sheet at their fair values as at the date of acquisition.

(3) The income and expenditure of the undertaking acquired must be brought into the group accounts only as from the date of the acquisition.

(4) There must be set off against the acquisition cost of the interest in the shares of the undertaking held by the parent LLP and its subsidiary undertakings the interest of the parent LLP and its subsidiary undertakings in the adjusted capital and reserves of the undertaking acquired.

(5) The resulting amount if positive must be treated as goodwill, and if negative as a negative consolidation difference.

10. The conditions for accounting for an acquisition as a merger are that adoption of the merger method of accounting accords with generally accepted accounting principles or practice.

11.—(1) Where an LLP adopts the merger method of accounting, it must comply with this paragraph, and with generally accepted accounting principles or practice.

(2) The assets and liabilities of the undertaking acquired must be brought into the group accounts at the figures at which they stand in the undertaking's accounts, subject to any adjustment authorised or required by this Schedule.

(3) The income and expenditure of the undertaking acquired must be included in the group accounts for the entire financial year, including the period before the acquisition.

(4) The group accounts must show corresponding amounts relating to the previous financial year as if the undertaking acquired had been included in the consolidation throughout that year.

12.—(1) Where a group is acquired, paragraphs 9 to 11 apply with the following adaptations.

(2) References to shares of the undertaking acquired are to be construed as references to shares of the parent undertaking of the group.

(3) Other references to the undertaking acquired are to be construed as references to the group; and references to the assets and liabilities, income and expenditure and capital and reserves of the undertaking acquired must be construed as references to the assets and liabilities, income and expenditure and capital and reserves of the group after making the set-offs and other adjustments required by this Schedule in the case of group accounts.

13.—(1) The following information with respect to acquisitions taking place in the financial year must be given in a note to the accounts.

(2) There must be stated—

(a) the name of the undertaking acquired or, where a group was acquired, the name of the parent undertaking of that group, and

(b) whether the acquisition has been accounted for by the acquisition or the merger method of accounting;

and in relation to an acquisition which significantly affects the figures shown in the group accounts, the following further information must be given.

(3) The composition and fair value of the consideration for the acquisition given by the parent LLP and its subsidiary undertakings must be stated.

(4) Where the acquisition method of accounting has been adopted, the book values immediately prior to the acquisition, and the fair values at the date of acquisition, of each class of assets and liabilities of the undertaking or group acquired must be stated in tabular form, including a statement of the amount of any goodwill or negative consolidation difference arising on the acquisition, together with an explanation of any significant adjustments made.

(5) In ascertaining for the purposes of sub-paragraph (4) the profit or loss of a group, the book values and fair values of assets and liabilities of a group or the amount of the assets and liabilities of a group, the set-offs and other adjustments required by this Schedule in the case of group accounts must be made.

14.—(1) There must also be stated in a note to the accounts the cumulative amount of goodwill resulting from acquisitions in that and earlier financial years which has been written off otherwise than in the consolidated profit and loss account for that or any earlier financial year.

(2) That figure must be shown net of any goodwill attributable to subsidiary undertakings or businesses disposed of prior to the balance sheet date.

15. Where during the financial year there has been a disposal of an undertaking or group which significantly affects the figures shown in the group accounts, there must be stated in a note to the accounts—

(a) the name of that undertaking or, as the case may be, of the parent undertaking of that group, and

(b) the extent to which the profit or loss shown in the group accounts is attributable to profit or loss of that undertaking or group.

16. The information required by paragraph 13, 14 or 15 need not be disclosed with respect to an undertaking which—

    (a)   is established under the law of a country outside the United Kingdom, or

    (b)   carries on business outside the United Kingdom,

if in the opinion of the members of the parent LLP the disclosure would be seriously prejudicial to the business of that undertaking or to the business of the parent LLP or any of its subsidiary undertakings and the Secretary of State agrees that the information should not be disclosed.

Minority interests

17.—(1) The formats set out in Schedule 1 to these Regulations have effect in relation to group accounts with the following additions.

(2) In the Balance Sheet Formats there must be shown, as a separate item and under an appropriate heading, the amount of capital and reserves attributable to shares in subsidiary undertakings included in the consolidation held by or on behalf of persons other than the parent LLP and its subsidiary undertakings.

(3) In the Profit and Loss Account Formats there must be shown, as a separate item and under an appropriate heading—

    (a)   the amount of any profit or loss on ordinary activities, and

    (b)   the amount of any profit or loss on extraordinary activities,

attributable to shares in subsidiary undertakings included in the consolidation held by or on behalf of persons other than the parent LLP and its subsidiary undertakings.

(4) For the purposes of paragraph 4 of Schedule 1 (power to adapt or combine items)—

    (a)   the additional item required by sub-paragraph (2) above is treated as one to which a letter is assigned, and

    (b)   the additional items required by sub-paragraph (3)(a) and (b) above are treated as ones to which an Arabic number is assigned.

Joint ventures

18.—(1) Where an undertaking included in the consolidation manages another undertaking jointly with one or more undertakings not included in the consolidation, that other undertaking ("the joint venture") may, if it is not—

    (a)   a body corporate, or

    (b)   a subsidiary undertaking of the parent LLP,

be dealt with in the group accounts by the method of proportional consolidation.

(2) The provisions of this Schedule relating to the preparation of consolidated accounts apply, with any necessary modifications, to proportional consolidation under this paragraph.

Associated undertakings

19.—(1) An "associated undertaking" means an undertaking in which an undertaking included in the consolidation has a participating interest and over whose operating and financial policy it exercises a significant influence, and which is not—

    (a)   a subsidiary undertaking of the parent LLP, or

    (b)   a joint venture dealt with in accordance with paragraph 18.

(2) Where an undertaking holds 20% or more of the voting rights in another undertaking, it is presumed to exercise such an influence over it unless the contrary is shown.

(3) The voting rights in an undertaking means the rights conferred on shareholders in respect of their shares or, in the case of an undertaking not having a share capital, on members, to vote at general meetings of the undertaking on all, or substantially all, matters.

(4) The provisions of paragraphs 5 to 11 of Schedule 7 to the 2006 Act (parent and subsidiary undertakings: rights to be taken into account and attribution of rights) apply in determining for the purposes of this paragraph whether an undertaking holds 20% or more of the voting rights in another undertaking.

20.—(1) The interest of an undertaking in an associated undertaking, and the amount of profit or loss attributable to such an interest, must be shown by the equity method of accounting (including dealing with any goodwill arising in accordance with paragraphs 17 to 20 and 22 of Schedule 1 to these Regulations).

(2) Where the associated undertaking is itself a parent undertaking, the net assets and profits or losses to be taken into account are those of the parent and its subsidiary undertakings (after making any consolidation adjustments).

(3) The equity method of accounting need not be applied if the amounts in question are not material for the purpose of giving a true and fair view.

PART 2

INFORMATION ABOUT RELATED UNDERTAKINGS WHERE LLP PREPARING GROUP ACCOUNTS (NON-IAS OR IAS GROUP ACCOUNTS)

Introduction and interpretation

21. In this Part of this Schedule "the group" means the group consisting of the parent LLP and its subsidiary undertakings.

Subsidiary undertakings

22.—(1) The following information must be given with respect to the undertakings that are subsidiary undertakings of the parent LLP at the end of the financial year.

(2) The name of each undertaking must be stated.

(3) There must be stated—

(a) if the undertaking is incorporated outside the United Kingdom, the country in which it is incorporated,

(b) if it is unincorporated, the address of its principal place of business.

(4) It must also be stated whether the subsidiary undertaking is included in the consolidation and, if it is not, the reasons for excluding it from consolidation must be given.

(5) It must be stated with respect to each subsidiary undertaking by virtue of which of the conditions specified in section 1162(2) or (4) of the 2006 Act it is a subsidiary undertaking of its immediate parent undertaking.

That information need not be given if the relevant condition is that specified in subsection (2)(a) of that section (holding of a majority of the voting rights) and the immediate parent undertaking holds the same proportion of the shares in the undertaking as it holds voting rights.

Holdings in subsidiary undertakings

23.—(1) The following information must be given with respect to the shares of a subsidiary undertaking held—

(a) by the parent LLP, and

(b) by the group,

and the information under paragraphs (a) and (b) must (if different) be shown separately.

(2) There must be stated—

(a) the identity of each class of shares held, and

(b) the proportion of the nominal value of the shares of that class represented by those shares.

Financial information about subsidiary undertakings not included in the consolidation

24.—(1) There must be shown with respect to each subsidiary undertaking not included in the consolidation—

(a) the aggregate amount of its capital and reserves as at the end of its relevant financial year, and

(b) its profit or loss for that year.

(2) That information need not be given if the group's investment in the undertaking is included in the accounts by way of the equity method of valuation or if—

(a) the undertaking is not required by any provision of the 2006 Act to deliver a copy of its balance sheet for its relevant financial year and does not otherwise publish that balance sheet in the United Kingdom or elsewhere, and

(b) the holding of the group is less than 50% of the nominal value of the shares in the undertaking.

(3) Information otherwise required by this paragraph need not be given if it is not material.

(4) For the purposes of this paragraph the "relevant financial year" of a subsidiary undertaking is—

(a) if its financial year ends with that of the LLP, that year, and

(b) if not, its financial year ending last before the end of the LLP's financial year.

Joint ventures

25.—(1) The following information must be given where an undertaking is dealt with in the consolidated accounts by the method of proportional consolidation in accordance with paragraph 18 of this Schedule (joint ventures)—

(a) the name of the undertaking,

(b) the address of the principal place of business of the undertaking,

(c) the factors on which joint management of the undertaking is based, and

(d) the proportion of the capital of the undertaking held by undertakings included in the consolidation.

(2) Where the financial year of the undertaking did not end with that of the LLP, there must be stated the date on which a financial year of the undertaking last ended before that date.

Associated undertakings

26.—(1) The following information must be given where an undertaking included in the consolidation has an interest in an associated undertaking.

(2) The name of the associated undertaking must be stated.

(3) There must be stated—

    (a) if the undertaking is incorporated outside the United Kingdom, the country in which it is incorporated,

    (b) if it is unincorporated, the address of its principal place of business.

(4) The following information must be given with respect to the shares of the undertaking held—

    (a) by the parent LLP, and

    (b) by the group,

and the information under paragraphs (a) and (b) must be shown separately.

(5) There must be stated—

    (a) the identity of each class of shares held, and

    (b) the proportion of the nominal value of the shares of that class represented by those shares.

(6) In this paragraph "associated undertaking" has the meaning given by paragraph 19 of this Schedule; and the information required by this paragraph must be given notwithstanding that paragraph 20(3) of this Schedule (materiality) applies in relation to the accounts themselves.

Other significant holdings of parent LLP or group

27.—(1) The information required by paragraphs 28 and 29 must be given where at the end of the financial year the parent LLP has a significant holding in an undertaking which is not one of its subsidiary undertakings and does not fall within paragraph 25 (joint ventures) or paragraph 26 (associated undertakings).

(2) A holding is significant for this purpose if—

    (a) it amounts to 20% or more of the nominal value of any class of shares in the undertaking, or

    (b) the amount of the holding (as stated or included in the LLP's individual accounts) exceeds 20% of the amount of its assets (as so stated).

28.—(1) The name of the undertaking must be stated.

(2) There must be stated—

    (a) if the undertaking is incorporated outside the United Kingdom, the country in which it is incorporated,

    (b) if it is unincorporated, the address of its principal place of business.

(3) The following information must be given with respect to the shares of the undertaking held by the parent LLP.

(4) There must be stated—

    (a) the identity of each class of shares held, and

    (b) the proportion of the nominal value of the shares of that class represented by those shares.

29.—(1) There must also be stated—

    (a) the aggregate amount of the capital and reserves of the undertaking as at the end of its relevant financial year, and

    (b) its profit or loss for that year.

(2) That information need not be given in respect of an undertaking if—

    (a) the undertaking is not required by any provision of the 2006 Act to deliver a copy of its balance sheet for its relevant financial year and does not otherwise publish that balance sheet in the United Kingdom or elsewhere, and

    (b) the LLP's holding is less than 50% of the nominal value of the shares in the undertaking.

(3) Information otherwise required by this paragraph need not be given if it is not material.

(4) For the purposes of this paragraph the "relevant financial year" of an undertaking is—

    (a) if its financial year ends with that of the LLP, that year, and

    (b) if not, its financial year ending last before the end of the LLP's financial year.

30.—(1) The information required by paragraphs 31 and 32 must be given where at the end of the financial year the group has a significant holding in an undertaking which is not a subsidiary undertaking of the parent LLP and does not fall within paragraph 25 (joint ventures) or paragraph 26 (associated undertakings).

(2) A holding is significant for this purpose if—

    (a) it amounts to 20% or more of the nominal value of any class of shares in the undertaking, or

    (b) the amount of the holding (as stated or included in the group accounts) exceeds 20% of the amount of the group's assets (as so stated).

31.—(1) The name of the undertaking must be stated.

(2) There must be stated—

    (a) if the undertaking is incorporated outside the United Kingdom, the country in which it is incorporated,

    (b) if it is unincorporated, the address of its principal place of business.

(3) The following information must be given with respect to the shares of the undertaking held by the group.

(4) There must be stated—

    (a) the identity of each class of shares held, and

    (b) the proportion of the nominal value of the shares of that class represented by those shares.

32.—(1) There must also be stated—

    (a) the aggregate amount of the capital and reserves of the undertaking as at the end of its relevant financial year, and

    (b) its profit or loss for that year.

(2) That information need not be given if—

    (a) the undertaking is not required by any provision of the 2006 Act to deliver a copy of its balance sheet for its relevant financial year and does not otherwise publish that balance sheet in the United Kingdom or elsewhere, and

    (b) the holding of the group is less than 50% of the nominal value of the shares in the undertaking.

(3) Information otherwise required by this paragraph need not be given if it is not material.

(4) For the purposes of this paragraph the "relevant financial year" of an outside undertaking is—

    (a) if its financial year ends with that of the parent LLP, that year, and

    (b) if not, its financial year ending last before the end of the parent LLP's financial year.

Parent undertaking drawing up accounts for larger group

33.—(1) Where the parent LLP is itself a subsidiary undertaking, the following information must be given with respect to that parent undertaking of the LLP which heads—

    (a) the largest group of undertakings for which group accounts are drawn up and of which that LLP is a member, and

    (b) the smallest such group of undertakings.

(2) The name of the parent undertaking must be stated.

(3) There must be stated—

    (a) if the undertaking is incorporated outside the United Kingdom, the country in which it is incorporated,

    (b) if it is unincorporated, the address of its principal place of business.

(4) If copies of the group accounts referred to in sub-paragraph (1) are available to the public, there must also be stated the addresses from which copies of the accounts can be obtained.

Identification of ultimate parent

34.—(1) Where the parent LLP is itself a subsidiary undertaking, the following information must be given with respect to the body corporate (if any) regarded by the members as being that LLP's ultimate parent.

(2) The name of that body corporate must be stated.

(3) If that body corporate is incorporated outside the United Kingdom, the country in which it is incorporated must be stated (if known to the members).

Construction of references to shares held by parent LLP or group

35.—(1) References in this Part of this Schedule to shares held by the parent LLP or the group are to be construed as follows.

(2) For the purposes of paragraphs 23, 26(4) and (5) and 27 to 29 (information about holdings in subsidiary and other undertakings)—

    (a) there must be attributed to the parent LLP shares held on its behalf by any person; but

    (b) there must be treated as not held by the parent LLP shares held on behalf of a person other than the LLP.

(3) References to shares held by the group are to any shares held by or on behalf of the parent LLP or any of its subsidiary undertakings; but any shares held on behalf of a person other than the parent LLP or any of its subsidiary undertakings are not to be treated as held by the group.

(4) Shares held by way of security must be treated as held by the person providing the security—

    (a) where apart from the right to exercise them for the purpose of preserving the value of the security, or of realising it, the rights attached to the shares are exercisable only in accordance with his instructions, and

    (b) where the shares are held in connection with the granting of loans as part of normal business activities and apart from the right to exercise them for the purpose of preserving the value of the security, or of realising it, the rights attached to the shares are exercisable only in his interests.

SCHEDULE 5

Regulation 8

GENERAL INTERPRETATION

Financial instruments

1. References to "derivatives" include commodity-based contracts that give either contracting party the right to settle in cash or in some other financial instrument, except where such contracts—

    (a) were entered into for the purpose of, and continue to meet, the LLP's expected purchase, sale or usage requirements,

    (b) were designated for such purpose at their inception, and

    (c) are expected to be settled by delivery of the commodity.

2.—(1) The expressions listed in sub-paragraph (2) have the same meaning as they have in Council Directive 78/660/EEC on the annual accounts of certain types of companies**(a)**.

(2) Those expressions are "available for sale financial asset", "business combination", "commodity-based contracts", "derivative", "equity instrument", "exchange difference", "fair value hedge accounting system", "financial fixed asset", "financial instrument", "foreign entity", "hedge accounting", "hedge accounting system", "hedged items", "hedging instrument", "held for trading purposes", "held to maturity", "monetary item", "receivables", "reliable market" and "trading portfolio".

Fixed and current assets

3. "Fixed assets" means assets of an LLP which are intended for use on a continuing basis in the LLP's activities, and "current assets" means assets not intended for such use.

Historical cost accounting rules

4. References to the historical cost accounting rules are to be read in accordance with paragraph 30 of Schedule 1 to these Regulations.

Listed investments

5.—(1) "Listed investment" means an investment as respects which there has been granted a listing on—

    (a) a recognised investment exchange other than an overseas investment exchange, or

    (b) a stock exchange of repute outside the United Kingdom.

(2) "Recognised investment exchange" and "overseas investment exchange" have the meaning given in Part 18 of the Financial Services and Markets Act 2000**(b)**.

Loans

6. A loan is treated as falling due for repayment, and an instalment of a loan is treated as falling due for payment, on the earliest date on which the lender could require repayment or (as the case may be) payment, if he exercised all options and rights available to him.

(a) O.J. L222 of 14.8.1978, page 11, as amended in particular by Directives 2001/65/EEC, 2003/51/EEC and 2006/46/EEC of the European Parliament and of the Council (O.J. L238 of 27.12.2001, page 28, O.J. L178 of 17.7.2003, page 16 and O.J. L224 of 16.8.2006, page 1).
(b) 2000 c.8.

Materiality

7. Amounts which in the particular context of any provision of Schedule 1 to these Regulations are not material may be disregarded for the purposes of that provision.

Participating interests

8.—(1) A "participating interest" means an interest held by an undertaking in the shares of another undertaking which it holds on a long-term basis for the purpose of securing a contribution to its activities by the exercise of control or influence arising from or related to that interest.

(2) A holding of 20% or more of the shares of the undertaking is to be presumed to be a participating interest unless the contrary is shown.

(3) The reference in sub-paragraph (1) to an interest in shares includes—

    (a) an interest which is convertible into an interest in shares, and

    (b) an option to acquire shares or any such interest,

and an interest or option falls within paragraph (a) or (b) notwithstanding that the shares to which it relates are, until the conversion or the exercise of the option, unissued.

(4) For the purposes of this paragraph an interest held on behalf of an undertaking is to be treated as held by it.

(5) In the balance sheet and profit and loss formats set out in Part 1 of Schedule 1 and Part 1 of Schedule 3 to these Regulations, "participating interest" does not include an interest in a group undertaking.

(6) For the purpose of this paragraph as it applies in relation to the expression "participating interest"—

    (a) in those formats as they apply in relation to group accounts, and

    (b) in paragraph 19 of Schedule 4 (group accounts: undertakings to be accounted for as associated undertakings),

the references in sub-paragraphs (1) to (4) to the interest held by, and the purposes and activities of, the undertaking concerned are to be construed as references to the interest held by, and the purposes and activities of, the group (within the meaning of paragraph 1 of that Schedule).

Provisions

9.—(1) References to provisions for depreciation or diminution in value of assets are to any amount written off by way of providing for depreciation or diminution in value of assets.

(2) Any reference in the profit and loss account formats set out in Part 1 of Schedule 1 to these Regulations to the depreciation of, or amounts written off, assets of any description is to any provision for depreciation or diminution in value of assets of that description.

10. References to provisions for liabilities are to any amount retained as reasonably necessary for the purpose of providing for any liability the nature of which is clearly defined and which is either likely to be incurred, or certain to be incurred but uncertain as to amount or as to the date on which it will arise.

Purchase price

11. "Purchase price", in relation to an asset of an LLP or any raw materials or consumables used in the production of such an asset, includes any consideration (whether in cash or otherwise) given by the LLP in respect of that asset or those materials or consumables, as the case may be.

Staff costs

12.—(1) "Social security costs" means any contributions by the LLP to any state social security or pension scheme, fund or arrangement.

(2) "Pension costs" includes—

    (a) any costs incurred by the LLP in respect of any pension scheme established for the purpose of providing pensions for persons currently or formerly employed by the LLP,

    (b) any sums set aside for the future payment of pensions directly by the LLP to current or former employees, and

    (c) any pensions paid directly to such persons without having first been set aside.

(3) Any amount stated in respect of the item "social security costs" or in respect of the item "wages and salaries" in the LLP's profit and loss account must be determined by reference to payments made or costs incurred in respect of all persons employed by the LLP during the financial year under contracts of service.

EXPLANATORY NOTE

(This note is not part of the Regulations)

These Regulations specify the form and content of the accounts of limited liability partnerships (LLPs) subject to the small LLPs regime under Part 15 of the Companies Act 2006 (c.46) ("the 2006 Act") as applied to LLPs with modifications by the Limited Liability Partnerships (Accounts and Audit) (Application of Companies Act 2006) Regulations 2008 (S.I. 2008/1911). They do so by applying to LLPs, with modifications, provisions of the Small Companies and Groups (Accounts and Directors' Report) Regulations 2008 (S.I. 2008/409).

Section 381 of the 2006 Act as applied to LLPs defines what is meant by "small LLPs regime". The accounts of large and medium-sized LLPs are dealt with separately in the Large and Medium-sized Limited Liability Partnerships (Accounts) Regulations 2008 (S.I. 2008/1913).

The Regulations replace provisions previously contained in the Schedules to Part 7 of the Companies Act 1985 (c.6) ("the 1985 Act") and in the Schedules to Part 8 of the Companies (Northern Ireland) Order 1986 (S.I. 1986/1032 (N.I. 6)) ("the 1986 Order") as applied to LLPs with modifications by the Limited Liability Partnerships Regulations 2001 (S.I. 2001/1090) and the Limited Liability Partnerships Regulations (Northern Ireland) 2004 (SR (NI) 2004/307). The Regulations extend to the whole of the United Kingdom, reflecting the extent of the 2006 Act.

The Regulations come into force on 1st October 2008, and apply to financial years beginning on or after that date (regulation 2). The corresponding provisions of the 1985 Act or the 1986 Order as applied to LLPs with modifications continue to apply to accounts for financial years beginning before that date.

Regulation 3 of, and Schedule 1 to, the Regulations specify the form and content of the individual accounts of an LLP which is subject to the small LLPs regime and the members of which are preparing non-IAS individual accounts (as defined in section 395 of the 2006 Act as applied to LLPs). Schedule 1 re-enacts Schedule 8 to the 1985 Act and Schedule 8 to the 1986 Order as applied to LLPs, with one substantive modification. Paragraph 36(4) of Schedule 1 gives LLPs the option of including financial instruments in the accounts at a fair value provided that they may be so included under international accounting standards adopted under the IAS Regulation (as defined in section 474(1) of the 2006 Act as applied to LLPs) on or before 5th September 2006, and provided that the disclosures required by such standards are made.

Regulation 4 of, and Schedule 2 to, the Regulations re-enact the requirements of Part 1 of Schedule 5 to the 1985 Act and Part 1 of Schedule 5 to the 1986 Order for small LLPs. They concern information about related undertakings which must be provided in the notes to an LLP's individual accounts, whether they are non-IAS accounts or IAS accounts.

Regulation 5 of, and Schedule 3 to, the Regulations make provision about non-IAS individual accounts which may be delivered to the registrar of companies for a small LLP under section 444 of the 2006 Act as applied to LLPs. Schedule 3 re-enacts Schedule 8A to the 1985 Act and Schedule 8A to the 1986 Order as applied to LLPs.

Regulation 6 of, and Part 1 of Schedule 4 to, the Regulations specify the form and content of non- IAS group accounts which a parent LLP subject to the small LLPs regime may choose to prepare, although not required to do so (see section 398 of the 2006 Act as applied to LLPs). Part 1 of Schedule 4 re-enacts Schedule 4A to the 1985 Act and Schedule 4A to the 1986 Order as they apply to small LLPs, save that paragraphs 9, 13 and 17 have been simplified to facilitate convergence with international accounting standards.

Regulation 7 of, and Part 2 of Schedule 4 to, the Regulations concern information about related undertakings which must be included in the notes to IAS and non-IAS group accounts which the directors of a small parent LLP choose to prepare. Part 2 of Schedule 4 re-enacts Part 2 of Schedule 5 to the 1985 Act and Part 2 of Schedule 5 to the 1986 Order as applied to LLPs.

Regulation 8 of, and Schedule 5 to, the Regulations contain general interpretation provisions.

An Impact Assessment of the effect that these Regulations will have on the costs of business, charities or voluntary bodies has been prepared and is available from the Department for Business, Enterprise and Regulatory Reform, Corporate Law and Governance Directorate, 1 Victoria Street, London SW1H OET. It is also available electronically at http://www.berr.gov.uk/bbf/llp/page39897.html. Copies have also been placed in the libraries of both Houses of Parliament.

Appendix D Large and Medium-sized Limited Liability Partnerships (Accounts) Regulations 2008 (SI 2008/1913)

This appendix reproduces in full SI 2008/1913 *Large and Medium-sized Limited Liability Partnerships (Accounts) Regulations* 2008. It is also available at: www.legislation.gov.uk/uksi/2008/1913/contents/made

In summary, as set out in the Contents below, the statutory instrument comprises:

Part 1 Introduction

Part 2 Form and content of accounts

Part 3 Interpretation

Schedule 1 – Non-IAS individual accounts

Schedule 2 – Information on related undertakings required whether preparing non-IAS or IAS accounts

Schedule 3 – Non-IAS group accounts

Schedule 4 – General interpretation

S T A T U T O R Y   I N S T R U M E N T S

2008 No. 1913

LIMITED LIABILITY PARTNERSHIPS

The Large and Medium-sized Limited Liability Partnerships
(Accounts) Regulations 2008

Made - - - -	*17th July 2008*
Coming into force - -	*1st October 2008*

CONTENTS

PART 1

INTRODUCTION

PART 2

FORM AND CONTENT OF ACCOUNTS

PART 3

INTERPRETATION

The Secretary of State makes the following Regulations in exercise of the powers conferred by sections 15 and 17 of the Limited Liability Partnerships Act 2000(**a**).

In accordance with section 17(4) and (5)(b) of the Limited Liability Partnerships Act 2000 a draft of this instrument was laid before Parliament and approved by a resolution of each House of Parliament.

PART 1

INTRODUCTION

Citation and interpretation

1.—(1) These Regulations may be cited as the Large and Medium-sized Limited Liability Partnerships (Accounts) Regulations 2008.

(2) In these Regulations—

"the 2006 Act" means the Companies Act 2006(**b**);

"the Large and Medium-sized Companies Accounts Regulations" means the Large and Medium-sized Companies and Groups (Accounts and Reports) Regulations 2008(**c**);

"LLP" means a limited liability partnership formed under the Limited Liability Partnerships Act 2000 or the Limited Liability Partnerships Act (N.I.) 2002(**d**).

(3)   Any reference in these Regulations to a numbered Part or section of the 2006 Act is a reference to that Part or section as applied to LLPs by the Limited Liability Partnerships (Accounts and Audit) (Application of Companies Act 2006) Regulations 2008(**e**).

Commencement and application

2.—(1) These Regulations come into force on 1st October 2008.

(2) They apply in relation to financial years beginning on or after 1st October 2008.

(3) They apply to LLPs, with modifications, provisions of the Large and Medium-sized Companies Accounts Regulations.

(4) They do not apply to LLPs which are subject to the small LLPs regime under Part 15 of the 2006 Act.

(**a**) 2000 c. 12.
(**b**) 2006 c.46.
(**c**) S.I. 2008/410.
(**d**) 2002 (N.I.) (c. 12).
(**e**) S.I. 2008/1911.

PART 2

FORM AND CONTENT OF ACCOUNTS

Non-IAS individual accounts

3.—(1) Regulation 3 of the Large and Medium-sized Companies Accounts Regulations applies to LLPs, modified so that it reads as follows—

"Non-IAS individual accounts

3.—(1) Subject to regulation 4, non-IAS individual accounts under section 396 of the 2006 Act (non-IAS individual accounts) must comply with the provisions of Schedule 1 to the Large and Medium-sized Limited Liability Partnerships (Accounts) Regulations 2008(a) as to the form and content of the balance sheet and profit and loss account, and additional information to be provided by way of notes to the accounts.

(2) The profit and loss account of an LLP that falls within section 408 of the 2006 Act (individual profit and loss account where group accounts prepared)(b) need not contain the information specified in paragraphs 62 to 67 of Schedule 1 to the Large and Medium-sized Limited Liability Partnerships (Accounts) Regulations 2008 (information supplementing the profit and loss account)."

(2) The provisions of Schedule 1 to the Large and Medium-sized Companies Accounts Regulations apply to LLPs, modified so that they are the provisions set out in Schedule 1 to these Regulations.

Medium-sized LLPs: exemptions for non-IAS individual accounts

4. Regulation 4 of the Large and Medium-sized Companies Accounts Regulations applies to LLPs, modified so that it reads as follows—

"Medium-sized LLPs: exemptions for non-IAS individual accounts

4.—(1) This regulation applies to an LLP—

(a) which qualifies as medium-sized in relation to a financial year under section 465 of the 2006 Act(c), and

(b) the members of which are preparing non-IAS individual accounts under section 396 of that Act for that year.

(2) The individual accounts for the year need not comply with the following provisions of Schedule 1 to the Large and Medium-sized Limited Liability Partnerships (Accounts) Regulations 2008—

(a) paragraph 45 (disclosure with respect to compliance with accounting standards), and

(b) paragraph 70 (related party transactions).

(3) The members of the LLP may deliver to the registrar of companies a copy of the accounts for the year—

(a) which includes a profit and loss account in which the following items listed in the profit and loss account formats set out in Schedule 1 to the Large and Medium- sized Limited Liability Partnerships (Accounts) Regulations 2008 are combined as one item—

items 2, 3 and 6 in format 1;

(a) S.I. 2008/1913.
(b) Section 408 is amended by regulation 10 of S.I. 2008/393.
(c) Section 465 is amended by regulation 4(1) of S.I. 2008/393.

items 2 to 5 in format 2;

(b) which does not contain the information required by paragraph 65 of Schedule 1 to those Regulations (particulars of turnover)."

Information about related undertakings (non-IAS or IAS individual or group accounts)

5.—(1) Regulation 7 of the Large and Medium-sized Companies Accounts Regulations applies to LLPs, modified so that it reads as follows—

"Information about related undertakings (non-IAS or IAS individual or group accounts

7.—(1) Non-IAS or IAS individual or group accounts must comply with the provisions of Schedule 2 to the Large and Medium-sized Limited Liability Partnerships (Accounts) Regulations 2008 as to information about related undertakings to be given in notes to the LLP's accounts.

(2) In Schedule 2 to the Large and Medium-sized Limited Liability Partnerships (Accounts) Regulations 2008—

Part 1 contains provisions applying to all LLPs

Part 2 contains provisions applying only to LLPs not required to prepare group accounts

Part 3 contains provisions applying only to LLPs required to prepare group accounts.

(3) Information otherwise required to be given by Schedule 2 need not be disclosed with respect to an undertaking that—

(a) is established under the law of a country outside the United Kingdom, or

(b) carries on business outside the United Kingdom,

if the conditions specified in section 409(4) of the 2006 Act are met (see section 409(5) of the 2006 Act for disclosure required where advantage taken of this exemption)."

(2) The provisions of Schedule 4 to the Large and Medium-sized Companies Accounts Regulations apply to LLPs, modified so that they are the provisions set out in Schedule 2 to these Regulations.

Non-IAS group accounts

6.—(1) Regulation 9 of the Large and Medium-sized Companies Accounts Regulations applies to LLPs, modified so that it reads as follows—

"Non-IAS group accounts

9. Where the members of a parent LLP prepare non-IAS group accounts under section 403 of the 2006 Act (group accounts: applicable accounting framework), those accounts must comply with the provisions of Schedule 3 to the Large and Medium-sized Limited Liability Partnerships (Accounts) Regulations 2008 as to the form and content of the consolidated balance sheet and consolidated profit and loss account, and additional information to be provided by way of notes to the accounts."

(2) The provisions of Part 1 of Schedule 6 to the Large and Medium-sized Companies Accounts Regulations apply to LLPs, modified so that they are the provisions set out in Schedule 3 to these Regulations.

PART 3

INTERPRETATION

General interpretation

7.—(1) Regulation 13 of the Large and Medium-sized Companies Accounts Regulations applies to LLPs, modified so that it reads as follows—

> **"General interpretation**
>
> **13.** Schedule 4 to the Large and Medium-sized Limited Liability Partnerships (Accounts) Regulations 2008 contains general definitions for the purposes of these Regulations as applied to LLPs."

(2) The provisions of Schedule 10 to the Large and Medium-sized Companies Accounts Regulations apply to LLPs, modified so that they are the provisions set out in Schedule 4 to these Regulations.

Gareth Thomas
Parliamentary Under Secretary of State for Trade and Consumer Affairs,
17th July 2008   Department for Business, Enterprise and Regulatory Reform

SCHEDULE 1   Regulation 3

NON-IAS INDIVIDUAL ACCOUNTS

PART 1

GENERAL RULES AND FORMATS

SECTION A

GENERAL RULES

1.—(1) Subject to the following provisions of this Schedule—

(a) every balance sheet of an LLP must show the items listed in either of the balance sheet formats in Section B of this Part, and

(b) every profit and loss account must show the items listed in either of the profit and loss account formats in Section B.

(2)   References in this Schedule to the items listed in any of the formats in Section B are to those items read together with any of the notes following the formats which apply to those items.

(3)   The items must be shown in the order and under the headings and sub-headings given in the particular format used, but—

(a) the notes to the formats may permit alternative positions for any particular items, and

(b) the heading or sub-heading for any item does not have to be distinguished by any letter or number assigned to that item in the format used.

2.—(1) Where in accordance with paragraph 1 an LLP's balance sheet or profit and loss account for any financial year has been prepared by reference to one of the formats in Section B, the members of the LLP must use the same format in preparing non-IAS individual accounts for subsequent financial years, unless in their opinion there are special reasons for a change.

(2) Particulars of any such change must be given in a note to the accounts in which the new format is first used, and the reasons for the change must be explained.

3.—(1) Any item required to be shown in an LLP's balance sheet or profit and loss account may be shown in greater detail than required by the particular format used.

(2) The balance sheet or profit and loss account may include an item representing or covering the amount of any asset or liability, income or expenditure not otherwise covered by any of the items listed in the format used, save that none of the following may be treated as assets in any balance sheet—

(a) preliminary expenses,

(b) expenses of, and commission on, any issue of debentures, and

(c) costs of research.

4.—(1) Where the special nature of the LLP's business requires it, the members of the LLP must adapt the arrangement, headings and sub-headings otherwise required in respect of items given an Arabic number in the balance sheet or profit and loss account format used.

(2) The members may combine items to which Arabic numbers are given in any of the formats in Section B if—

(a) their individual amounts are not material to assessing the state of affairs or profit or loss of the LLP for the financial year in question, or

(b) the combination facilitates that assessment.

(3) Where sub-paragraph (2)(b) applies, the individual amounts of any items which have been combined must be disclosed in a note to the accounts.

5.—(1) Subject to sub-paragraph (2), the members must not include a heading or sub-heading corresponding to an item in the balance sheet or profit and loss account format used if there is no amount to be shown for that item for the financial year to which the balance sheet or profit and loss account relates.

(2) Where an amount can be shown for the item in question for the immediately preceding financial year that amount must be shown under the heading or sub-heading required by the format for that item.

6. Every profit and loss account must show the amount of an LLP's profit or loss on ordinary activities before taxation.

7.—(1) For every item shown in the balance sheet or profit and loss account the corresponding amount for the immediately preceding financial year must also be shown.

(2) Where that corresponding amount is not comparable with the amount to be shown for the item in question in respect of the financial year to which the balance sheet or profit and loss account relates, the former amount may be adjusted, and particulars of the non-comparability and of any adjustment must be disclosed in a note to the accounts.

8. Amounts in respect of items representing assets or income may not be set off against amounts in respect of items representing liabilities or expenditure (as the case may be), or vice versa.

9. The members of the LLP must, in determining how amounts are presented within items in the profit and loss account and balance sheet, have regard to the substance of the reported transaction or arrangement, in accordance with generally accepted accounting principles or practice.

SECTION B

THE REQUIRED FORMATS FOR ACCOUNTS(a)

Balance sheet formats

Format 1

A. Fixed assets
  I. Intangible assets
    1. Development costs
    2. Concessions, patents, licences, trade marks and similar rights and assets *(1)*
    3. Goodwill *(2)*
    4. Payments on account
  II. Tangible assets
    1. Land and buildings
    2. Plant and machinery
    3. Fixtures, fittings, tools and equipment
    4. Payments on account and assets in course of construction
  III. Investments
    1. Shares in group undertakings
    2. Loans to group undertakings
    3. Participating interests

(a) A number in brackets following any item is a reference to the note of that number in the notes following the formats.

    4.   Loans to undertakings in which the LLP has a participating interest
    5.   Other investments other than loans
    6.   Other loans

B.   Current assets
   I.   Stocks
      1.   Raw materials and consumables
      2.   Work in progress
      3.   Finished goods and goods for resale
      4.   Payments on account
   II. Debtors *(3)*
      1.   Trade debtors
      2.   Amounts owed by group undertakings
      3.   Amounts owed by undertakings in which the LLP has a participating interest
      4.   Other debtors
      5.   Prepayments and accrued income *(4)*
   III. Investments
      1.   Shares in group undertakings
      2.   Other investments
   IV. Cash at bank and in hand

C.   Prepayments and accrued income *(4)*

D.   Creditors: amounts falling due within one year
      1.   Debenture loans *(5)*
      2.   Bank loans and overdrafts
      3.   Payments received on account *(6)*
      4.   Trade creditors
      5.   Bills of exchange payable
      6.   Amounts owed to group undertakings
      7.   Amounts owed to undertakings in which the LLP has a participating interest
      8.   Other creditors including taxation and social security *(7)*
      9.   Accruals and deferred income *(8)* ·

E.   Net current assets (liabilities) *(9)*

F.   Total assets less current liabilities

G.   Creditors: amounts falling due after more than one year
      1.   Debenture loans *(5)*
      2.   Bank loans and overdrafts
      3.   Payments received on account *(6)*
      4.   Trade creditors
      5.   Bills of exchange payable
      6.   Amounts owed to group undertakings
      7.   Amounts owed to undertakings in which the LLP has a participating interest
      8.   Other creditors including taxation and social security *(7)*
      9.   Accruals and deferred income *(8)*

H.   Provisions for liabilities
      1.   Pensions and similar obligations
      2.   Taxation, including deferred taxation
      3.   Other provisions

I.   Accruals and deferred income *(8)*

J. Loans and other debts due to members *(10)*

K. Members' other interests
    I. Members' capital
    II. Revaluation reserve
    III. Other reserves

Balance sheet formats

Format 2

ASSETS

A. Fixed assets
    I. Intangible assets
        1. Development costs
        2. Concessions, patents, licences, trade marks and similar rights and assets *(1)*
        3. Goodwill *(2)*
        4. Payments on account
    II. Tangible assets
        1. Land and buildings
        2. Plant and machinery
        3. Fixtures, fittings, tools and equipment
        4. Payments on account and assets in course of construction
    III. Investments
        1. Shares in group undertakings
        2. Loans to group undertakings
        3. Participating interests
        4. Loans to undertakings in which the LLP has a participating interest
        5. Other investments other than loans
        6. Other loans

B. Current assets
    I. Stocks
        1. Raw materials and consumables
        2. Work in progress
        3. Finished goods and goods for resale
        4. Payments on account
    II. Debtors *(3)*
        1. Trade debtors
        2. Amounts owed by group undertakings
        3. Amounts owed by undertakings in which the LLP has a participating interest
        4. Other debtors
        5. Prepayments and accrued income *(4)*
    III. Investments
        1. Shares in group undertakings
        2. Other investments
        3. Cash at bank and in hand

C. Prepayments and accrued income *(4)*

LIABILITIES

A.   Loans and other debts due to members *(10)*

B.   Members' other interests
          I.   Members' capital
         II. Revaluation reserve
       III. Other reserves

C.   Provisions for liabilities
          1. Pensions and similar obligations
          2. Taxation, including deferred taxation
          3. Other provisions

D.   Creditors *(11)*
          1. Debenture loans *(5)*
          2. Bank loans and overdrafts
          3. Payments received on account *(6)*
          4. Trade creditors
          5. Bills of exchange payable
          6. Amounts owed to group undertakings
          7. Amounts owed to undertakings in which the LLP has a participating interest
          8. Other creditors including taxation and social security *(7)*
          9. Accruals and deferred income *(8)*

E.   Accruals and deferred income *(8)*

Notes on the balance sheet formats

(1)   *Concessions, patents, licences, trade marks and similar rights and assets*

(Formats 1 and 2, item A.I.2.)

Amounts in respect of assets are only to be included in an LLP's balance sheet under this item if either—
    (a) the assets were acquired for valuable consideration and are not required to be shown under goodwill, or
    (b) the assets in question were created by the LLP itself.

(2)   *Goodwill*

(Formats 1 and 2, item A.I.3.)

Amounts representing goodwill are only to be included to the extent that the goodwill was acquired for valuable consideration.

(3)   *Debtors*

(Formats 1 and 2, items B.II.I to 5.)

The amount falling due after more than one year must be shown separately for each item included under debtors.

(4)   Prepayments and accrued income

(Formats 1 and 2, items B.II.5 and C.)

  This item may be shown in either of the two positions given in Formats 1 and 2.

(5)   Debenture loans

(Format 1, items D.I and G.I and Format 2, item D.I.)

  The amount of any convertible loans must be shown separately.

(6)   Payments received on account

(Format 1, items D.3 and G.3 and Format 2, item D.3.)

  Payments received on account of orders must be shown for each of these items in so far as they are not shown as deductions from stocks.

(7)   Other creditors including taxation and social security

(Format 1, items D.8 and G.8 and Format 2, item D.8.)

  The amount for creditors in respect of taxation and social security must be shown separately from the amount for other creditors.

(8)   Accruals and deferred income

(Format 1, items D.9, G.9 and I and Format 2, items D.9 and E.)

  The two positions given for this item in Format 1 at D.9 and G.9 are an alternative to the position at I, but if the item is not shown in a position corresponding to that at I it may be shown in either or both of the other two positions (as the case may require).

  The two positions given for this item in Format 2 are alternatives.

(9)   Net current assets (liabilities)

(Format 1, item E.)

  In determining the amount to be shown for this item any amounts shown under "prepayments and accrued income" must be taken into account wherever shown.

(10)   Loans and other debts due to members

(Format 1, item J and Format 2, Liabilities item A.)

  The following amounts must be shown separately under this item—
    (a) the aggregate amount of money advanced to the LLP by the members by way of loan,
    (b) the aggregate amount of money owed to members by the LLP in respect of profits,
    (c) any other amounts.

(11)   Creditors

(Format 2, items D.I to 9.)

Amounts falling due within one year and after one year must be shown separately for each of these items and for the aggregate of all of these items.

Profit and loss account formats(a)

Format 1
(see note (15) below)

1.   Turnover

2.   Cost of sales *(12)*

3.   Gross profit or loss

4.   Distribution costs *(12)*

5.   Administrative expenses *(12)*

6.   Other operating income

7.   Income from shares in group undertakings

8.   Income from participating interests

9.   Income from other fixed asset investments *(13)*

10.   Other interest receivable and similar income *(13)*

11.   Amounts written off investments

12.   Interest payable and similar charges *(14)*

13.   Tax on profit or loss on ordinary activities

14.   Profit or loss on ordinary activities after taxation

15.   Extraordinary income

16.   Extraordinary charges

17.   Extraordinary profit or loss

18.   Tax on extraordinary profit or loss

19.   Other taxes not shown under the above items

20.   Profit or loss for the financial year before members' remuneration and profit shares

---

(a) See regulation 4(3)(a) for exemption for medium-sized LLP in accounts delivered to registrar of companies.

Profit and loss account formats(a)

Format 2

1.   Turnover

2.   Change in stocks of finished goods and in work in progress

3.   Own work capitalised

4.   Other operating income

5.   (a)   Raw materials and consumables

     (b)   Other external charges

6.   Staff costs

     (a)   wages and salaries

     (b)   social security costs

     (c)   other pension costs

7.   (a)   Depreciation and other amounts written off tangible and intangible fixed assets

     (b)   Exceptional amounts written off current assets

8.   Other operating charges

9.   Income from shares in group undertakings

10. Income from participating interests

11. Income from other fixed asset investments *(13)*

12. Other interest receivable and similar income *(13)*

13. Amounts written off investments

14. Interest payable and similar charges *(14)*

15. Tax on profit or loss on ordinary activities

16. Profit or loss on ordinary activities after taxation

17. Extraordinary income

18. Extraordinary charges

19. Extraordinary profit or loss

20. Tax on extraordinary profit or loss

21. Other taxes not shown under the above items

22. Profit or loss for the financial year before members' remuneration and profit shares

---

(a) See regulation 4(3)(a) for exemption for medium-sized LLP in accounts delivered to registrar of companies.

Notes on the profit and loss account formats

(12)   Cost of sales: distribution costs: administrative expenses

(Format 1, items 2, 4 and 5.)

These items must be stated after taking into account any necessary provisions for depreciation or diminution in value of assets.

(13)   Income from other fixed asset investments: other interest receivable and similar income

(Format 1, items 9 and 10; Format 2, items 11 and 12.)

Income and interest derived from group undertakings must be shown separately from income and interest derived from other sources. Interest receivable from members must not be included under this item.

(14)   Interest payable and similar charges

(Format 1, item 12; Format 2, item 14.)

The amount payable to group undertakings must be shown separately. Interest payable to members must not be included under this item.

(15)   Format 1

The amount of any provisions for depreciation and diminution in value of tangible and intangible fixed assets falling to be shown under item 7(a) in Format 2 must be disclosed in a note to the accounts in any case where the profit and loss account is prepared using Format 1.

PART 2

ACCOUNTING PRINCIPLES AND RULES

SECTION A

ACCOUNTING PRINCIPLES

Preliminary

10.—(1) The amounts to be included in respect of all items shown in an LLP's accounts must be determined in accordance with the principles set out in this Section.

(2) But if it appears to the LLP's members that there are special reasons for departing from any of those principles in preparing the LLP's accounts in respect of any financial year they may do so, in which case particulars of the departure, the reasons for it and its effect must be given in a note to the accounts.

Accounting principles

11. The LLP is presumed to be carrying on business as a going concern.

12. Accounting policies must be applied consistently within the same accounts and from one financial year to the next.

13. The amount of any item must be determined on a prudent basis, and in particular—
   (a) only profits realised at the balance sheet date are to be included in the profit and loss account, and

(b) all liabilities which have arisen in respect of the financial year to which the accounts relate or a previous financial year must be taken into account, including those which only become apparent between the balance sheet date and the date on which it is signed on behalf of the members in accordance with section 414 of the 2006 Act (approval and signing of accounts).

14. All income and charges relating to the financial year to which the accounts relate must be taken into account, without regard to the date of receipt or payment.

15. In determining the aggregate amount of any item, the amount of each individual asset or liability that falls to be taken into account must be determined separately.

SECTION B

HISTORICAL COST ACCOUNTING RULES

Preliminary

16. Subject to Sections C and D of this Part of this Schedule, the amounts to be included in respect of all items shown in an LLP's accounts must be determined in accordance with the rules set out in this Section.

Fixed assets

General rules

17.—(1) The amount to be included in respect of any fixed asset must be its purchase price or production cost.

(2) This is subject to any provision for depreciation or diminution in value made in accordance with paragraphs 18 to 20.

Rules for depreciation and diminution in value

18. In the case of any fixed asset which has a limited useful economic life, the amount of—

(a) its purchase price or production cost, or

(b) where it is estimated that any such asset will have a residual value at the end of the period of its useful economic life, its purchase price or production cost less that estimated residual value,

must be reduced by provisions for depreciation calculated to write off that amount systematically over the period of the asset's useful economic life.

19.—(1) Where a fixed asset investment falling to be included under item A.III of either of the balance sheet formats set out in Part 1 of this Schedule has diminished in value, provisions for diminution in value may be made in respect of it and the amount to be included in respect of it may be reduced accordingly.

(2) Provisions for diminution in value must be made in respect of any fixed asset which has diminished in value if the reduction in its value is expected to be permanent (whether its useful economic life is limited or not), and the amount to be included in respect of it must be reduced accordingly.

(3) Any provisions made under sub-paragraph (1) or (2) which are not shown in the profit and loss account must be disclosed (either separately or in aggregate) in a note to the accounts.

20.—(1) Where the reasons for which any provision was made in accordance with paragraph 19 have ceased to apply to any extent, that provision must be written back to the extent that it is no longer necessary.

(2) Any amounts written back in accordance with sub-paragraph (1) which are not shown in the profit and loss account must be disclosed (either separately or in aggregate) in a note to the accounts.

Development costs

21.—(1) Notwithstanding that an item in respect of "development costs" is included under "fixed assets" in the balance sheet formats set out in Part 1 of this Schedule, an amount may only be included in an LLP's balance sheet in respect of development costs in special circumstances.

(2) If any amount is included in an LLP's balance sheet in respect of development costs the following information must be given in a note to the accounts—

  (a) the period over which the amount of those costs originally capitalised is being or is to be written off, and

  (b) the reasons for capitalising the development costs in question.

Goodwill

22.—(1) The application of paragraphs 17 to 20 in relation to goodwill (in any case where goodwill is treated as an asset) is subject to the following.

(2) Subject to sub-paragraph (3), the amount of the consideration for any goodwill acquired by an LLP must be reduced by provisions for depreciation calculated to write off that amount systematically over a period chosen by the members of the LLP.

(3) The period chosen must not exceed the useful economic life of the goodwill in question.

(4) In any case where any goodwill acquired by an LLP is shown or included as an asset in the LLP's balance sheet there must be disclosed in a note to the accounts—

  (a) the period chosen for writing off the consideration for that goodwill, and

  (b) the reasons for choosing that period.

Current assets

23. Subject to paragraph 24, the amount to be included in respect of any current asset must be its purchase price or production cost.

24.—(1) If the net realisable value of any current asset is lower than its purchase price or production cost, the amount to be included in respect of that asset must be the net realisable value.

(2) Where the reasons for which any provision for diminution in value was made in accordance with sub-paragraph (1) have ceased to apply to any extent, that provision must be written back to the extent that it is no longer necessary.

Miscellaneous and supplementary provisions

Excess of money owed over value received as an asset item

25.—(1) Where the amount repayable on any debt owed by an LLP is greater than the value of the consideration received in the transaction giving rise to the debt, the amount of the difference may be treated as an asset.

(2) Where any such amount is so treated—

  (a) it must be written off by reasonable amounts each year and must be completely written off before repayment of the debt, and

  (b) if the current amount is not shown as a separate item in the LLP's balance sheet, it must be disclosed in a note to the accounts.

Assets included at a fixed amount

26.—(1) Subject to sub-paragraph (2), assets which fall to be included—

(a) amongst the fixed assets of an LLP under the item "tangible assets", or

(b) amongst the current assets of an LLP under the item "raw materials and consumables",

may be included at a fixed quantity and value.

(2) Sub-paragraph (1) applies to assets of a kind which are constantly being replaced where—

(a) their overall value is not material to assessing the LLP's state of affairs, and

(b) their quantity, value and composition are not subject to material variation.

Determination of purchase price or production cost

27.—(1) The purchase price of an asset is to be determined by adding to the actual price paid any expenses incidental to its acquisition.

(2) The production cost of an asset is to be determined by adding to the purchase price of the raw materials and consumables used the amount of the costs incurred by the LLP which are directly attributable to the production of that asset.

(3) In addition, there may be included in the production cost of an asset—

(a) a reasonable proportion of the costs incurred by the LLP which are only indirectly attributable to the production of that asset, but only to the extent that they relate to the period of production, and

(b) interest on capital borrowed to finance the production of that asset, to the extent that it accrues in respect of the period of production,

provided, however, in a case within paragraph (b), that the inclusion of the interest in determining the cost of that asset and the amount of the interest so included is disclosed in a note to the accounts.

(4) In the case of current assets distribution costs may not be included in production costs.

28.—(1) The purchase price or production cost of—

(a) any assets which fall to be included under any item shown in an LLP's balance sheet under the general item "stocks", and

(b) any assets which are fungible assets (including investments),

may be determined by the application of any of the methods mentioned in sub-paragraph (2) in relation to any such assets of the same class, provided that the method chosen is one which appears to the members to be appropriate in the circumstances of the LLP.

(2) Those methods are—

(a) the method known as "first in, first out" (FIFO),

(b) the method known as "last in, first out" (LIFO),

(c) a weighted average price, and

(d) any other method similar to any of the methods mentioned above.

(3) Where in the case of any LLP—

(a) the purchase price or production cost of assets falling to be included under any item shown in the LLP's balance sheet has been determined by the application of any method permitted by this paragraph, and

(b) the amount shown in respect of that item differs materially from the relevant alternative amount given below in this paragraph,

the amount of that difference must be disclosed in a note to the accounts.

(4) Subject to sub-paragraph (5), for the purposes of sub-paragraph (3)(b), the relevant alternative amount, in relation to any item shown in an LLP's balance sheet, is the amount which would have been shown in respect of that item if assets of any class included under that item at an

amount determined by any method permitted by this paragraph had instead been included at their replacement cost as at the balance sheet date.

(5) The relevant alternative amount may be determined by reference to the most recent actual purchase price or production cost before the balance sheet date of assets of any class included under the item in question instead of by reference to their replacement cost as at that date, but only if the former appears to the members of the LLP to constitute the more appropriate standard of comparison in the case of assets of that class.

(6) "Fungible assets" means assets of any description which are substantially indistinguishable one from another.

Substitution of original stated amount where price or cost unknown

29.—(1) This paragraph applies where—

   (a)   there is no record of the purchase price or production cost of any asset of an LLP or of any price, expenses or costs relevant for determining its purchase price or production cost in accordance with paragraph 27, or

   (b)   any such record cannot be obtained without unreasonable expense or delay.

(2) In such a case, the purchase price or production cost of the asset must be taken, for the purposes of paragraphs 17 to 24, to be the value ascribed to it in the earliest available record of its value made on or after its acquisition or production by the LLP.

SECTION C

ALTERNATIVE ACCOUNTING RULES

Preliminary

30.—(1) The rules set out in Section B are referred to below in this Schedule as the historical cost accounting rules.

(2) Those rules, with the omission of paragraphs 16, 22 and 26 to 29, are referred to below in this Part of this Schedule as the depreciation rules; and references below in this Schedule to the historical cost accounting rules do not include the depreciation rules as they apply by virtue of paragraph 33.

31. Subject to paragraphs 33 to 35, the amounts to be included in respect of assets of any description mentioned in paragraph 32 may be determined on any basis so mentioned.

Alternative accounting rules

32.—(1) Intangible fixed assets, other than goodwill, may be included at their current cost.

(2) Tangible fixed assets may be included at a market value determined as at the date of their last valuation or at their current cost.

(3) Investments of any description falling to be included under item A III of either of the balance sheet formats set out in Part 1 of this Schedule may be included either—

   (a)   at a market value determined as at the date of their last valuation, or

   (b)   at a value determined on any basis which appears to the members to be appropriate in the circumstances of the LLP.

But in the latter case particulars of the method of valuation adopted and of the reasons for adopting it must be disclosed in a note to the accounts.

(4) Investments of any description falling to be included under item B III of either of the balance sheet formats set out in Part 1 of this Schedule may be included at their current cost.

(5) Stocks may be included at their current cost.

Application of the depreciation rules

33.—(1) Where the value of any asset of an LLP is determined on any basis mentioned in paragraph 32, that value must be, or (as the case may require) be the starting point for determining, the amount to be included in respect of that asset in the LLP's accounts, instead of its purchase price or production cost or any value previously so determined for that asset.

The depreciation rules apply accordingly in relation to any such asset with the substitution for any reference to its purchase price or production cost of a reference to the value most recently determined for that asset on any basis mentioned in paragraph 32.

(2) The amount of any provision for depreciation required in the case of any fixed asset by paragraphs 18 to 20 as they apply by virtue of sub-paragraph (1) is referred to below in this paragraph as the adjusted amount, and the amount of any provision which would be required by any of those paragraphs in the case of that asset according to the historical cost accounting rules is referred to as the historical cost amount.

(3) Where sub-paragraph (1) applies in the case of any fixed asset the amount of any provision for depreciation in respect of that asset—

(a) included in any item shown in the profit and loss account in respect of amounts written off assets of the description in question, or

(b) taken into account in stating any item so shown which is required by note (12) of the notes on the profit and loss account formats set out in Part 1 of this Schedule to be stated after taking into account any necessary provision for depreciation or diminution in value of assets included under it,

may be the historical cost amount instead of the adjusted amount, provided that the amount of any difference between the two is shown separately in the profit and loss account or in a note to the accounts.

Additional information to be provided in case of departure from historical cost accounting rules

34.—(1) This paragraph applies where the amounts to be included in respect of assets covered by any items shown in an LLP's accounts have been determined on any basis mentioned in paragraph 32.

(2) The items affected and the basis of valuation adopted in determining the amounts of the assets in question in the case of each such item must be disclosed in a note to the accounts.

(3) In the case of each balance sheet item affected (except stocks) either—

(a) the comparable amounts determined according to the historical cost accounting rules, or

(b) the differences between those amounts and the corresponding amounts actually shown in the balance sheet in respect of that item,

must be shown separately in the balance sheet or in a note to the accounts.

(4) In sub-paragraph (3), references in relation to any item to the comparable amounts determined as there mentioned are references to—

(a) the aggregate amount which would be required to be shown in respect of that item if the amounts to be included in respect of all the assets covered by that item were determined according to the historical cost accounting rules, and

(b) the aggregate amount of the cumulative provisions for depreciation or diminution in value which would be permitted or required in determining those amounts according to those rules.

Revaluation reserve

35.—(1) With respect to any determination of the value of an asset of an LLP on any basis mentioned in paragraph 32, the amount of any profit or loss arising from that determination (after allowing, where appropriate, for any provisions for depreciation or diminution in value made otherwise than by reference to the value so determined and any adjustments of any such provisions made in the light of that determination) must be credited or (as the case may be) debited to a separate reserve ("the revaluation reserve").

(2) The amount of the revaluation reserve must be shown in the LLP's balance sheet under a separate sub-heading in the position given for the item "revaluation reserve" in Format 1 or 2 of the balance sheet formats set out in Part 1 of this Schedule, but need not be shown under that name.

(3) The treatment for taxation purposes of amounts credited or debited to the revaluation reserve must be disclosed in a note to the accounts.

SECTION D

FAIR VALUE ACCOUNTING

Inclusion of financial instruments at fair value

36.—(1) Subject to sub-paragraphs (2) to (5), financial instruments (including derivatives) may be included at fair value.

(2) Sub-paragraph (1) does not apply to financial instruments that constitute liabilities unless—

    (a)   they are held as part of a trading portfolio,

    (b)   they are derivatives, or

    (c)   they are financial instruments falling within sub-paragraph (4).

(3) Unless they are financial instruments falling within sub-paragraph (4), sub-paragraph (1) does not apply to—

    (a)   financial instruments (other than derivatives) held to maturity,

    (b)   loans and receivables originated by the LLP and not held for trading purposes,

    (c)   interests in subsidiary undertakings, associated undertakings and joint ventures,

    (d)   equity instruments issued by the LLP,

    (e)   contracts for contingent consideration in a business combination, or

    (f)   other financial instruments with such special characteristics that the instruments, according to generally accepted accounting principles or practice, should be accounted for differently from other financial instruments.

(4) Financial instruments that, under international accounting standards adopted by the European Commission on or before 5th September 2006 in accordance with the IAS Regulation, may be included in accounts at fair value, may be so included, provided that the disclosures required by such accounting standards are made.

(5) If the fair value of a financial instrument cannot be determined reliably in accordance with paragraph 37, sub-paragraph (1) does not apply to that financial instrument.

(6) In this paragraph—

"associated undertaking" has the meaning given by paragraph 19 of Schedule 3 to these Regulations;

"joint venture" has the meaning given by paragraph 18 of that Schedule.

Determination of fair value

37.—(1) The fair value of a financial instrument is its value determined in accordance with this paragraph.

(2) If a reliable market can readily be identified for the financial instrument, its fair value is determined by reference to its market value.

(3) If a reliable market cannot readily be identified for the financial instrument but can be identified for its components or for a similar instrument, its fair value is determined by reference to the market value of its components or of the similar instrument.

(4) If neither sub-paragraph (2) nor (3) applies, the fair value of the financial instrument is a value resulting from generally accepted valuation models and techniques.

(5) Any valuation models and techniques used for the purposes of sub-paragraph (4) must ensure a reasonable approximation of the market value.

Hedged items

38. An LLP may include any assets and liabilities, or identified portions of such assets or liabilities, that qualify as hedged items under a fair value hedge accounting system at the amount required under that system.

Other assets that may be included at fair value

39.—(1) This paragraph applies to—

    (a)   investment property, and

    (b)   living animals and plants,

that, under international accounting standards, may be included in accounts at fair value.

(2) Such investment property and such living animals and plants may be included at fair value, provided that all such investment property or, as the case may be, all such living animals and plants are so included where their fair value can reliably be determined.

(3) In this paragraph, "fair value" means fair value determined in accordance with relevant international accounting standards.

Accounting for changes in value

40.—(1) This paragraph applies where a financial instrument is valued in accordance with paragraph 36 or 38 or an asset is valued in accordance with paragraph 39.

(2) Notwithstanding paragraph 13 in this Part of this Schedule, and subject to sub-paragraphs (3) and (4), a change in the value of the financial instrument or of the investment property or living animal or plant must be included in the profit and loss account.

(3) Where—

    (a)   the financial instrument accounted for is a hedging instrument under a hedge accounting system that allows some or all of the change in value not to be shown in the profit and loss account, or

    (b)   the change in value relates to an exchange difference arising on a monetary item that forms part of an LLP's net investment in a foreign entity,

the amount of the change in value must be credited to or (as the case may be) debited from a separate reserve ("the fair value reserve").

(4) Where the instrument accounted for—

    (a)   is an available for sale financial asset, and

    (b)   is not a derivative,

the change in value may be credited to or (as the case may be) debited from the fair value reserve.

The fair value reserve

41.—(1) The fair value reserve must be adjusted to the extent that the amounts shown in it are no longer necessary for the purposes of paragraph 40(3) or (4).

(2) The treatment for taxation purposes of amounts credited or debited to the fair value reserve must be disclosed in a note to the accounts.

PART 3
NOTES TO THE ACCOUNTS

Preliminary

42. Any information required in the case of any LLP by the following provisions of this Part of this Schedule must (if not given in the LLP's accounts) be given by way of a note to the accounts.

General

Reserves

43. Any amount set aside or proposed to be set aside to, or withdrawn or proposed to be withdrawn from, reserves must be stated.

Disclosure of accounting policies

44. The accounting policies adopted by the LLP in determining the amounts to be included in respect of items shown in the balance sheet and in determining the profit or loss of the LLP must be stated (including such policies with respect to the depreciation and diminution in value of assets).

45. It must be stated whether the accounts have been prepared in accordance with applicable accounting standards and particulars of any material departure from those standards and the reasons for it must be given (see regulation 4 for exemption for medium-sized LLPs).

Information supplementing the balance sheet

46. Paragraphs 47 to 61 require information which either supplements the information given with respect to any particular items shown in the balance sheet or is otherwise relevant to assessing the LLP's state of affairs in the light of the information so given.

Loans and other debts due to members

47. The following information must be given—
  (a) the aggregate amount of loans and other debts due to members as at the date of the beginning of the financial year,
  (b) the aggregate amounts contributed by members during the financial year,
  (c) the aggregate amounts transferred to or from the profit and loss account during that year,
  (d) the aggregate amounts withdrawn by members or applied on behalf of members during that year,
  (e) the aggregate amount of loans and other debts due to members as at the balance sheet date, and
  (f) the aggregate amount of loans and other debts due to members that fall due after one year.

Debentures

48.—(1) If the LLP has issued any debentures during the financial year to which the accounts relate, the following information must be given—
  (a) the classes of debentures issued, and
  (b) as respects each class of debentures, the amount issued and the consideration received by the LLP for the issue.

(2) Where any of the LLP's debentures are held by a nominee of or trustee for the LLP, the nominal amount of the debentures and the amount at which they are stated in the accounting records kept by the LLP in accordance with section 386 of the 2006 Act (duty to keep accounting records) must be stated.

Fixed assets

49.—(1) In respect of each item which is or would but for paragraph 4(2)(b) be shown under the general item "fixed assets" in the LLP's balance sheet the following information must be given—

    (a)   the appropriate amounts in respect of that item as at the date of the beginning of the financial year and as at the balance sheet date respectively,

    (b)   the effect on any amount shown in the balance sheet in respect of that item of—
        (i)   any revision of the amount in respect of any assets included under that item made during that year on any basis mentioned in paragraph 32,
        (ii) acquisitions during that year of any assets,
        (iii) disposals during that year of any assets, and
        (iv) any transfers of assets of the LLP to and from that item during that year.

(2) The reference in sub-paragraph (l)(a) to the appropriate amounts in respect of any item as at any date there mentioned is a reference to amounts representing the aggregate amounts determined, as at that date, in respect of assets falling to be included under that item on either of the following bases, that is to say—

    (a)   on the basis of purchase price or production cost (determined in accordance with paragraphs 27 and 28), or

    (b)   on any basis mentioned in paragraph 32,

(leaving out of account in either case any provisions for depreciation or diminution in value).

(3) In respect of each item within sub-paragraph (1) there must also be stated—

    (a)   the cumulative amount of provisions for depreciation or diminution in value of assets included under that item as at each date mentioned in sub-paragraph (l)(a),

    (b)   the amount of any such provisions made in respect of the financial year,

    (c)   the amount of any adjustments made in respect of any such provisions during that year in consequence of the disposal of any assets, and

    (d)   the amount of any other adjustments made in respect of any such provisions during that year.

50. Where any fixed assets of the LLP (other than listed investments) are included under any item shown in the LLP's balance sheet at an amount determined on any basis mentioned in paragraph 32, the following information must be given—

    (a)   the years (so far as they are known to the members) in which the assets were severally valued and the several values, and

    (b)   in the case of assets that have been valued during the financial year, the names of the persons who valued them or particulars of their qualifications for doing so and (whichever is stated) the bases of valuation used by them.

51.—(1) In relation to any amount which is or would but for paragraph 4(2)(b) be shown in respect of the item "land and buildings" in the LLP's balance sheet there must be stated—

    (a)   how much of that amount is ascribable to land of freehold tenure and how much to land of leasehold tenure, and

    (b)   how much of the amount ascribable to land of leasehold tenure is ascribable to land held on long lease and how much to land held on short lease.

(2) In this paragraph—

(a) "long lease" means a lease in the case of which the portion of the term for which it was granted remaining unexpired at the end of the financial year is not less than 50 years,

(b) "short lease" means a lease which is not a long lease, and

(c) "lease" includes an agreement for a lease.

(3) In the application of this regulation to Scotland, "land of freehold tenure" means land in respect of which the LLP is the owner; "land of leasehold tenure" means land of which the company is the tenant under a lease.

Investments

52.—(1) In respect of the amount of each item which is or would but for paragraph 4(2)(b) be shown in the LLP's balance sheet under the general item "investments" (whether as fixed assets or as current assets) there must be stated how much of that amount is ascribable to listed investments.

(2) Where the amount of any listed investments is stated for any item in accordance with subparagraph (1), the following amounts must also be stated—

(a) the aggregate market value of those investments where it differs from the amount so stated, and

(b) both the market value and the stock exchange value of any investments of which the former value is, for the purposes of the accounts, taken as being higher than the latter.

Information about fair value of assets and liabilities

53.—(1) This paragraph applies where financial instruments have been valued in accordance with paragraph 36 or 38.

(2) There must be stated—

(a) the significant assumptions underlying the valuation models and techniques used where the fair value of the instruments has been determined in accordance with paragraph 37(4),

(b) for each category of financial instrument, the fair value of the instruments in that category and the changes in value—

(i) included in the profit and loss account, or

(ii) credited to or (as the case may be) debited from the fair value reserve,

in respect of those instruments, and

(c) for each class of derivatives, the extent and nature of the instruments, including significant terms and conditions that may affect the amount, timing and certainty of future cash flows.

(3) Where any amount is transferred to or from the fair value reserve during the financial year, there must be stated in tabular form—

(a) the amount of the reserve as at the date of the beginning of the financial year and as at the balance sheet date respectively,

(b) the amount transferred to or from the reserve during that year, and

(c) the source and application respectively of the amounts so transferred.

54. Where the LLP has derivatives that it has not included at fair value, there must be stated for each class of such derivatives—

(a) the fair value of the derivatives in that class, if such a value can be determined in accordance with paragraph 37, and

(b) the extent and nature of the derivatives.

55.—(1) This paragraph applies if—

(a) the LLP has financial fixed assets that could be included at fair value by virtue of paragraph 36,

231

    (b)   the amount at which those items are included under any item in the LLP's accounts is in excess of their fair value, and

    (c)   the LLP has not made provision for diminution in value of those assets in accordance with paragraph 19(1) of this Schedule.

(2) There must be stated—

    (a)   the amount at which either the individual assets or appropriate groupings of those individual assets are included in the LLP's accounts,

    (b)   the fair value of those assets or groupings, and

    (c)   the reasons for not making a provision for diminution in value of those assets, including the nature of the evidence that provides the basis for the belief that the amount at which they are stated in the accounts will be recovered.

Information where investment property and living animals and plants included at fair value

56.—(1) This paragraph applies where the amounts to be included in an LLP's accounts in respect of investment property or living animals and plants have been determined in accordance with paragraph 39.

(2) The balance sheet items affected and the basis of valuation adopted in determining the amounts of the assets in question in the case of each such item must be disclosed in a note to the accounts.

(3) In the case of investment property, for each balance sheet item affected there must be shown, either separately in the balance sheet or in a note to the accounts—

    (a)   the comparable amounts determined according to the historical cost accounting rules, or

    (b)   the differences between those amounts and the corresponding amounts actually shown in the balance sheet in respect of that item.

(4) In sub-paragraph (3), references in relation to any item to the comparable amounts determined in accordance with that sub-paragraph are to—

    (a)   the aggregate amount which would be required to be shown in respect of that item if the amounts to be included in respect of all the assets covered by that item were determined according to the historical cost accounting rules, and

    (b)   the aggregate amount of the cumulative provisions for depreciation or diminution in value which would be permitted or required in determining those amounts according to those rules.

Reserves and provisions

57.—(1) This paragraph applies where any amount is transferred—

    (a)   to or from any reserves, or

    (b)   to any provision for liabilities, or

    (c)   from any provision for liabilities otherwise than for the purpose for which the provision was established,

and the reserves or provisions are or would but for paragraph 4(2)(b) be shown as separate items in the LLP's balance sheet.

(2) The following information must be given in respect of the aggregate of reserves or provisions included in the same item—

    (a)   the amount of the reserves or provisions as at the date of the beginning of the financial year and as at the balance sheet date respectively,

    (b)   any amounts transferred to or from the reserves or provisions during that year, and

    (c)   the source and application respectively of any amounts so transferred.

(3) Particulars must be given of each provision included in the item "other provisions" in the LLP's balance sheet in any case where the amount of that provision is material.

Provision for taxation

58. The amount of any provision for deferred taxation must be stated separately from the amount of any provision for other taxation.

Details of indebtedness

59.—(1) For the aggregate of all items shown under "creditors" in the LLP's balance sheet there must be stated the aggregate of the following amounts—

(a) the amount of any debts included under "creditors" which are payable or repayable otherwise than by instalments and fall due for payment or repayment after the end of the period of five years beginning with the day next following the end of the financial year, and

(b) in the case of any debts so included which are payable or repayable by instalments, the amount of any instalments which fall due for payment after the end of that period.

(2) Subject to sub-paragraph (3), in relation to each debt falling to be taken into account under sub-paragraph (1), the terms of payment or repayment and the rate of any interest payable on the debt must be stated.

(3) If the number of debts is such that, in the opinion of the members, compliance with subparagraph (2) would result in a statement of excessive length, it is sufficient to give a general indication of the terms of payment or repayment and the rates of any interest payable on the debts.

(4) In respect of each item shown under "creditors" in the LLP's balance sheet there must be stated—

(a) the aggregate amount of any debts included under that item in respect of which any security has been given by the LLP, and

(b) an indication of the nature of the securities so given.

(5) References above in this paragraph to an item shown under "creditors" in the LLP's balance sheet include references, where amounts falling due to creditors within one year and after more than one year are distinguished in the balance sheet—

(a) in a case within sub-paragraph (1), to an item shown under the latter of those categories, and

(b) in a case within sub-paragraph (4), to an item shown under either of those categories.

References to items shown under "creditors" include references to items which would but for paragraph 4(2)(b) be shown under that heading.

Guarantees and other financial commitments

60.—(1) Particulars must be given of any charge on the assets of the LLP to secure the liabilities of any other person, including, where practicable, the amount secured.

(2) The following information must be given with respect to any other contingent liability not provided for—

(a) the amount or estimated amount of that liability,

(b) its legal nature, and

(c) whether any valuable security has been provided by the LLP in connection with that liability and if so, what.

(3) There must be stated, where practicable, the aggregate amount or estimated amount of contracts for capital expenditure, so far as not provided for.

(4) Particulars must be given of—

    (a) any pension commitments included under any provision shown in the LLP's balance sheet, and

    (b) any such commitments for which no provision has been made,

and where any such commitment relates wholly or partly to pensions payable to past members of the LLP separate particulars must be given of that commitment so far as it relates to such pensions.

(5) Particulars must also be given of any other financial commitments that—

    (a) have not been provided for, and

    (b) are relevant to assessing the LLP's state of affairs.

Miscellaneous matters

61. Particulars must be given of any case where the purchase price or production cost of any asset is for the first time determined under paragraph 29.

Information supplementing the profit and loss account

62. Paragraphs 63 to 67 require information which either supplements the information given with respect to any particular items shown in the profit and loss account or otherwise provides particulars of income or expenditure of the LLP or of circumstances affecting the items shown in the profit and loss account (see regulation 3 for exemption for LLP falling within section 408 of the 2006 Act (individual profit and loss account where group accounts prepared)).

Separate statement of certain items of income and expenditure

63.—(1) Subject to sub-paragraph (2), there must be stated the amount of the interest on or any similar charges in respect of bank loans and overdrafts, and loans of any other kind made to the LLP.

(2) Sub-paragraph (1) does not apply to interest or charges on loans to the LLP from group undertakings, but, with that exception, it applies to interest or charges on all loans, whether made on the security of debentures or not.

Particulars of tax

64.—(1) Particulars must be given of any special circumstances which affect liability in respect of taxation of profits, income or capital gains for the financial year or liability in respect of taxation of profits, income or capital gains for succeeding financial years.

(2) The following amounts must be stated—

    (a) the amount of the charge for United Kingdom corporation tax,

    (b) if that amount would have been greater but for relief from double taxation, the amount which it would have been but for such relief,

    (c) the amount of the charge for United Kingdom income tax, and

    (d) the amount of the charge for taxation imposed outside the United Kingdom of profits, income and (so far as charged to revenue) capital gains.

These amounts must be stated separately in respect of each of the amounts which is or would but for paragraph 4(2)(b) be shown under the items "tax on profit or loss on ordinary activities" and "tax on extraordinary profit or loss" in the profit and loss account.

Particulars of turnover

65.—(1) If in the course of the financial year the LLP has carried on business of two or more classes that, in the opinion of the members, differ substantially from each other, the amount of the turnover attributable to each class must be stated and the class described (see regulation 4(3)(b) for exemption for medium-sized LLP in accounts delivered to registrar).

(2) If in the course of the financial year the LLP has supplied markets that, in the opinion of the members, differ substantially from each other, the amount of the turnover attributable to each such market must also be stated.

In this paragraph "market" means a market delimited by geographical bounds.

(3) In analysing for the purposes of this paragraph the source (in terms of business or in terms of market) of turnover, the members of the LLP must have regard to the manner in which the LLP's activities are organised.

(4) For the purposes of this paragraph—

(a) classes of business which, in the opinion of the members, do not differ substantially from each other must be treated as one class, and

(b) markets which, in the opinion of the members, do not differ substantially from each other must be treated as one market,

and any amounts properly attributable to one class of business or (as the case may be) to one market which are not material may be included in the amount stated in respect of another.

(5) Where in the opinion of the members the disclosure of any information required by this paragraph would be seriously prejudicial to the interests of the LLP, that information need not be disclosed, but the fact that any such information has not been disclosed must be stated.

Particulars of members

66.—(1) Particulars must be given of the average number of members of the LLP in the financial year, which number is to be determined by dividing the relevant annual number by the number of months in the financial year.

(2) The relevant annual number is to be determined by ascertaining for each month in the financial year the number of members of the LLP for all or part of that month, and adding together all the monthly numbers.

(3) Where the amount of the profit of the LLP for the financial year before members' remuneration and profit shares exceeds £200,000, there must be disclosed the amount of profit (including remuneration) which is attributable to the member with the largest entitlement to profit (including remuneration).

(4) For the purpose of determining the amount to be disclosed under sub-paragraph (3), "remuneration" includes any emoluments specified in paragraph 1(1)(a), (c) or (d) of Schedule 5 to the Large and Medium-sized Companies and Groups (Accounts and Reports) Regulations 2008 (**a**) receivable from—

(a) the LLP,

(b) the LLP's subsidiary undertakings, and

(c) any other person.

Miscellaneous matters

67.— (1) Where any amount relating to any preceding financial year is included in any item in the profit and loss account, the effect must be stated.

(2) Particulars must be given of any extraordinary income or charges arising in the financial year.

(3) The effect must be stated of any transactions that are exceptional by virtue of size or incidence though they fall within the ordinary activities of the LLP.

(**a**) S.I. 2008/410.

Sums denominated in foreign currencies

68. Where any sums originally denominated in foreign currencies have been brought into account under any items shown in the balance sheet format or profit and loss account formats, the basis on which those sums have been translated into sterling (or the currency in which the accounts are drawn up) must be stated.

Dormant LLPs acting as agents

69. Where the members of an LLP take advantage of the exemption conferred by section 480 of the 2006 Act (dormant LLPs: exemption from audit), and the LLP has during the financial year in question acted as an agent for any person, the fact that it has so acted must be stated.

Related party transactions

70.—(1) Particulars may be given of transactions which the LLP has entered into with related parties, and must be given if such transactions are material and have not been concluded under normal market conditions (see regulation 4 for exemption for medium-sized LLPs).

(2) The particulars of transactions required to be disclosed by sub-paragraph (1) must include—

(a)   the amount of such transactions,

(b)   the nature of the related party relationship, and

(c)   other information about the transactions necessary for an understanding of the financial position of the LLP.

(3) Information about individual transactions may be aggregated according to their nature, except where separate information is necessary for an understanding of the effects of related party transactions on the financial position of the LLP.

(4) Particulars need not be given of transactions entered into between two or more members of a group, provided that any subsidiary undertaking which is a party to the transaction is wholly- owned by such a member.

(5) In this paragraph, "related party" has the same meaning as in international accounting standards.

PART 4

SPECIAL PROVISION WHERE LLP IS A PARENT LLP OR SUBSIDIARY UNDERTAKING

LLP's own accounts: guarantees and other financial commitments in favour of group undertakings

71. Commitments within any of sub-paragraphs (1) to (5) of paragraph 60 (guarantees and other financial commitments) which are undertaken on behalf of or for the benefit of—

(a)   any parent undertaking or fellow subsidiary undertaking, or

(b)   any subsidiary undertaking of the LLP,

must be stated separately from the other commitments within that paragraph, and commitments within paragraph (a) must also be stated separately from those within paragraph (b).

SCHEDULE 2   Regulation 5

INFORMATION ON RELATED UNDERTAKINGS REQUIRED
WHETHER PREPARING NON-IAS OR IAS ACCOUNTS

PART 1

PROVISIONS APPLYING TO ALL LLPs

Subsidiary undertakings

1.—(1) The following information must be given where at the end of the financial year the LLP has subsidiary undertakings.

(2) The name of each subsidiary undertaking must be stated.

(3) There must be stated with respect to each subsidiary undertaking—

   (a)   if it is incorporated outside the United Kingdom, the country in which it is incorporated,

   (b)   if it is unincorporated, the address of its principal place of business.

Financial information about subsidiary undertakings

2.—(1) There must be disclosed with respect to each subsidiary undertaking not included in consolidated accounts by the LLP—

   (a)   the aggregate amount of its capital and reserves as at the end of its relevant financial year, and

   (b)   its profit or loss for that year.

(2) That information need not be given if the LLP is exempt by virtue of section 400 or 401 of the 2006 Act from the requirement to prepare group accounts (parent LLP included in accounts of larger group).

(3) That information need not be given if the LLP's investment in the subsidiary undertaking is included in the LLP's accounts by way of the equity method of valuation.

(4) That information need not be given if—

   (a)   the subsidiary undertaking is not required by any provision of the 2006 Act to deliver a copy of its balance sheet for its relevant financial year and does not otherwise publish that balance sheet in the United Kingdom or elsewhere, and

   (b)   the LLP's holding is less than 50% of the nominal value of the shares in the undertaking.

(5) Information otherwise required by this paragraph need not be given if it is not material.

(6) For the purposes of this paragraph the "relevant financial year" of a subsidiary undertaking is—

   (a)   if its financial year ends with that of the LLP, that year, and

   (b)   if not, its financial year ending last before the end of the LLP's financial year.

Significant holdings in undertakings other than subsidiary undertakings

3.—(1) The information required by paragraphs 4 and 5 must be given where at the end of the financial year the LLP has a significant holding in an undertaking which is not a subsidiary undertaking of the LLP, and which does not fall within paragraph 16 (joint ventures) or 17 (associated undertakings).

(2) A holding is significant for this purpose if—

(a) it amounts to 20% or more of the nominal value of any class of shares in the undertaking, or

(b) the amount of the holding (as stated or included in the LLP's individual accounts) exceeds one-fifth of the amount (as so stated) of the LLP's assets.

4.—(1) The name of the undertaking must be stated.

(2) There must be stated—

(a) if the undertaking is incorporated outside the United Kingdom, the country in which it is incorporated,

(b) if it is unincorporated, the address of its principal place of business.

(3) There must also be stated—

(a) the identity of each class of shares in the undertaking held by the LLP, and

(b) the proportion of the nominal value of the shares of that class represented by those shares.

5.—(1) Subject to paragraph 12, there must also be stated—

(a) the aggregate amount of the capital and reserves of the undertaking as at the end of its relevant financial year, and

(b) its profit or loss for that year.

(2) That information need not be given in respect of an undertaking if—

(a) the undertaking is not required by any provision of the 2006 Act to deliver a copy of its balance sheet for its relevant financial year and does not otherwise publish that balance sheet in the United Kingdom or elsewhere, and

(b) the LLP's holding is less than 50% of the nominal value of the shares in the undertaking.

(3) Information otherwise required by this paragraph need not be given if it is not material.

(4) For the purposes of this paragraph the "relevant financial year" of an undertaking is—

(a) if its financial year ends with that of the LLP, that year, and

(b) if not, its financial year ending last before the end of the LLP's financial year.

Parent undertaking drawing up accounts for larger group

6.—(1) Where the LLP is a subsidiary undertaking, the following information must be given with respect to the parent undertaking of—

(a) the largest group of undertakings for which group accounts are drawn up and of which the LLP is a member, and

(b) the smallest such group of undertakings.

(2) The name of the parent undertaking must be stated.

(3) There must be stated—

(a) if the undertaking is incorporated outside the United Kingdom, the country in which it is incorporated,

(b) if it is unincorporated, the address of its principal place of business.

(4) If copies of the group accounts referred to in sub-paragraph (1) are available to the public, there must also be stated the addresses from which copies of the accounts can be obtained.

Identification of ultimate parent

7.—(1) Where the LLP is a subsidiary undertaking, the following information must be given with respect to the body corporate (if any) regarded by the members as being the LLP's ultimate parent.

(2) The name of that body corporate must be stated.

(3) If that body corporate is incorporated outside the United Kingdom, the country in which it is incorporated must be stated (if known to the members).

PART 2

LLP NOT REQUIRED TO PREPARE GROUP ACCOUNTS

Reason for not preparing group accounts

8.—(1) The reason why the LLP is not required to prepare group accounts must be stated.

(2) If the reason is that all the subsidiary undertakings of the LLP fall within the exclusions provided for in section 405 of the 2006 Act (non-IAS group accounts: subsidiary undertakings included in the consolidation), it must be stated with respect to each subsidiary undertaking which of those exclusions applies.

Holdings in subsidiary undertakings

9.—(1) There must be stated in relation to shares of each class held by the LLP in a subsidiary undertaking—

  (a) the identity of the class, and

  (b) the proportion of the nominal value of the shares of that class represented by those shares.

(2) The shares held by or on behalf of the LLP itself must be distinguished from those attributed to the LLP which are held by or on behalf of a subsidiary undertaking.

Financial years of subsidiary undertakings

10. Where—

  (a) disclosure is made under paragraph 2(1) with respect to a subsidiary undertaking, and

  (b) that undertaking's financial year does not end with that of the LLP,

there must be stated in relation to that undertaking the date on which its last financial year ended (last before the end of the LLP's financial year).

Exemption from giving information about significant holdings in non-subsidiary undertakings

11. The information otherwise required by paragraph 3 (significant holdings in undertakings other than subsidiary undertaking) need not be given if—

  (a) the LLP is exempt by virtue of section 400 or 401 of the 2006 Act from the requirement to prepare group accounts (parent LLP included in accounts of larger group), and

  (b) the investment of the LLP in all undertakings in which it has such a holding as is mentioned in sub-paragraph (1) is shown, in aggregate, in the notes to the accounts by way of the equity method of valuation.

Construction of references to shares held by LLP

12.—(1) References in Parts 1 and 2 of this Schedule to shares held by an LLP are to be construed as follows.

(2) For the purposes of paragraphs 2, 9 and 10 (information about subsidiary undertakings)—

  (a) there must be attributed to the LLP any shares held by a subsidiary undertaking, or by a person acting on behalf of the LLP or a subsidiary undertaking; but

  (b) there must be treated as not held by the LLP any shares held on behalf of a person other than the LLP or a subsidiary undertaking.

(3) For the purposes of paragraphs 3 to 5 (information about undertakings other than subsidiary undertakings)—

    (a) there must be attributed to the LLP shares held on its behalf by any person; but

    (b) there must be treated as not held by an LLP shares held on behalf of a person other than the LLP.

(4) For the purposes of any of those provisions, shares held by way of security must be treated as held by the person providing the security—

    (a) where apart from the right to exercise them for the purpose of preserving the value of the security, or of realising it, the rights attached to the shares are exercisable only in accordance with that person's instructions, and

    (b) where the shares are held in connection with the granting of loans as part of normal business activities and apart from the right to exercise them for the purpose of preserving the value of the security, or of realising it, the rights attached to the shares are exercisable only in that person's interests.

PART 3

LLP REQUIRED TO PREPARE GROUP ACCOUNTS

Introductory

13. In this Part of this Schedule "the group" means the group consisting of the parent LLP and its subsidiary undertakings.

Subsidiary undertakings

14.—(1) In addition to the information required by paragraph 2, the following information must also be given with respect to the undertakings which are subsidiary undertakings of the parent LLP at the end of the financial year.

(2) It must be stated whether the subsidiary undertaking is included in the consolidation and, if it is not, the reasons for excluding it from consolidation must be given.

(3) It must be stated with respect to each subsidiary undertaking by virtue of which of the conditions specified in section 1162(2) or (4) of the 2006 Act it is a subsidiary undertaking of its immediate parent undertaking.

That information need not be given if the relevant condition is that specified in subsection (2)(a) of that section (holding of a majority of the voting rights) and the immediate parent undertaking holds the same proportion of the shares in the undertaking as it holds voting rights.

Holdings in subsidiary undertakings

15.—(1) The following information must be given with respect to the shares of a subsidiary undertaking held—

    (a) by the parent LLP, and

    (b) by the group,

and the information under paragraphs (a) and (b) must (if different) be shown separately.

(2) There must be stated—

    (a) the identity of each class of shares held, and

    (b) the proportion of the nominal value of the shares of that class represented by those shares.

Joint ventures

16.—(1) The following information must be given where an undertaking is dealt with in the consolidated accounts by the method of proportional consolidation in accordance with paragraph 18 of Schedule 3 to these Regulations (joint ventures)—

   (a)   the name of the undertaking,

   (b)   the address of the principal place of business of the undertaking,

   (c)   the factors on which joint management of the undertaking is based, and

   (d)   the proportion of the capital of the undertaking held by undertakings included in the consolidation.

(2) Where the financial year of the undertaking did not end with that of the LLP, there must be stated the date on which a financial year of the undertaking last ended before that date.

Associated undertakings

17.—(1) The following information must be given where an undertaking included in the consolidation has an interest in an associated undertaking.

(2) The name of the associated undertaking must be stated.

(3) There must be stated—

   (a)   if the undertaking is incorporated outside the United Kingdom, the country in which it is incorporated,

   (b)   if it is unincorporated, the address of its principal place of business.

(4) The following information must be given with respect to the shares of the undertaking held—

   (a)   by the parent LLP, and

   (b)   by the group,

and the information under paragraphs (a) and (b) must be shown separately.

(5)   There must be stated—

   (a)   the identity of each class of shares held, and

   (b)   the proportion of the nominal value of the shares of that class represented by those shares.

(6) In this paragraph "associated undertaking" has the meaning given by paragraph 19 of Schedule 3 to these Regulations; and the information required by this paragraph must be given notwithstanding that paragraph 21(3) of that Schedule (materiality) applies in relation to the accounts themselves.

Requirement to give information about other significant holdings of parent LLP or group

18.—(1) The information required by paragraphs 4 and 5 must also be given where at the end of the financial year the group has a significant holding in an undertaking which is not a subsidiary undertaking of the parent LLP and does not fall within paragraph 16 (joint ventures) or 17 (associated undertakings), as though the references to the LLP in those paragraphs were a reference to the group.

(2) A holding is significant for this purpose if—

   (a)   it amounts to 20% or more of the nominal value of any class of shares in the undertaking, or

   (b)   the amount of the holding (as stated or included in the group accounts) exceeds one-fifth of the amount of the group's assets (as so stated).

(3) For the purposes of those paragraphs as applied to a group the "relevant financial year" of an outside undertaking is—

(a)   if its financial year ends with that of the parent LLP, that year, and

(b)   if not, its financial year ending last before the end of the parent LLP's financial year.

Construction of references to shares held by parent LLP or group

19.—(1) References in Parts 1 and 3 of this Schedule to shares held by that parent LLP or group are to be construed as follows.

(2) For the purposes of paragraphs 3 to 5, 15 and 17(4) and (5) (information about holdings in subsidiary and other undertakings)—

(a)   there must be attributed to the parent LLP shares held on its behalf by any person; but

(b)   there must be treated as not held by the parent LLP shares held on behalf of a person other than the LLP.

(3) References to shares held by the group are to any shares held by or on behalf of the parent LLP or any of its subsidiary undertakings; but any shares held on behalf of a person other than the parent LLP or any of its subsidiary undertakings are not to be treated as held by the group.

(4) Shares held by way of security must be treated as held by the person providing the security—

(a)   where apart from the right to exercise them for the purpose of preserving the value of the security, or of realising it, the rights attached to the shares are exercisable only in accordance with his instructions, and

(b)   where the shares are held in connection with the granting of loans as part of normal business activities and apart from the right to exercise them for the purpose of preserving the value of the security, or of realising it, the rights attached to the shares are exercisable only in his interests.

SCHEDULE 3   Regulation 6

NON-IAS GROUP ACCOUNTS

General rules

1. Group accounts must comply so far as practicable with the provisions of Schedule 1 to these Regulations as if the undertakings included in the consolidation ("the group") were a single LLP.

2.—(1)The consolidated balance sheet and profit and loss account must incorporate in full the information contained in the individual accounts of the undertakings included in the consolidation, subject to the adjustments authorised or required by the following provisions of this Schedule and to such other adjustments (if any) as may be appropriate in accordance with generally accepted accounting principles or practice.

(2) If the financial year of a subsidiary undertaking included in the consolidation does not end with that of the parent LLP, the group accounts must be made up—

(a)   from the accounts of the subsidiary undertaking for its financial year last ending before the end of the parent LLP's financial year, provided that year ended no more than three months before that of the parent LLP, or

(b)   from interim accounts prepared by the subsidiary undertaking as at the end of the parent LLP's financial year.

3.—(1) Where assets and liabilities to be included in the group accounts have been valued or otherwise determined by undertakings according to accounting rules differing from those used for the group accounts, the values or amounts must be adjusted so as to accord with the rules used for the group accounts.

(2) If it appears to the members of the parent LLP that there are special reasons for departing from sub-paragraph (1) they may do so, but particulars of any such departure, the reasons for it and its effect must be given in a note to the accounts.

(3) The adjustments referred to in this paragraph need not be made if they are not material for the purpose of giving a true and fair view.

4. Any differences of accounting rules as between a parent LLP's individual accounts for a financial year and its group accounts must be disclosed in a note to the latter accounts and the reasons for the difference given.

5. Amounts that in the particular context of any provision of this Schedule are not material may be disregarded for the purposes of that provision.

Elimination of group transactions

6.—(1) Debts and claims between undertakings included in the consolidation, and income and expenditure relating to transactions between such undertakings, must be eliminated in preparing the group accounts.

(2) Where profits and losses resulting from transactions between undertakings included in the consolidation are included in the book value of assets, they must be eliminated in preparing the group accounts.

(3) The elimination required by sub-paragraph (2) may be effected in proportion to the group's interest in the shares of the undertakings.

(4) Sub-paragraphs (1) and (2) need not be complied with if the amounts concerned are not material for the purpose of giving a true and fair view.

Acquisition and merger accounting

7.—(1) The following provisions apply where an undertaking becomes a subsidiary undertaking of the parent LLP.

(2) That event is referred to in those provisions as an "acquisition", and references to the "undertaking acquired" are to be construed accordingly.

8. An acquisition must be accounted for by the acquisition method of accounting unless the conditions for accounting for it as a merger are met and the merger method of accounting is adopted.

9.—(1) The acquisition method of accounting is as follows.

(2) The identifiable assets and liabilities of the undertaking acquired must be included in the consolidated balance sheet at their fair values as at the date of acquisition.

(3) The income and expenditure of the undertaking acquired must be brought into the group accounts only as from the date of the acquisition.

(4) There must be set off against the acquisition cost of the interest in the shares of the undertaking held by the parent LLP and its subsidiary undertakings the interest of the parent LLP and its subsidiary undertakings in the adjusted capital and reserves of the undertaking acquired.

(5) The resulting amount if positive must be treated as goodwill, and if negative as a negative consolidation difference.

10. The conditions for accounting for an acquisition as a merger are that adoption of the merger method of accounting accords with generally accepted accounting principles or practice.

11.—(1) Where an LLP adopts the merger method of accounting it must comply with this paragraph, and with generally accepted accounting principles or practice.

(2) The assets and liabilities of the undertaking acquired must be brought into the group accounts at the figures at which they stand in the undertaking's accounts, subject to any adjustment authorised or required by this Schedule.

(3) The income and expenditure of the undertaking acquired must be included in the group accounts for the entire financial year, including the period before the acquisition.

(4) The group accounts must show corresponding amounts relating to the previous financial year as if the undertaking acquired had been included in the consolidation throughout that year.

12.—(1) Where a group is acquired, paragraphs 9 to 11 apply with the following adaptations.

(2) References to shares of the undertaking acquired are to be construed as references to shares of the parent undertaking of the group.

(3) Other references to the undertaking acquired are to be construed as references to the group; and references to the assets and liabilities, income and expenditure and capital and reserves of the undertaking acquired must be construed as references to the assets and liabilities, income and expenditure and capital and reserves of the group after making the set-offs and other adjustments required by this Schedule in the case of group accounts.

13.—(1) The following information with respect to acquisitions taking place in the financial year must be given in a note to the accounts.

(2) There must be stated—

  (a) the name of the undertaking acquired or, where a group was acquired, the name of the parent undertaking of that group, and

  (b) whether the acquisition has been accounted for by the acquisition or the merger method of accounting;

and in relation to an acquisition which significantly affects the figures shown in the group accounts, the following further information must be given.

(3) The composition and fair value of the consideration for the acquisition given by the parent LLP and its subsidiary undertakings must be stated.

(4) Where the acquisition method of accounting has been adopted, the book values immediately prior to the acquisition, and the fair values at the date of acquisition, of each class of assets and liabilities of the undertaking or group acquired must be stated in tabular form, including a statement of the amount of any goodwill or negative consolidation difference arising on the acquisition, together with an explanation of any significant adjustments made.

(5) In ascertaining for the purposes of sub-paragraph (4) the profit or loss of a group, the book values and fair values of assets and liabilities of a group or the amount of the assets and liabilities of a group, the set-offs and other adjustments required by this Schedule in the case of group accounts must be made.

14.—(1) There must also be stated in a note to the accounts the cumulative amount of goodwill resulting from acquisitions in that and earlier financial years which has been written off otherwise than in the consolidated profit and loss account for that or any earlier financial year.

(2) That figure must be shown net of any goodwill attributable to subsidiary undertakings or businesses disposed of prior to the balance sheet date.

15. Where during the financial year there has been a disposal of an undertaking or group which significantly affects the figure shown in the group accounts, there must be stated in a note to the accounts—

(a) the name of that undertaking or, as the case may be, of the parent undertaking of that group, and

(b) the extent to which the profit or loss shown in the group accounts is attributable to profit or loss of that undertaking or group.

16. The information required by paragraph 13, 14 or 15 need not be disclosed with respect to an undertaking which—

(a) is established under the law of a country outside the United Kingdom, or

(b) carries on business outside the United Kingdom,

if in the opinion of the members of the parent LLP the disclosure would be seriously prejudicial to the business of that undertaking or to the business of the parent LLP or any of its subsidiary undertakings and the Secretary of State agrees that the information should not be disclosed.

Minority interests

17.—(1) The formats set out in Schedule 1 to these Regulations have effect in relation to group accounts with the following additions.

(2) In the balance sheet formats there must be shown, as a separate item and under an appropriate heading, the amount of capital and reserves attributable to shares in subsidiary undertakings included in the consolidation held by or on behalf of persons other than the parent LLP and its subsidiary undertakings.

(3) In the profit and loss account formats there must be shown, as a separate item and under an appropriate heading—

(a) the amount of any profit or loss on ordinary activities, and

(b) the amount of any profit or loss on extraordinary activities,

attributable to shares in subsidiary undertakings included in the consolidation held by or on behalf of persons other than the parent LLP and its subsidiary undertakings.

(4) For the purposes of paragraph 4 of Schedule 1 (power to adapt or combine items)—

(a) the additional item required by sub-paragraph (2) above is treated as one to which a letter is assigned, and

(b) the additional items required by sub-paragraph (3)(a) and (b) above are treated as ones to which an Arabic number is assigned.

Joint ventures

18.—(1) Where an undertaking included in the consolidation manages another undertaking jointly with one or more undertakings not included in the consolidation, that other undertaking ("the joint venture") may, if it is not—

(a) a body corporate, or

(b) a subsidiary undertaking of the parent LLP,

be dealt with in the group accounts by the method of proportional consolidation.

(2) The provisions of this Schedule relating to the preparation of consolidated accounts apply, with any necessary modifications, to proportional consolidation under this paragraph.

Associated undertakings

19.—(1) An "associated undertaking" means an undertaking in which an undertaking included in the consolidation has a participating interest and over whose operating and financial policy it exercises a significant influence, and which is not—

(a) a subsidiary undertaking of the parent LLP, or

(b) a joint venture dealt with in accordance with paragraph 18.

(2) Where an undertaking holds 20% or more of the voting rights in another undertaking, it is presumed to exercise such an influence over it unless the contrary is shown.

(3) The voting rights in an undertaking means the rights conferred on shareholders in respect of their shares or, in the case of an undertaking not having a share capital, on members, to vote at general meetings of the undertaking on all, or substantially all, matters.

(4) The provisions of paragraphs 5 to 11 of Schedule 7 to the 2006 Act (parent and subsidiary undertakings: rights to be taken into account and attribution of rights) apply in determining for the purposes of this paragraph whether an undertaking holds 20% or more of the voting rights in another undertaking.

20.— (1) The formats set out in Schedule 1 to these Regulations have effect in relation to group accounts with the following modifications.

(2) In the balance sheet formats replace the items headed "Participating interests", that is—

(a) in format 1, item A.III.3, and

(b) in format 2, item A.III.3 under the heading "ASSETS",

by two items: "Interests in associated undertakings" and "Other participating interests".

(3) In the profit and loss account formats replace the items headed "Income from participating interests", that is—

(a) in format 1, item 8, and

(b) in format 2, item 10,

by two items: "Income from interests in associated undertakings" and "Income from other participating interests".

21. —(1) The interest of an undertaking in an associated undertaking, and the amount of profit or loss attributable to such an interest, must be shown by the equity method of accounting (including dealing with any goodwill arising in accordance with paragraphs 17 to 20 and 22 of Schedule 1 to these Regulations).

(2) Where the associated undertaking is itself a parent undertaking, the net assets and profits or losses to be taken into account are those of the parent and its subsidiary undertakings (after making any consolidation adjustments).

(3) The equity method of accounting need not be applied if the amounts in question are not material for the purpose of giving a true and fair view.

Related party transactions

22. Paragraph 70 of Schedule 1 to these Regulations applies to transactions which the parent LLP, or other undertakings included in the consolidation, have entered into with related parties, unless they are intra group transactions.

SCHEDULE 4 Regulation 7

GENERAL INTERPRETATION

Financial instruments

1. References to "derivatives" include commodity-based contracts that give either contracting party the right to settle in cash or in some other financial instrument, except where such contracts—

(a) were entered into for the purpose of, and continue to meet, the LLP's expected purchase, sale or usage requirements,

(b) were designated for such purpose at their inception, and

(c) are expected to be settled by delivery of the commodity.

2.—(1) The expressions listed in sub-paragraph (2) have the same meaning as they have in Council Directive 78/660/EEC on the annual accounts of certain types of companies(**a**).

(2) Those expressions are "available for sale financial asset", "business combination", "commodity-based contracts", "derivative", "equity instrument", "exchange difference", "fair value hedge accounting system", "financial fixed asset", "financial instrument", "foreign entity", "hedge accounting", "hedge accounting system", "hedged items", "hedging instrument", "held for trading purposes", "held to maturity", "monetary item", "receivables", "reliable market" and "trading portfolio".

Fixed and current assets

3. "Fixed assets" means assets of an LLP which are intended for use on a continuing basis in the LLP's activities, and "current assets" means assets not intended for such use.

Historical cost accounting rules

4. References to the historical cost accounting rules are to be read in accordance with paragraph 30 of Schedule 1 to these Regulations.

Listed investments

5.—(1) "Listed investment" means an investment as respects which there has been granted a listing on—

(a) a recognised investment exchange other than an overseas investment exchange, or

(b) a stock exchange of repute outside the United Kingdom.

(2) "Recognised investment exchange" and "overseas investment exchange" have the meaning given in Part 18 of the Financial Services and Markets Act 2000(**b**).

Loans

6. A loan or advance (including a liability comprising a loan or advance) is treated as falling due for repayment, and an instalment of a loan or advance is treated as falling due for payment, on the earliest date on which the lender could require repayment or (as the case may be) payment, if he exercised all options and rights available to him.

(**a**) O.J. L222 of 14.8.1978, page 11, as amended in particular by Directives 2001/65/EEC, 2003/51/EEC and 2006/46/EEC of the European Parliament and of the Council (O.J. L238 of 27.12.2001, page 28, O.J. L178 of 17.7.2003, page 16 and O.J. L224 of 16.8.2006, page 1).
(**b**) 2000 c.8.

Materiality

7. Amounts which in the particular context of any provision of Schedule 1 to these Regulations are not material may be disregarded for the purposes of that provision.

Participating interests

8.—(1) A"participating interest" means an interest held by an undertaking in the shares of another undertaking which it holds on a long-term basis for the purpose of securing a contribution to its activities by the exercise of control or influence arising from or related to that interest.

(2) A holding of 20% or more of the shares of the undertaking is to be presumed to be a participating interest unless the contrary is shown.

(3) The reference in sub-paragraph (1) to an interest in shares includes—

   (a)   an interest which is convertible into an interest in shares, and

   (b)   an option to acquire shares or any such interest,

and an interest or option falls within paragraph (a) or (b) notwithstanding that the shares to which it relates are, until the conversion or the exercise of the option, unissued.

(4) For the purposes of this paragraph an interest held on behalf of an undertaking is to be treated as held by it.

(5) In the balance sheet and profit and loss formats set out in Schedule 1 to these Regulations, "participating interest" does not include an interest in a group undertaking.

(6) For the purpose of this paragraph as it applies in relation to the expression "participating interest"—

   (a)   in those formats as they apply in relation to group accounts, and

   (b)   in paragraph 19 of Schedule 3 (group accounts: undertakings to be accounted for as associated undertakings),

the references in sub-paragraphs (1) to (4) to the interest held by, and the purposes and activities of, the undertaking concerned are to be construed as references to the interest held by, and the purposes and activities of, the group (within the meaning of paragraph 1 of that Schedule).

Provisions

9.—(1) References to provisions for depreciation or diminution in value of assets are to any amount written off by way of providing for depreciation or diminution in value of assets.

(2) Any reference in the profit and loss account formats set out in Schedule 1 to these Regulations to the depreciation of, or amounts written off, assets of any description is to any provision for depreciation or diminution in value of assets of that description.

10. References to provisions for liabilities are to any amount retained as reasonably necessary for the purpose of providing for any liability the nature of which is clearly defined and which is either likely to be incurred, or certain to be incurred but uncertain as to amount or as to the date on which it will arise.

Purchase price

11. "Purchase price", in relation to an asset of an LLP or any raw materials or consumables used in the production of such an asset, includes any consideration (whether in cash or otherwise) given by the LLP in respect of that asset or those materials or consumables, as the case may be.

Staff costs

12.—(1) "Social security costs" means any contributions by the LLP to any state social security or pension scheme, fund or arrangement.

(2)"Pension costs" includes—

(a) any costs incurred by the LLP in respect of any pension scheme established for the purpose of providing pensions for persons currently or formerly employed by the LLP,

(b) any sums set aside for the future payment of pensions directly by the LLP to current or former employees, and

(c) any pensions paid directly to such persons without having first been set aside.

(3) Any amount stated in respect of the item "social security costs" or in respect of the item "wages and salaries" in the LLP's profit and loss account must be determined by reference to payments made or costs incurred in respect of all persons employed by the LLP during the financial year under contracts of service.

EXPLANATORY NOTE

(This note is not part of the Regulations)

These Regulations specify the form and content of the accounts of limited liability partnerships (LLPs), other than those subject to the small LLPs regime, under Part 15 of the Companies Act 2006 (c.46) ("the 2006 Act"), as applied to LLPs with modifications by the Limited Liability Partnerships (Accounts and Audit) (Application of Companies Act 2006) Regulations 2008 (S.I. 2008/1911). They do so by applying to LLPs, with modifications, provisions of the Large and Medium-sized Companies and Groups (Accounts and Reports) Regulations 2008 (S.I. 2008/410).

The accounts of small LLPs are dealt with separately in the Small Limited Liability Partnerships (Accounts) Regulations 2008 (S.I. 2008/1912).

The Regulations replace provisions previously contained in the Schedules to Part 7 of the Companies Act 1985 (c.6) ("the 1985 Act") and in the Schedules to Part 8 of the Companies (Northern Ireland) Order 1986 (S.I. 1986/1032 (N.I. 6)) ("the 1986 Order") as applied to LLPs with modifications by the Limited Liability Partnerships Regulations 2001 (S.I. 2001/1090) and the Limited Liability Partnerships Regulations (Northern Ireland) 2004 (SR (NI) 2004/307). The Regulations extend to the whole of the United Kingdom, reflecting the extent of the 2006 Act.

The Regulations come into force on 1st October 2008 and apply to financial years beginning on or after that date (regulation 2). The corresponding provisions of the 1985 Act or the 1986 Order as applied to LLPs with modifications continue to apply to accounts for financial years beginning before that date.

Regulation 3 of, and Schedule 1 to, the Regulations specify the form and content of the individual accounts of an LLP the members of which are preparing non-IAS individual accounts (as defined in section 395 of the 2006 Act as applied to LLPs). Schedule 1 re-enacts Schedule 4 to the 1985 Act and Schedule 4 to the 1986 Order as applied to LLPs, with two substantive modifications. Paragraph 36(4) of Schedule 1 gives LLPs the option of including financial instruments in the accounts at a fair value provided that they may be so included under international accounting standards adopted under the IAS Regulation (as defined in section 474(1) of the 2006 Act as applied to LLPs) on or before 5th September 2006, and provided that the disclosures required by such standards are made. Paragraph 70 requires LLPs to make certain disclosures about transactions with related parties.

Regulation 4 specifies certain exemptions for medium-sized LLPs the members of which are preparing non-IAS individual accounts. It re-enacts the exemptions in section 246A of the 1985 Act and in Article 254A of the 1986 Order as applied to LLPs, save that medium-sized LLPs are required to disclose their turnover in the accounts delivered to the registrar of companies. Medium-sized LLPs are exempted from making the disclosures about related party transactions required by paragraph 70 of Schedule 1 to the Regulations.

Regulation 5 of, and Schedule 2 to, the Regulations specify information about related undertakings which the members of an LLP must include in the notes to the individual or group accounts, whether they are non-IAS or IAS individual accounts. The Schedule re-enacts Schedule 5 to the 1985 Act and Schedule 5 to the 1986 Order as applied to LLPs.

Regulation 6 of, and Schedule 3 to, the Regulations specify the form and content of non-IAS group accounts (as defined in section 403 of the 2006 Act as applied to LLPs). The Schedule re-enacts Schedule 4A to the 1985 Act and Schedule 4A to the 1986 Order as applied to LLPs, save that paragraphs 9, 13 and 17 have been simplified to facilitate convergence with international accounting standards.

Regulation 7 of, and Schedule 4 to, the Regulations contain general interpretation provisions.

An Impact Assessment of the effect that these Regulations will have on the costs of business, charities or voluntary bodies has been prepared and is available from the Department for Business, Enterprise and Regulatory Reform, Corporate Law and Governance Directorate, 1 Victoria Street, London SW1H 0ET. It is also available electronically at http://www.berr.gov.uk/bbf/llp/page39897.html. Copies have also been placed in the libraries of both Houses of Parliament.

Appendix E Decision chart to determine size qualification

The decision chart below is designed to determine whether an LLP qualifies in any particular year to be treated as small or medium-sized, and hence whether it is entitled to certain provisions in the preparation of its annual accounts, and whether it is entitled to prepare and file abbreviated accounts.

Decision chart to determine size qualification

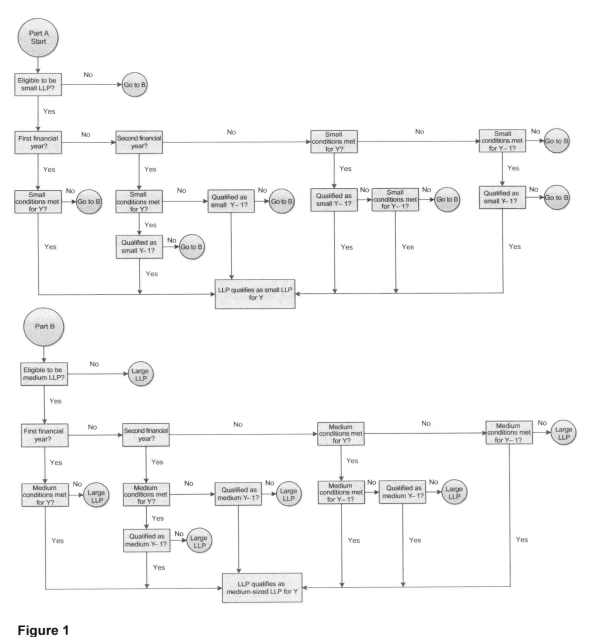

Figure 1

Terms, expressions, etc. used in the chart are explained as follows.

253

1 'Eligible to be small LLP?'

The following LLPs are not eligible to be small and are therefore not entitled to prepare accounts under the small LLPs regime or to file small abbreviated accounts or to be exempt from audit, irrespective of size:

s. 384

- an LLP whose securities are admitted to trading on a regulated market in an EEA state;
- an LLP which is a member of an 'ineligible' group;

s. 384(1)

- an LLP carrying on an insurance market activity; and
- an LLP that is an authorised insurance company, a banking LLP, an e-money issuer, a MiFID investment firm or a UCITS management company.

A group is ineligible if any of its members is a public company, a body corporate (other than a company) whose shares are admitted to trading on a regulated market in an EEA State, a person (other than a small company or small LLP) who has permission under Pt. 4A of FSMA 2000 to carry on a regulated activity, an e-money issuer, a small company or small LLP that is an authorised insurance company, a banking company or banking LLP, a MiFID investment firm or a UCITS management company, or a person who carries on insurance market activity.

s. 384(2)

An LLP is a 'small LLP' for the purpose of ineligibility if it qualified as small in relation to its last financial year ending on or before the end of the financial year to which the accounts relate.

2 'Eligible to be medium LLP'

The following LLPs are not eligible to be medium sized and were therefore not entitled to the accounting exemptions available to medium sized LLPs or to file medium sized abbreviated accounts, irrespective of size:

s. 467

- an LLP whose securities are admitted to trading on a regulated market in an EEA state;
- an LLP which is a member of an ineligible group;
- an LLP carrying on an insurance market activity;

s. 467(1)

- an LLP that has permission under Pt. 4A of FSMA 2000 to carry on a regulated activity; and
- an LLP which is an e-money issuer.

The definition of an ineligible group is the same as for small LLP eligibility.

3 Years

Y = current financial year

Y − 1 = preceding financial year

4 'First financial year?'

In an LLP's first year of incorporation, it will qualify as small or medium-sized, as appropriate, provided it meets the qualifying conditions in its first financial year.

5   Qualifying conditions

In order to qualify as small or medium-sized, as the case may be, the qualifying conditions set out in **Chapter 4 at 4.2** must be satisfied.

Note: Part B of the chart should only be used after following the logic route of Part A.

6   'Qualified as small (medium)?'

Did the LLP qualify as small (or medium-sized)?

7   'Large LLP'

The LLP, being neither small nor medium-sized, is not entitled to prepare accounts in accordance with the relevant provisions. The term 'large' is not used in the legislation.

Appendix F Decision chart to determine LLP Audit exemption

The decision chart below is designed to determine whether an LLP qualifies in any particular year to exemption from audit.

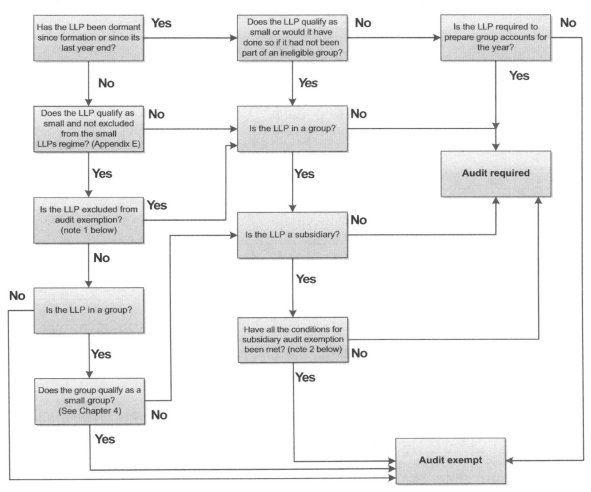

Note 1 – LLPs excluded from audit exemption

An LLP is not entitled to the small LLPs audit exemption conferred by CA 2006, s. 477 as applied to LLPs, if it was at any time within the financial year in question:

s. 478

- a public company (LLPs cannot be 'public' so this would not apply); or
- an authorised insurance company, a banking company, an e-money issuer, a MiFID investment firm or a UCITS management company, or an entity that carries on insurance market activity; or
- a special register body (as defined under the *Trade Union and Labour Relations (Consolidation) Act* 1992) or an employers' association (as defined under the *Industrial Relations (Northern Ireland) Order* 1992).

Note that the first two bullet points above would also exclude the LLP from the small LLPs regime and thus render it ineligible for the small LLPs audit exemption on that basis as well.

Note 2 – Subsidiaries of EEA companies – audit exemption

In accordance with CA 2006, s. 479A, as applied to LLPs, an LLP which is a subsidiary (irrespective of its size) is exempt from audit if it fulfils all of the following conditions:

(a)   its parent undertaking is established under the law of an EEA state;

(b)   all of the subsidiary's members agree the exemption in respect of the financial year in question;

(c)   the parent gives a guarantee (under s. 479C) of all the outstanding liabilities to which the subsidiary is subject at the end of the financial year until they are satisfied in full;

(d)   the subsidiary is included in the consolidated accounts drawn up by the parent undertaking. These accounts must be prepared in accordance with Directive 83/349/EEC (the Seventh Company Law Directive) or international accounting standards;

(e)   the consolidated accounts drawn up by the parent must disclose the use of the exemption by the subsidiary;

(f)   the designated members of the subsidiary must file the following documents at Companies House on or before the date that they file the subsidiary's accounts:

(i)   written notice of the agreement in (b);

(ii)   a written statement by the parent of the guarantee in (c);

(iii)   a copy of the consolidated annual report and accounts referred to in (d) and the auditor's report on those accounts;

(g)   the subsidiary is not an authorised insurance company, a banking LLP, an e-money issuer, a MiFID investment firm or a UCITS management company, or carries on insurance market activity; and

(h)   the subsidiary is not an employers' association (as defined under the *Trade Union and Labour Relations (Consolidation) Act* 1992 or the *Industrial Relations (Northern Ireland) Order* 1992).

Appendix G LLP SORP disclosure checklist

The table below contains a financial statements disclosure checklist derived from the LLP SORP and can be used for financial statements.

		SORP para	Tick or N/A
	The definitions set out in **Appendix A section 4** apply within this checklist;		
1	**THE CONTENTS OF THE ANNUAL REPORT AND FINANCIAL STATEMENTS**		
	Does the Annual Report comprise:	**25**	
	(a) the financial statements?	**25**	
	(b) a statement of members' responsibilities in relation to the production of financial statements?	**25**	
	(c) a report on the financial statements by a registered auditor, if required by the Regulations? and	**26**	
	Subject to the exemptions for small and medium-sized entities, do the financial statements, as defined by the Regulations and accounting standards comprise:	**26**	
	(a) either: • a single statement of comprehensive income displaying all items of income and expense recognised during the period including those items recognised in determining profit or loss and items of other comprehensive income; or • a separate income statement and a separate statement of comprehensive income Consolidated in the case of a group preparing consolidated accounts?	**26**	
	(b) a statement of changes in equity, consolidated in the case of a group preparing consolidated accounts?	**26**	
	(c) a statement of cash flows, consolidated in the case of a group preparing consolidated accounts?	**26**	
	(d) a statement of financial position for the LLP and, if it prepares group accounts, a consolidated balance sheet? and	**26**	
	(e) notes to the above financial statements?	**26**	
	Accounting by smaller LLPs		
	Note that where the LLP is applying FRSSE and there are conflicting requirements between those of the SORP and those of the FRSSE, the requirements of the FRSSE take precedence.	**27–28**	

		SORP para	Tick or N/A
	Information about the LLP		
	Is the following information disclosed:	30	
	(a) the principal activities of the LLP and its subsidiary undertakings, indicating any significant changes during the year?	30	
	(b) an indication of the existence of any branches outside of the UK? (branches are defined by CA 2006, s.1046(3))	30	
	(c) the identity of anyone who was a designated member during the year? and	30	
	(d) the policy of the LLP regarding members' drawings and the subscription and repayment of amounts subscribed or otherwise contributed by members?	30 69	
2	**MEMBERS' REMUNERATION AND INTERESTS**		
	Analysing members' participation rights		
	Have members' participation rights in the earnings or assets of an LLP been analysed (based on the terms of the members' agreement) as either:	32	
	(a) a financial liability where the LLP is contractually obliged to transfer cash (or other asset) to the member? or	33	
	(b) equity where the LLP has an unconditional right to avoid delivering cash or other assets to the member (i.e. the right to any payment or repayment being at the LLP's discretion)? or	33	
	(c) equity where certain conditions are met for puttable instruments or amounts payable on liquidation? (Note that where the conditions are met for puttable instruments and amounts payable on liquidation, such instruments will be classified partly or wholly as equity even though the LLP does not have an unconditional right to avoid delivering cash or other asset to the member.)	33	
	Have participation rights in respect of amounts subscribed or otherwise contributed been analysed separately from those in respect of remuneration?	34	
	Have any non-discretionary amounts becoming due to members in respect ofparticipation rights in the profits of the LLP been included as an expense within the profit and loss account within the heading 'Members'' remuneration charged as an expense')?	35	
	Have any amounts becoming due to members in respect of equity participation rights, following a discretionary division of profits been debited directly to equity in the year in which the division occurs (and excluded from expenditure within the profit and loss account)?	36	
	Have any discretionary divisions of profit that took place after the balance sheet date been treated as a non adjusting event?	36	

	SORP para	Tick or N/A
Puttable instruments		
Have puttable financial instruments and obligations arising on liquidation been treated correctly?	**40–45**	
Division of profits		
Where there are no equity participation rights in the profits for the year, have all amounts becoming due to members, in respect of those profits, been presented within members' remuneration and charged as an expense?	**47, 51**	
Have profits that are automatically divided as they arise or are determined, so that the LLP does not have an unconditional right to refuse the payment, been included as liabilities in the balance sheet? Have these amounts also been treated as an expense in the profit and loss account in the relevant year?	**48–50**	
If profits are not automatically divided and the LLP has an unconditional right to refuse payment have these profits been classed as an appropriation of equity rather than an expense? Have they been shown as a residual amount available for appropriation in the profit and loss account?	**48–50**	
Members' remuneration: presentation and disclosure		
Does the profit and loss account disclose a sub-total, being 'Profit or loss for the financial year before members' remuneration and profit shares'?	**51**	
Has the total 'Members' remuneration charged as an expense' (as defined in **Appendix A section 4**) been disclosed separately and deducted from the balance stated above?	**51, 53**	
Does the 'Members' remuneration charged as an expense' only include automatic division of profits, remuneration that is paid under an employment contract or other payments, arising from components of members' participation rights in the profits for the year that give rise to liabilities (such as mandatory interest payments)?	**54**	
Have any share of profits arising from a division of profits that is discretionary on the part of the LLP (i.e. where the decision to divide the profits is taken after the profits have been made) been treated as an allocation of profit?	**54**	
Has the basis on which each element of remuneration (as defined) that was treated in the accounts been disclosed and explained by note?	**52**	
Where it is considered that it will assist an understanding of the financial performance of the LLP, has the 'Members' remuneration charged as an expense' been analysed further within the notes to the financial statements (e.g. between that which is paid under a contract of employment and that which relates to amounts arising from participation rights that give rise to a liability)?	**54**	

261

		SORP para	Tick or N/A
	Members' interests: presentation and disclosure		
	Have 'Loans and other debts due to members' (balance sheet item J) and 'Members' other interests' (balance sheet item K) been disclosed separately on the face of the balance sheet?	**55**	
	In respect of balance sheet item J (which is a financial liability) is there disclosure on the face of the balance sheet of the amounts relevant to the component parts of this balance (i.e. 'Loans and other debts due to members' and 'Members' capital (which has been classified as a liability)')?	**55**	
	In respect of balance sheet item K (which is equity) is there disclosure on the face of the balance sheet of the amounts relevant to the component parts of this balance (i.e. 'Members' capital (which has been classified as equity)', 'Revaluation reserve' and 'Other reserves')?	**55–57**	
	Does the balance for 'Loans and other debts due to members' include any unpaid element of 'Members' remuneration charged as an expense' together with any unpaid allocated profits arising from a discretionary division of profits during the year?	**56**	
	Does the face of the balance sheet show the net assets attributable to members of the LLP (i.e. the sum of balance sheet items B to I in Format 1)?	**58**	
	Is 'Total members' interests' (being the total of balance sheet items J and K (as noted above) less any amounts due from members in debtors) disclosed as a memorandum item on the face of the balance sheet?	**58**	
	Do the accounts include a reconciliation of movement in members' interests, analysed between 'Members' other interests' and 'Loans and other debts due to members' showing the amount brought forward from the previous year, the changes arising in the financial year and the balance carried forward at the end of the year?	**60**	
	Has either the reconciliation of movement in members interests or a statement of changes in equity been included as a primary statement?	**59 60A**	
	Have any unallocated profits been presented under 'Other reserves' on the balance sheet? Have any losses for the financial year not allocated to members been deducted from 'Other reserves'?	**61–62**	
	Do the notes to the accounts explain where amounts in 'Loans and other debts due to members' would rank in relation to other creditors who are unsecured in the event of winding up? Does this note include details of any protection afforded to creditors in such an event which is legally enforceable and cannot be revoked atwill by the members? Where no such protection is afforded, has that fact been disclosed?	**63–64**	
	Have all loans and other debts due to members falling due after more than one year been disclosed separately?	**65**	

	SORP para	Tick or N/A
Has the aggregate amount of money advanced by members by way of loan, the aggregate amount of money owed to members in respect of profits and any other amounts owed to members been separately disclosed?	**66**	
Has the amount of debts owing to the LLP by members been disclosed (without being offset against amounts due by the LLP to the members)?	**67–68**	
Other disclosures		
Does the LLP disclose the overall policy followed in relation to members' drawings, including an indication of policy applicable where the cash requirements of the business compete with the need to allow cash drawings by members?	**69**	
Does the above disclosure include any transfers of members' interests from equity to debt (and vice versa) during the year and up to the date the accounts are approved?	**69**	
Has the policy under which members contribute or subscribe amounts to the LLP by way of equity or debt and the policy under which their contributions and subscriptions are repayable by the LLP been disclosed?	**69**	
For large and medium-sized LLPs, has disclosure been made of the average number of members in the financial year? This should be calculated by dividing the aggregate number of members of the LLP for each month or part thereof in the financial year by the number of months in the financial year rounded to the nearest whole number.	**70**	
For large and medium-sized LLPs where the profit for the year before members' remuneration and profit shares exceeds £200,000, is there disclosure of the profit (including remuneration) that is attributable to the member with the largest entitlement to profit (including remuneration)? (The identity of the member need not be disclosed). Has the policy been disclosed for determining the disclosable amount?	**71–72**	
Where the LLP has chosen to disclose the average members' remuneration, has this been calculated by dividing the 'Profit before members' remuneration and profit shares' by the average numbers of members as discussed in paragraph 70 of the SORP?	**73**	
Cash flow statement presentation		
In the LLP's cash flow statement, have all cash flows been classified as operating, investing or financing, with transactions with members disclosed as follows:	**74**	
(a) Remuneration paid under an employment contract – operating?	**74A**	
(b) Other remuneration (discretionary or non-discretionary) for services provided – operating?	**74A**	

		SORP para	Tick or N/A
(c)	Post-retirement payments to former members – operating?	74A	
(d)	Capital introduced by members (classified as equity or liability) – financing?	74A	
(e)	Repayment of capital or debt to members – financing?	74A	
(f)	Payments to members that represent a return on amounts subscribed or otherwise contributed – financing?	74A	
	Have cash flows from transactions with members (and former members) been disclosed separately from those with non-members?	74B	
Retirement benefits			
	Have retirement benefits provided to employees been accounted for in accordance with section 28 of FRS 102 *Employee Benefits*? Does this include retirement benefits payable to members that are based on any salary paid to the member under an employment contract?	75	
	In respect of contractual or constructive obligations to make payments to members following their retirement/ceasing to be a member, has a liability been recognised in respect of the annuity due where the LLP has no discretion to withhold payment?	76–82	
	Have any such constructive or contractual obligations been analysed between:		
(a)	Those that meet the definition of an insurance contract and, therefore, fall within the scope of FRS 103 *Insurance contracts*?	76	
(b)	Those that give rise to financial liabilities falling within the scope of section 11 *Basic Financial Instruments* of FRS 102?	76	
(b)	Those that give rise to financial liabilities falling within the scope of section 12 *Other Financial Instruments Issues* of FRS 102? and	76	
(b)	Those that give rise to non-financial liabilities of uncertain timing and amount falling within the scope of section 21 *Provisions and Contingencies* of FRS 102?	76	
	Where the rights to an annuity build over the period of service by the member, have the costs been recognised over that period?	83	
	Where the liability falls within the scope of section 21, does the year end estimate of the liability reflect the latest expectations in respect of:	85–86	
(a)	The likely date of ceasing to be a member? and		

	SORP para	Tick or N/A
(b) The amounts likely to be payable from that date?		
Has the liability been recalculated annually to take account of changes in membership, eligibility for post-retirement payments, financial estimates and actuarial assumptions.	87	
Post-retirement benefits: presentation		
Have any post-retirement payments recognised in respect of current members been charged to the profit and loss account within 'Members' remuneration charged as an expense'?	88	
Have the amounts charged to the profit and loss account in respect of changes to the liability for post-retirement payments been split between those in respect of current members and those in respect of former members as follows:	88	
(a) Any changes in the liability for post-retirement payments in respect of current members should be charged to the profit and loss account as 'Members' remuneration charged as an expense'.	88	
(b) Any changes in the liability for post-retirement payments in respect of former members should be charged to the profit and loss account within a relevant expense item which is not 'members' remuneration'.	88	
Has the liability shown on the balance sheet for post-retirement payments been split between those in respect of current members and those in respect of former members as follows:	89	
(a) The liability in respect of former members should be shown in the balance sheet under 'Provision for liabilities' or 'Creditors' as appropriate.	89	
(b) The liability in respect of current members should be shown in the balance sheet separately if material, as a component of 'Loans and other debts due to members'.	89	
Where the liability has been discounted, has the unwinding of the discount:	90	
(a) Been presented next to the 'Interest cost' line in the profit and loss account where it relates to the liability in respect of former members? or	90	
(b) Been included in 'Members' remuneration charged as an expense' where it relates to the liability in respect of current members?	90	
Have any additional annuities granted after the date of a member's retirement been recognised in full in the profit and loss account within operating profit as soon as the award was granted to the former member?	91	
Post-retirement benefits: disclosure:		
Do the accounting policy notes disclose the LLP's policy in respect of post-retirement benefit payments to members?	92	
On transitions of a partnership or other undertaking to an LLP.		

		SORP para	Tick or N/A
	In respect of payments to members of a predecessor partnership or other organisation:	**93–94**	
	(a) Where an actual or constructive liability exists, has this been recorded on the balance sheet of the LLP? or	**93–94**	
	(b) Where this is merely recourse to the LLP in the event of a default of a third party and such default has not occurred and is not probable, has this been disclosed as a contingent liability?	**93–94**	
	Taxation		
	Has any personal tax liability (current or deferred) to be paid on members' remuneration been excluded from the profit and loss account and included instead within 'Members interests' ('Loans and other debts due to members') on the balance sheet? Have amounts retained for tax been included in 'Loans and other debts due to members'?	**95–96**	
	Has tax withheld from members who subsequently retire from membership been dealt with in the same way as other balances due to former members?	**97**	
	For LLPs that are subject to tax on profits arising in jurisdictions where LLPs are taxed as corporate entities, have such taxes been reported in their accounts as required by section 29 of FRS 102?	**98**	
	For group accounts of an LLP which include entities or organisations that are not partnerships or LLPs, such as companies, have the tax liabilities of such entities been recorded in the profit and loss account under the relevant heading and any related liability carried as a creditor in the balance sheet?	**99**	
	INVENTORIES (STOCKS)		
	In respect of stock, have the cost of the members' time and related overheads been accounted for in accordance with section 13 *Inventories* of FRS 102? Have contracts been accounted for in accordance with section 23 *Revenue* of FRS 102?	**100**	
	In respect of the cost of stock or work in progress, does the cost of members' time only include those elements that would have been expensed in the profit and loss account (i.e. 'Members' remuneration charged as an expense')?	**101**	
	BUSINESS COMBINATIONS AND GROUP ACCOUNTS		
	Entity and group accounts		
	Have rules on the requirement to prepare group accounts (and the exemptions therefrom) and the contents of the group accounts (and on inclusion and exclusion of subsidiaries) set out in section 9 of FRS 102 and the relevant sections of the Regulations been followed?	**102**	

	SORP para	Tick or N/A
Accounting for business combinations		
Has the application of GAAP with respect to mergers and acquisitions been considered in the context of both the group accounts and the entity accounts of the LLP? (When two LLPs combine, there may be only one surviving LLP, or a new LLP may be created or one LLP may become a member of the other. The recommended accounting treatment may therefore apply both to the entity's individual accounts and, if relevant, to its group accounts.)	103, 104	
Has consideration been given to whether a particular business combination represents a group reconstruction which may be accounted for using the merger method?	105	
Acquisition accounting		
Has the purchase method been used to account for a combination where the conditions for accounting for as a group reconstruction as set out in paragraph 19.27 of FRS 102 are not met?	106	
Where the purchase method is used, has the profit share promised to the new members in the enlarged LLP been assessed to determine whether any portion of that remuneration represents consideration for the business acquired, rather than future members' remuneration? For example, if members of the purchased entity were awarded an increased profit share for a limited period of time after the acquisition, falling back to 'normal' remuneration levels thereafter, this could indicate that the short-term excess amounts were part of the purchase consideration.	107	
Where it is not possible to value the consideration given in accordance with the requirements of paragraph 19.11 of FRS 102, has the best estimate of its value been obtained by valuing the entity acquired?	108	
Group reconstructions		
Has the transfer of all or the majority of the assets, liabilities and business of a partnership into an LLP incorporated for that purpose been dealt with as a group reconstruction, except where the requirements of paragraph 19.27 of FRS 102 are not met?	112	
Where the net asset transfer has been dealt with as a group reconstruction (and merger accounting has been used), does the initial 'opening' balance sheet follow the accounting policies of the LLP?	112	
Where a single entity LLP is formed through the transfer or incorporation of existing undertakings, and the initial transfer is dealt with using merger accounting, do the accounts reflect the transfer of the undertakings at book value at the date of transfer and disclose comparative *pro forma* amounts in the financial statements of the first period after incorporation?	115	

		SORP para	Tick or N/A
	The restatement of comparatives to consistent accounting policies will often result in a difference between the total interests of partners in the predecessor firm shown by its final balance sheet, and the members' interests in the opening balance sheet of the LLP. Have such differences been excluded from the financial statements of the LLP?	117	
	Where the comparatives have been restated to create consistency in the application of accounting policies, has disclosure been made of the nature and amount of any significant accounting adjustments as required by section 19 of FRS 102.	118	
	In respect of existing groups that have used merger accounting under a group reconstruction to put a new LLP at the top of the group (whether in order to convert to an LLP or as part of a group reconstruction), have the corresponding amounts in the financial statements of the period of the merger been presented, as required by paragraph 19.30 of FRS 102?	119	
	PROVISIONS AND OTHER IMPLICATIONS OF SECTION 21 OF FRS 102		
	For an LLP that has entered into any guarantee or indemnity with respect to the borrowings of a member or members personally, has the existence of such a guarantee or indemnity where material either been disclosed as a note to the accounts (where it is unlikely that the guarantee or indemnity would be called) or been provided for in the primary statements where there is an actual or constructive liability defined under section 21 of FRS 102 and it is probable that the guarantee or indemnity will be called?	124–127	
	RELATED PARTIES		
	Have predecessor partnerships of the LLP been treated as related parties of the LLP?	128	
	Has the nature and extent of members' involvement in the management of the LLP been considered, to determine whether a member is related to the LLP?	129–130	
	Have the controlling party and ultimate controlling party of an LLP, if one exists, been disclosed?	131	
	Compliance statement		
	Does the note to the financial statements which deals with accounting policies refer to the LLP's compliance with SORP, or detail areas of non-compliance and any reason therefor?	132	

Appendix H Selected reading and reference material

This appendix provides a selection of the literature to which this book might form a companion.

Legislation and regulation

The Limited Liability Partnerships Act 2000	www.legislation.gov.uk
Companies (Late Filing Penalties) and Limited Liability Partnerships (Filing Periods and Late Filing Penalties) Regulations 2008 (SI 2008/497)	www.legislation.gov.uk
Limited Liability Partnerships (Accounts and Audit) (Application of the Companies Act 2006) Regulations 2008 (SI 2008/1911)	www.legislation.gov.uk
Small Limited Liability Partnerships (Accounts) Regulations 2008 (SI 2008/1912)	www.legislation.gov.uk
Large and Medium-sized Limited Liability Partnerships (Accounts) Regulations 2008 (SI 2008/1913)	www.legislation.gov.uk
Limited Liability Partnerships (Application of the Companies Act 2006) Regulations 2009 (SI 2009/1804)	www.legislation.gov.uk
Companies and Limited Liability Partnerships (Accounts and Audit Exemptions and Change of Accounting Framework) Regulations 2012	www.legislation.gov.uk

Accounting and Auditing Standards

Accounting Standards 2015/2016		Wolters Kluwer (UK) Ltd
Financial Reporting Standard for Smaller Entities (effective January 2015)		FRC Publications
Statement of Recommended Practice 'Accounting by Limited Liability Partnerships'	CCAB (Consultative Committee of Accountancy Bodies)	
International Accounting Standards		

2016 International Financial Reporting Standards		IASB
Auditing Standards		Wolters Kluwer (UK) Limited

Checklists and further guidance

Company Accounts Disclosure Checklist (which includes requirements for LLPs)	SWAT UK Ltd	Wolters Kluwer (UK) Limited
FRS 101 Reduced Disclosure Framework		Wolters Kluwer (UK) Limited
Applying New UK GAAP 2015–16 (formerly CCH New UK GAAP In-depth)		Wolters Kluwer (UK) Limited

Financial Reporting Council

The Special Auditor's Report on Abbreviated Accounts in the United Kingdom	APB Bulletin 2008/4 (April 2008)
Miscellaneous Reports by Auditors Required by the United Kingdom *Companies Act* 2006	APB Bulletin 2008/9 (October 2008)
Compendium of Illustrative Auditor's Reports on Financial Statements in the United Kingdom Private Sector Financial Statements for periods ended on or after 15 December 2010 (Revised)	APB Bulletin 2010/2 (revised March 2012)

Useful websites

International Accounting Standard Board	www.ifrs.org
Financial Reporting Council	www.frc.org.uk
International Auditing and Assurance Standards Board	www.ifac.org/IAASB
BIS (Department for Business, Innovation and Skills)	www.gov.uk/government/organisations/department-for-business-innovation-skills
Companies House	
– *Life of a Limited Liability Partnership – GPLLP2*	www.gov.uk/government/publications/life-of-a-limited-liability-partnership
Institute of Chartered Accountants	
– in England and Wales	www.icaew.com
– of Scotland	www.icas.org.uk
Accountancy Magazine	www.accountancymagazine.com

Index

271